Paris in American Literatures

Paris in American Literatures

On Distance as a Literary Resource

Edited by Jeffrey Herlihy-Mera and Vamsi K. Koneru

FAIRLEIGH DICKINSON UNIVERSITY PRESS
Madison • Teaneck

Published by Fairleigh Dickinson University Press
Co-published with The Rowman & Littlefield Publishing Group, Inc.
4501 Forbes Boulevard, Suite 200, Lanham, Maryland 20706
www.rowman.com

10 Thornbury Road, Plymouth PL6 7PP, United Kingdom

British Library Cataloguing in Publication Information Available

Library of Congress Cataloging-in-Publication Data
Paris in American literatures : on distance as a literary resource / edited by Jeffrey Herlihy-Mera and Vamsi K. Koneru.
pages cm
Includes bibliographical references and index.
ISBN 978-1-61147-607-1 (cloth)—ISBN 978-1-61147-608-8 (electronic)
1. American literature—History and criticism. 2. Paris (France)—In literature. 3. American literature—French influences. I. Herlihy-Mera, Jeffrey, editor of compilation. II. Koneru, Vamsi K. editor of compilation.
PS159.F5P37 2013
810.9'324436—dc23
2013004913
ISBN 978-1-61147-810-5(pbk)

In Memoriam:

George Langlands Wilson

22-3-1950–11-1-2012

A man who treasured a poem as much as plunder.

Contents

Acknowledgments

This project has come together with the support of several institutions, scholars, and friends. We are indebted to Harry Keyishian and Kirk Curnutt for their advice and sharp insights on revising our preliminary manuscripts. We also are grateful for the encouragement we have received over the years from several scholars, all of whom were indirectly involved with this project; among those not listed here, we would like to thank Amarilis Mello, Arturo Mera-Cardozo, Angelo Anthony Casso, Amy Weisman de Mamani, and Prasad Koneru, for their generosity, support, and confidence in our work.

We must also note here our appreciation for the organizations and institutions whose support made this project possible. We recognize the National Endowment for the Humanities, the Fulbright Commission, the Ernest Hemingway Foundation, the Clarence VerSteeg Foundation, Universidad de Puerto Rico, Albright College, Yale School of Medicine's Hispanic Services Clinic, Harvard Medical School, Morningside College, and Universidad del Azuay.

And most important, we would like to express our profound gratitude to our family and friends who contributed many intangible parts to this book. We would like to mention the contributions of Jenny and George Wilson; Joanna, Paola, Kathy, and María-Augusta Mera; Nelly, Iván, and Rodrigo Pereira; Anne, Ravi, and Miles Koneru; Sebastián and Sofía Zalamea; Jorge and Jorge-Daniel Mogrovejo; Pablo and María-Eduarda Dávila; Amy Herlihy; William, Boo, Faith, and Jay Barrass; Jennifer, Edward, Bella, Grace, and Rosemary Rakeman; Francis and Gladys Tolsma; Donna and Miguel Herlihy; and Bob and Lakshmi Koneru.

Introduction: On Distance as a Literary Resource

Jeffrey Herlihy-Mera and Vamsi K. Koneru

"Paris" could be the first word of an epic poem. For the visitor, it is a city that offers the qualities of a cultural texture, a life-frame, and social character external to one's own, and the stimulation of that social distance has long been used as a creative well for thought, writing, and inspiration. For centuries the Parisian urbanscape has drawn writers, artists, and émigrés from many nations, and the place has helped forge some eminent aesthetic perspectives. Paris has served as an escape not only from political danger, social conflict, and war, but also from provinciality and the cultural stagnancy from which many artists suffer in their places of origin. For many Americans in the French capital, the distance from home— a distance that is at once geographic, cultural, social, linguistic, and aesthetic—has engendered renovation, renewal, and a drive for experiential growth. Maybe for these reasons travel is frequently a central component of an author's creative register. While there are many cultural pilgrimages in Western Arts (to The Alhambra, Venice, Mumbai, and Machu Picchu), Paris seems to stand above others, flourishing as an image of possibility and sophistication. The city has a rich history with foreign artists and writers, intellectual and political exiles, military leaders and philosophers; her streets have felt the footsteps of Napoleon and Che Guevara, Van Gogh and Picasso, Josephine Baker and Mozart, Barack Obama and Hemingway, and the city has left an indelible mark on each.

This collection examines Paris in American Literature with two principal ends: to examine the use of a foreign scene as a literary device; and to engage new perspectives on the expatriate writing process. A focus on distance as a literary resource might offer novel insights on the distribution of certain aesthetic patterns that we find in the literature and poetry, journalism, memoirs, and personal correspondence from or about the city. A discussion of Paris in American Literature should begin through the contexts of exile and identity, structures that define a writer with relation to his or her place and, possibly, fictional settings. The function of a far-off place like Paris for an American author often relies on preconceived images associated with the city and French people(s).[1] The writer's foreign register in France draws from the readers' (and his or her own) preconceptions, at once nuancing and interacting with them. The use of an exotic location can thus dramatize the protagonists' experiences, increasing the importance of the present.

In order to approach these topics in closer detail, we begin this introduction through questions that address foreignness and writing. In some sense, in order for a person to be an expatriate he or she must first be a patriot—and this point leads to a series of concerns regarding social and cultural registers: what transpires psychologically, culturally, and sociolinguistically when a person moves away from a native community? What if this move is permanent, a short escape, or a series of trips interspersed with time at home? What if the expatriate resides among compatriots, alone, with native residents, or with foreigners from other places? Does his or her daily language, French, English, or another tongue, shape their perceptions of self and surroundings? The authors treated in this collection dealt with these questions throughout their lives (or maybe just for short periods), and their work, too, demonstrates a diverse scope of interpretations of Parisian places, languages, peoples, and experiences. A common thread is that the Paris of their imaginations, and of their pages, derives from the stimulation of being away from origins.

THE STUDY OF PLACE AS LITERARY CRITICISM

Place as a forum of literary study is relatively new. As editors Peter Brown and Michael Irwin note in their 2008 study, *Literature and Place, 1800–2000*, the strand is yet "in its early stages of development" (15). Their volume regards place as "coloured or redefined by time, by war, by politics, by memory, by nostalgia, by subjectivity. . . . Thus the primary object of study is typically not 'nineteenth-century London' but 'Dickens's London,' not 'The Great Plains,' but 'Washington Irving's Great Plains'" (15–16). In the same way, several other reports in this subfield offer interpretations of the function of specific settings—like mountains, valleys, deserts, and the home, for example. In many cases, setting is treated as something transcendental and the function of place itself is generally considered symbolic.[2]

Among the leading monographs in this discipline is Leonard Lutwack's *The Role of Place in Literature* (1984), a text which considers a range of physical, geographic, and social elements on writers and their use of scenery. Lutwack endeavors to delineate how places function through preconceived notions such as geographical assumptions, popular images, and political narratives. He also examines the relationship between setting and character, pointing out how the actor forms traits by reacting to an environment over a period of time. One of the main tenets of his monograph is that a character "cannot fully exist without an environment" (17). All places, Lutwack argues, serve metaphorical purposes and therefore give up part of their solidity to accommodate human desires. This critic goes on to say that "the quality of a place in literature is subtly determined by the manner in which a character arrives in it, moves within it, and departs from it. The general impression of a place often depends on its position in a series of places visited by a journeying character, whose moving point of view confers comparison and climax on otherwise static places" (59). By detaching characters from their homes, argues Lutwack, they may live existentially, recreating themselves anew in the exotic place or through a series of movements from place to place. "If there is any place at all in the lives of this new breed of character," writes Lutwack, "it is the highway itself" (227). *The Role of Place in Literature* begins to grapple with a reality where (or when?) dislocation is the norm, not the exception. Lutwack asserts that modern writers who employ dislocation as a device also "portray the disorientation of the individual in a changing world and the possibilities of reorientation" (113).

PARIS IN AMERICAN LITERARY CRITICISM

There is a rich tradition of scholarly work on Paris in American Literature from North American, European, and other perspectives. This succinct review of Paris criticism offers the pulse of several prominent studies—it is not an exhaustive sample: above all, the texts discussed here have been influential scholarly germs for this volume. The proliferation of texts on American Paris written for scholars and nonacademic readers, attests to the widespread reputation that Paris enjoys in American art and literature. Moreover, as the number of books, films, and websites dedicated to Americans in Paris continues to grow each year, this would suggest that the expatriate scene remains a robust source of artistic inspiration. [3]

Several texts have examined American Paris since the colonial period,[4] but more common are the reports on the first half of the twentieth century—and within that scope, there has been a considerable emphasis on the 1920s. Among prominent studies on that range are: *Americans in Paris 1903–1939*, by George Wickes; *Writing the Lost Generation: Expatriate Autobiography and American Modernism*, by Craig Monk; and Noel Riley Fitch's *Sylvia Beach and the Lost Generation: A History of Literary Paris in the Twenties and Thirties*.[5] A notable semi-memoir concerning this period is *Exile's Return: A Literary Odyssey of the 1920s*, by Malcolm Cowley. From a firsthand perspective, Cowley interprets the motivations for expatriation, the details of day-to-day life in Paris for Americans, and the reasons for their eventual return to the United States. This scholar discusses extensively what he terms the "deracination" of the Americans—through reflection and social distance, argues Cowley, they enter into a discourse on identity and origin, on the value of culture, and on the place of self.

Indeed, Cowley's work in this capacity anticipated the transnational approaches that emerged decades later.

Shari Benstock's *Women of the Left Bank: Paris 1900–1940* (1987), is of particular importance to expatriate scholarship. Her work decentered a modernist critical canon that had been dominated by study of men through assessing the writing and biographies of female expatriates. The examination elucidates the work of twenty-two women in the scope of the modernist aesthetics and examined Paris as a source of inspiration, freedom, and experimentation. What is at times an unmentioned theme in Benstock's text is the use of expatriation by these authors as an expression in itself: that women (and the women in her volume, more concretely) "knew their place" — and it was one outside of the social prescriptions of the time. They were revolutionaries and an element in their break from restrictive cultural norms was the choice of residence, a decision that proved to be an important dimension of their creative work. Moreover, by placing these women writers in the context of one another, instead of in relation to their male counterparts, Benstock's work began a new way of contemplating American Paris.

Jean Méral's *Paris in American Literature*, originally published in French in 1983 (translated to English in 1989), surveys American writing in the City of Light from a European perspective. The text broadly catalogs American writing from Paris, illustrating the breadth of material to contemplate on the subject; Méral also executes an analysis of the American experience in France and the collective idealization of Paris. This critic believes that the seductiveness of the Parisian milieu resulted in a uniform way of writing about the city: "the same elements constantly recur, as if shaped by an autonomous group dynamic that functions almost independently of real circumstances, creating a common fiction" (240). Méral also structuralizes the American experience in Paris into two camps: one, the exotic and new in which authors revere the place, "simplifying and exaggerating as they do so"; the second American Paris for Méral is that of expatriate writer, whose work is constructed textually though the "dramatic development [of] the opposition between the Old World and the New" (240).

One text that focuses more centrally on the foreignness of Americans in Paris, on the role of place, and on the act of writing as an identifying device, is J. Gerald Kennedy's *Imaging Paris: Exile, Writing, and American Identity* (1994). While each of the studies thus far mentioned employs a rhetorical approach to consider writing and literature, Kennedy's text nuances this tendency, utilizing a base of empirical work on geography and place to supplement his argument. Indeed, his line of study begins to deconstruct the concepts of place and its use as a literary device, striving to comprehend how we understand relationships with our environment. It is a model of interdisciplinary study, treating our human urges toward territory and communal living (safety in numbers), and steering the critical axes toward comprehending the differentiation of "us" and "them" as well as "here" and "there." Kennedy's work begins to interpolate these categories, their construction and development, and his register uses concepts that he (along with Edward Relph) names "insideness" and "outsideness" to interpret the American experiences of Paris. While *Imagining Paris* examines principally Stein, Hemingway, and Fitzgerald, the work is a deft analysis of exilic themes in literature that offers an effective organizational pattern to scrutinize the cultural reactions which occur over an extended period of expatriation. Since expatriate status is universal in American Literature from Paris, Kennedy's study is one that begins to uncover the profound impact that foreign places have in American writing.

"I think, really, that I would stay in Spain forever," reflects Hella in *Giovanni's Room*, "if I had never seen Paris" (Baldwin 1956, 135) American Paris as a concept has been broadly celebrated in popular spheres, certainly, and this is also true to a certain extent in academic study. As Shari Benstock remarked, "we have romanticized those years [1900–1940]" (Benstock 1987, 4). Brian Bruce observed that "Today the phrase 'lost generation,' calls to mind romantic images of Hemingway scribbling in a notebook in a Paris café" (2006, xiii) and Brook Lindy Blower in *Becoming Americans in Paris* (2011), noted: "It is hard to resist . . romanticizing" (1). The critical tendencies often esteem the French capital, the expatriate literary community, and the foreignness of Americans, a frame that tends to treat the writers and Paris and France as static phenomena. The inclination at times limits investigative latitude to a generally positive and optimistic impression of American Paris. Our volume aims to complement this rich scholarly body through a nuanced examination of some negative aspects of expatriation, grounding the analysis in an empirical body of scholarship on the psychology of cultural displacement. A focus on these behavioral outcomes—instead of a strictly thematic or biographical approach—we feel will offer a novel understanding of how the pilgrimage to Paris has become a catalyst for creativity, the likes of which is almost unparalleled in Western culture.

FOREIGNNESS AND CREATIVITY

Traveling or moving abroad—and to Paris in particular—is an artistic rite of passage. Americans have monumentalized the French capital in novels, memoirs, poetry, painting, and film, such that the circumstance of being an American in Paris has developed into a cultural subgenre unto itself. Artists and writers have long been conscious of the benefits of life abroad; recent empirical studies in psychology and anthropology, too, have explored the social implications of a foreign residence. The empirical data thus far compiled notes some compelling facts about how expatriation can affect a person: while being abroad has obvious influences on the way we view the world and ourselves, it can also stimulate our brains to function in a different way.

Considering ingenuity and inventiveness as phenomena with variability, limits, and plastic dynamics is a relatively new hypothesis in cultural and behavioral study.[6] Creativity has been defined as the means to bring something new into existence that is unique, practical, or beautiful; in "Cultural Borders and Mental Barriers: The Relationship Between Living Abroad and Creativity," Maddux and Galinski (2009) note that there are several measurable factors that increase capacity for innovation. Some are: being a first- or second-generation immigrant; speaking more than one language; and experiencing multiple cultures on a daily basis (1048). These scholars carried out experiments involving construction, recognition, awareness, and negotiation, among other topics, aimed to determine if people with expatriate experience have different cognitive competences than those who have lived in a single environment. The results were clear: "The relationship between living abroad and creativity was consistent across a number of creativity measures (including those measuring insight, association, and generation) . . . both in the United States and Europe, demonstrating the robustness of this phenomenon" (1047). In addition, a longer experience abroad corresponded to a higher level of creativity in the given tasks. We should note here that, in what is likely a function of this circumstance, migrants are more than three times more likely to receive patents for new inventions than native-born residents in the United States (Greenstone and Loney, 2010, 11).[7]

In the realm of a native cohort group, for a person who has not lived abroad, language, social traditions, gastronomy, religious rites, and so on could be understood as ingrained habits that control reality and limit the capacity to perceive specific associations and possibilities which, when combined and synthesized, result in what has been called "creative" faculty. In a foreign context, then, the process of self-orientation within the multiple structures of social stimulation allows (or perhaps requires) an individual to explore multiple perceptions, realities, and cultural systems. The exposure to and immersion within distinct linguistic, sociocultural, and geographic contexts consequently results in a plurality of vision of sorts, and the associated competencies (in perception, synthesis, application) are facilitative components for a person's artistic vigor.

ABROAD THE ARTIST IS FREE FROM INVISIBLE SOCIAL LIMITS

The foreign context also offers social latitudes that would be productive for creative writing. "You could be as wild as you wanted to in Paris," observes Suzzanne Rodríguez, "if you were a foreigner" (Remerowski, 2006). For instance, if we consider the concept of a home-space as constrictive, our associations to families and friends, to our communities and their social norms, bind us and in a sense subordinate us to a set of behavioral expectations. These cultural prescriptions lay out how one is expected to behave and not behave, to think and not think, and so on. Breaking expectations is often necessary in order to perceive or create something new or different; however, social organizations tend to be resistant to individual deviation. In the home-space, therefore, atypical behavior and thought processes—actions that are aberrant to the cultural prescriptions—can cause stresses of ridicule, alienation, and undue tensions; these sentiments are generally unsuitable for creative development. The fact that the foreign artist is not part of the local community excludes him or her from the associated pressures to normalize.

In this way, many celebrated intellectuals who went to France from elsewhere—Van Gogh, Picasso, Einstein, Che Guevara, and Napoleon, for instance—benefitted from their distance from origins. In Paris, their respective disciplinary revelations (painting in bright colors; using geometric angles for body parts; raising a socialist revolution; or carrying out military attacks at night and in rain) circumvented undue social stresses precisely because they were realized far from communities who might criticize them as aberrations from "normalcy." Moreover, because the French capital has long accepted exiles, émigrés, and foreign artists, the urban public there presents a general receptiveness to atypical work. Thus, the Parisians would not pressure the foreign artists to purge the novel dimensions of their work (a reality which would not occur if the artist were in their community of origin) because they are social outsiders. Indeed, Paris itself is unique among foreign destinations, too, due to the rich history of radical art and writing that has been carried out there. If Picasso had released *Les demoiselles d'Avignon* in Boston or Shanghai as a foreign artist, those more conservative publics might respond with negativity to the canvas's revolutionary insights. Furthermore, if he had released the work in Málaga, the town of his birth, how might the Andalusian public have viewed the canvas? Under the close scrutiny of neighbors, family, and former teachers, if he'd never left, Picasso would have had to respond to the weight of their criticism in person on a daily basis—at his studio, buying bread, taking out the garbage. In Paris, too, the revelation of Cubist art was recognized gradually, but Picasso's distance from the cultural mores of Andalucía and immersion within Parisian society liberated him from some of the pervasive strains of home-ties.

WRITING PARISIAN GLOOM

In this dialogue Paris is an open space: it is where artists are free, unbound, and immersed in a community of (often also displaced) receptive minds, working in an array of creative disciplines. An amenable place for creation, art, and literature, as Gertrude Stein remarked, it is "where the twentieth century was." Another set of influences to have in mind, conversely, are the negative aspects of social displacement—some of which can be seriously destructive to both the mind and the body. "That's Paris," notes Pierre in the film *Paris* directed by Cédric Klapisch. "No one's ever happy. We grumble. We love that."

While it is true that many authors have written glowingly of the French capital, as several case studies herein note, much of the American writing about Paris has a considerably different tone. After the aesthetic delights of arrival, American Paris has also been a complicated situation wrought with tension, petulance, even revulsion[8]—and this often neglected dimension of migrant/expatriate life in Paris (even in the case of an aesthetic migrant) has significant literary outcomes. David McCullough has observed that for Americans, Parisian living "was not the romantic expatriate life commonly imagined" (2011, 345). Life in the cosmopolitan French capital (in the 1920s or today) may be a stimulating concept for many authors and artists, yet once abroad the person will have a change of sentiment and subsequently endure the strains of displacement. This transition has profound consequences, the dimensions of which are just beginning to be understood by psychologists and anthropologists. The psychiatric studies of displaced communities demonstrate destructive characteristics particular to displaced individuals, concepts crucial to consider when interpreting expatriate writing. While the openness of Parisian cafés and literary life is productive for inspiration, the process of cultural reorientation exposes and eventually subordinates the mover to another social structure, cultural framework, linguistic system, and canon of values—and this displacement brings about considerable physical and psychiatric problems. Migrants, regardless of their motivation for life abroad, suffer from higher rates of mental and sociocultural stresses in comparison to their cohort who remained in the place of origin; among the psychiatric reactions specific to intercultural immersion are higher frequencies of alcoholism, admission to psychiatric hospitals, diabetes, suicide, and other serious ailments.[9] Alcoholism aside, among the notable artists who fell to mental illness or suicide, or both, after moving to Paris in the last century we find Olive Thomas, Ivar Kreuger, Alexandre Stravinsky, Max Linder (and his wife), Daul Kim, Lucy Gordon, Kat Mckenzie, Hermann Guthmann, Henry Collett, Sadeq Hedayat, Ernest Hemingway, and Zelda Fitzgerald.

A critical locus of this inspection, then, explores a binding circumstance for all expatriate writing—cultural displacement—in order to elucidate how perceived social distance, in the forms of ethnic, linguistic, cultural, and social otherness, might shape a person's behavior, emotions, and self-perception. Interestingly the psychological studies of migrants from the last decade have been carried out concurrently with the emerging literary fields of transnational, postcolonial, and border studies.

While the two disciplines (literary and psychological study of migration) attempt to resolve very similar issues, the fields have remained separate—but there are some compelling interrelations that exist between them. Painting and writing, for instance, have been described as coping mechanisms for the stresses of migration. Engaging the empirical outcomes of foreign life as a theoretical apparatus to study fiction, poetry, and the writing/creative process itself, we argue that the drama realized in much expatriate writing depends to a very important degree upon the implications of cultural distance. A foreign-to-the-protagonist scenario—often read as an exotic backdrop or cosmopolitan milieu—is also a motivating factor in character action and a vehicle for dramatic irony.

There is a growing body of empirical research on the apparent phases of cultural immersion that we should bear in mind when considering American writing in and about Paris. Upon arrival in a new social context, the mover tends to experience a "honeymoon period," during which language and social obstacles are motivating rather than problematic. This stage has been described as a phase marked by "euphoria, enchantment, fascination and enthusiasm" (Eckerman et al. 2010, 124) while visitors are yet innocent to negativity related to the realities of life in the new place. "Visitors are open and curious, ready to accept whatever comes. They do not judge anything and suppress minor irritations. They concentrate on nice things . . . such as the food, landscape, people, and country" (Reisinger 2009, 217). In an artistic sense, in this context we should expect that an author's initial textual impressions of the city would be optimistic and sanguine, and later—after confronting the ills of social distance—that they would descend into more contemptuous or apathetic commentaries, possibly infused with sarcasm or cynicism.

After several months of residence, the American confronts the realities of day-to-day life in Paris—a city that has been undergoing an unprecedented demographic shift since the mid-nineteenth century. The population changes since 1870 have significantly altered the cultural, linguistic, and social environment of the urbanscape. The metropolitan area had a population of 1.8 million in 1870, a number that would swell to 3 million (9.3 million including *le petite couronne* or immediate suburbs) by 1914 (Ayers 2004, 16). By 1920 more than half the population of the capital was from the provinces and the regional identities within the city limits corresponded approximately with the rail lines termini (Jacobs 2009). "In effect, of every 100 Paris residents [in 1920], there are just 39 native-born Parisians, 50 or 51 born in the provinces, and 10 or 11 foreigners" (qtd. in Jacobs). Moreover, many of the provincial residents (until the 1930s) likely learned French in school as a second language, that is, if they spoke French at all.[10] While international migration has been shown to trigger the severe psychological strain thus far noted here, intra-national migrant cohorts also demonstrate similar outcomes.

While critics often treat the Parisian social and cultural demographic as a monolithic backdrop, amid which displaced Americans intermingle, as Walker Connor (1994) notes, "as late as World War I" throughout the political boundaries of France, many from rural areas "did not conceive themselves as members of a French nation" (154). Eugen Weber observed that as late as the first decades of the twentieth century, the country was yet "a France where many did not speak French or know (let alone use) the metric system, where *pistoles* and *écus* were better known than francs, where roads were few and markets distant, and where subsistence economy reflected the most common prudence" (Weber 1976, x). Due to the rapid migration to the capital, Paris was recently diversified by the cultures of these societies, communities that have different languages; ways of thinking, dressing, eating, and drinking; practicing religion and politics; and socializing; and these dynamics would have been retained in these ethnic enclaves of Paris.[11] Cabo and Molina argue that, like international migrants, the new Parisians would have assumed the provincial identity in Paris even "more naturally than in their places of origin" emphasizing cultural differences as a strategy to cope with the stresses of the new environment (Cabo and Molina 2009, 273).[12]

There are many noteworthy cases of provincials arriving in Paris to find the cultural distance from their place of origin as a cause of strife. Napoleon was a member of this subset, as were many authors and artists, such as Cézanne, Pisarro, Antoine Watteau, Rachilde (Marguerite Eymery), Nicolas Bergasse, Flaubert, and Louise Colet, among others. When we interpret American perceptions of Paris during these periods, we should bear in mind the transitory nature of the distinct populations of the city, which was made up in great part by peoples who were also cultural others in the capital. Employing cultural (instead of national) displacement as a register, Americans in Paris in the twentieth century were immersed in a dynamic multicultural community, one characterized by the diverse collective identities of its residents—and thus the social distance of each sector in relation to cultural norms of the metropole.

There are invisible hardships that weigh on all migrants to Paris—be they artists from the American Midwest or shopkeepers from Bretagne—and as this volume argues, these complicated resonances of social distance inform many American texts written in the city. Some seldom-cited passages from Lost Generation writers allude to these problems of expatriation, sentiments that contradict to a certain extent the common critical tones associated with Americans in Paris. Hadley Richardson, Ernest Hemingway's first wife, fought back tears as the young couple ate Christmas dinner, saying: "I didn't know Paris was [going to be] like this" (Hemingway 1985, 425). Hemingway, too, would later reflect on life in Paris with irony, writing on a notepad: "I do not know what I thought

Paris would be like but it was not that way. It rained nearly every day" (qtd. in Kennedy, 1994, 253; JFK Library item 186).

In the empirical fields foreignness is increasingly being treated as a condition that characterizes our psychological, cultural, and emotional states,[13] and its implications indeed influence the writer's craft in thematic and therapeutic senses. Writers explore foreign cities in their minds as they compose a textual consciousness. They mine their physical and social experiences of the city—their arrested or energetic acculturation—and their relational "I" is transposed through newness, otherness, and distance. What is evolving abroad is a new register, and in this way, writing is a social exercise, a signifying transmitter of belongingness to a people and, "to which people?" is a question layered by the affiliations of the past, present, and the individual's perceived future. The writing of exile often strives to constitute the author as an element within a history, and this dynamic is multicultural, connecting distance and loss but also rejuvenation and stimulation: the process of situating oneself through language on paper endeavors to heal the ruptures of distance and to express the dimensions of personal growth outside the limits of home. The writing is colored by absence and disorientation but also by adoptions (hybridizations) of new sentiments in aesthetic and cultural norms; the words and the narratives strive to depict these novel awarenesses; the texts can be understood as agencies of identification in a shifting, plastic sense of reality. Paris is the central interpretation of new reality for these writers, and inevitably, it represents a new beginning.

NOTES

1. For an in-depth discussion on the construction of collective imagery, cityscapes, and place, see chapter one of J. Gerald Kennedy's *Imagining Paris: Exile, Writing, and American Identity.*

2. In addition to Brown and Irwin's text, for more on this tendency. see: *Place and Literature* by Robert Dianotto and *Hard Facts: Setting and Form in the American Novel*, by Philip Fisher.

3. Many popular and scholarly cinemagraphic treatises that have emerged over the decades strive to locate the importance of American Paris through visual registers—such as *Midnight in Paris, Paris The Luminous Years: Toward the Making of the Modern,* and *Paris was a Woman.*

4. For more on this topic, see: *Paris in Mind: Three Centuries of American Writing on Paris,* by Jennifer Lee; *Cosmopolitan Patriots: Americans in Paris in the Age of Revolution,* by Philipp Ziesche; *Writers in Paris: Literary Lives and the City of Light,* by David Burke; *Literary Globalism: Anglo-American Fiction Set in France,* by Carolyn A. Durham; *American Expatriate Writing and the Paris Moment: Modernism and Place,* by Donald Pizer; *Becoming Americans in Paris: Transatlantic Politics and Culture between the World Wars,* by Brook L. Blower.

5. For more, see: *Geniuses Together: American Writers in Paris in the 1920s,* by Humphrey Carpenter; *Published in Paris: A Literary Chronicle of Paris in the 1920s and 1930s,* by Hugh Ford; *The Continual Pilgrimage: American Writers in Paris, 1944–1960,* Christopher Sawyer-LauCanno; *Modern Lives: A Cultural Re-Reading of the Lost Generation,* by Marc Dolan.

6. While this introduction focuses most closely on studies of psychological studies of migration and creativity, parallel investigations have been carried out on expatriate businesspeople. See, for instance, "What You Do Depends on Where You Are: Understanding Domestic and Expatriate Work Requirements Depend upon the Cultural Context" (Shin et al. 2007).

7. These circumstances have important economic consequences, particularly in technology. Some of Silicon Valley's top companies, including Google, Intel, and eBay, were founded or cofounded by immigrants.

8. See Jeffrey Herlihy-Mera's "When Hemingway Hated Paris: Divorce Proceedings, Contemplations of Suicide, and the First Drafts of *The Sun Also Rises*" in *Studies in the Novel*.

9. Some valuable peripheral studies of migrations and the psychological effects of dislocation are: *The Psychology of Culture Shock* by Stephen Bochner, Adrian Furnham, and Colleen Ward; *Acculturation: Advances in Theory, Measurement, and Applied Research* edited by Kevin M. Chun and Pamela Balls Organista; and *The Age of Migration: International Population Movements in the Modern World*, by Stephen Castles and Mark J. Miller.

10. John Merriman (2008) notes, in 1870 just 25 percent of the residents of the French political territory spoke French.

11. "France's attempts at becoming 'one and indivisible' were largely unsuccessful until well into the twentieth century" (Cabo and Molina 2009, 265).

12. While Breton, Basque, Corsican, Provencal, and other languages would have been heard colloquially around Lost Generation Paris, European and U.S. governments criminalized non-metropolitan cultural systems during the Cold War. In an attempt to homogenize popular sentiment against perceived threats from the east, regional languages were targeted: Charles De Gaulle intended to crush non-French languages like "grapes" (qtd. in Merriman 2008); Francisco Franco endeavored to re-create a Spanish society through mythic Castilian virtues, outlawing even his native tongue, *gallego*; in the United States, the number of Native Americans placed in schools in order to "civilize" them, through linguistic and other measures, peaked in the 1970s (Colmant 2000, 24–30). The systematized cultural cleansing almost decimated regional languages throughout the West. In France, 75 percent of western Bretons (and, presumably, the intra-national migrants in the capital) spoke Breton in 1945, a number that was reduced to 25 percent by 1990 (Texier and ÓNéill 2000, 1). Since the fall of the Berlin Wall, non-metropole identities and languages have been embraced throughout the West, but the marks from the past are severe.

13. "[P]erhaps home is not a place but simply an irrevocable condition" (Baldwin 1956, 119).

REFERENCES

Adato, Perry Miller, dir. *Paris: The Luminous Years—Towards the Making of the Modern*. TV movie. PBS, 2010.

Allen Woody, dir. *Midnight in Paris*. Gravier, 2011.

Ayers, Andrew. *The Architecture of Paris: An Architectural Guide*. London: Axel Menges, 2004.

Baldwin, James. *Giovanni's Room*. New York: Random House, 1956.

Benstock, Shari. *Women of the Left Bank: Paris 1900–1940*. Austin: University of Texas Press, 1987.

Bochner, Stephen, Adrian Furnham, and Collen Ward. *The Psychology of Culture Shock*. East Sussex, UK: Routledge, 2001.

Blower, Brooke Lindy. *Becoming Americans in Paris: Transatlantic Politics and Culture between the World Wars*. New York: Oxford, 2011.

Brown, Peter, and Michael Irwin, eds. *Literature and Place 1800–2000*. New York: Peter Lang, 2008.

Bruce, Brian. *Thomas Boyd: Lost Author of the Lost Generation.* Akron, OH: University of Akron Press, 2006.

Burke, David. *Writers in Paris: Literary Lives and the City of Light.* Berkeley, CA: Counterpoint, 2008.

Cabo, Miguel, and Fernando Molina. "The Long and Winding Road of Nationaliza-tion: Eugen Weber's *Peasants into Frenchmen* in Modern European History (1976–2006)." *European History Quarterly* 39 (2009): 264–86.

Carpenter, Humphrey. *Geniuses Together: American Writers in Paris in the 1920s.* New York: Houghton Mifflin, 1988.

Castles, Stephen, and Mark J. Miller. *The Age of Migration: International Population Movements in the Modern World.* New York: Macmillan, 1993.

Chun, Kevin M., Pamela Balls Organista, and Gerardo Marin, eds. *Acculturation: Advances in Theory, Measurement, and Applied Research.* Washington, DC: American Psychological Association, 2003, 139–61.

Colmant, S. A. "U.S. and Canadian Boarding Schools: A Review, Past and Present." *Native Americas Journal* 17, no. 4 (2000): 24–30.

Connor, Walker. "When Is a Nation?" In *Nationalism*, ed. John Hutchinson, and Anthony. D. Smith, 154–59. Oxford: Oxford University Press, 1994.

Cowley, Malcolm. *Exile's Return: A Literary Odyssey of the 1920s.* New York: Viking, 1934.

Dianotto, Robert. *Place and Literature.* Ithaca, NY: Cornell University Press, 2000.

Dolan, Marc. *Modern Lives: A Cultural Re-Reading of the Lost Generation.* West Lafayette, IN: Purdue University Press, 1996.

Durham, Carolyn A. *Literary Globalism: Anglo-American Fiction Set in France.* Lewisburg, PA: Bucknell University Press, 2005.

Eckerman, Ann-Katrin, Toni Dowd, Ena Chong, Lynette Nixon, Roy Gray, and Sally Johnson. *Binan Goonj: Bridging Cultures in Aboriginal Health.* Chatswood, Australia: Elsevier, 2010.

Fisher, Philip. *Hard Facts: Setting and Form in the American Novel.* New York: Oxford University Press, 1987.

Fitch, Noel Riley. *Sylvia Beach and the Lost Generation: A History of Literary Paris in the Twenties and Thirties.* New York: Norton, 1985.

Ford, Hugh. *Published in Paris: A Literary Chronicle of Paris in the 1920s and 1930s.* New York: Collier, 1988.

Greenstone, Michael, and Adam Loney. "Policy Memo: Ten Facts about Immigration." *The Hamilton Project.* Sept. 2010. www.immigrationpolicy.org/just-facts/value-added-immigrants-create-jobs-and-businesses-boost-wages-native-born-workers .

Hemingway, Ernest. *Byline Ernest Hemingway.* Ed. William White. New York: Scribner's, 1984.

———. *Dateline : Toronto.* Ed. William White. New York: Scribner's, 1985.

———. *The Ernest Hemingway Collection.* John F. Kennedy Library.

Herlihy-Mera, Jeffrey. "When Hemingway Hated Paris: Divorce Proceedings, Suicidal Tendencies, and the First Drafts of *The Sun Also Rises.*" *Studies in the Novel* 44, no. 1 (Spring 2012): 49–62.

Jacobs, Frank. "360 Urban Villages in Paris (1920)." *Strange Maps: Cartographic Curiosities.* http://bigthink.com/ideas/21413 .

Kennedy, J. Gerald. *Imagining Paris: Exile, Writing, and American Identity.* New Haven, CT: Yale, 1994.

Klapisch, Cédric, dir. *Paris.* Film. Studio Canal, 2008.

Lee, Jennifer. *Paris in Mind: Three Centuries of American Writing on Paris.* New York: Vintage, 2003.

Lutwack, Leonard. *The Role of Place in Literature.* Syracuse, NY: Syracuse University Press, 1984.

Maddux, William M. and Adam D. Galinsky, "Cultural Borders and Mental Barriers: The Relationship between Living Abroad and Creativity." *Journal of Personality and Social Psychology*, 96, no. 5 (2009): 1047–61.

McCullough, David. *The Greater Journey: Americans in Paris*. New York: Simon & Schuster, 2011.

Méral, Jean. *Paris in American Literature*. Trans. Laurette Long. Chapel Hill: University of North Carolina Press, 1989.

Merriman, John. "A Nation? Peasants, Language, and French Identity" Yale University. France Since 1871. Fall 2008. http://academicearth.org/lectures/peasants-language-french-identity .

Monk, Craig. *Writing the Lost Generation: Expatriate Autobiography and American Modernism*. Iowa City: University of Iowa Press, 2008.

Schiller, Greta, dir. *Paris was a Woman*. Film. Zeitgeist, 2003.

Pizer, Donald. *American Expatriate Writing and the Paris Moment: Modernism and Place*. Baton Rouge: Louisiana State University Press, 1996.

Reisinger, Yvette. *International Tourism: Cultures and Behavior*. Burlington, MA: Butterworth-Heinemann, 2009.

Remerowski, Ted, dir. *Legendary Sin Cities: Paris, Berlin and Shanghai*. TV series. Shanachi, 2006.

Sawyer-LauCanno, Christopher. *The Continual Pilgrimage: American Writers in Paris, 1944–1960*. Paris: City Lights Publisher, 2001.

Shin, S. J., Frederick P. Morgenson, and Michael A. Campion. "What You Do Depends on Where You Are: Understanding How Domestic and Expatriate Work Requirements Depend upon the Cultural Context" *Journal of International Business Studies* 38 January (2007): 64–83.

Texier, Marcel, and Diarmuid Ciaran ÓNéill. "The Nominoë Study of the Breton Language Compiled from Field Research." International Committee for the Defense of Breton Language (2000): http://icdbl.org/saozg/nominoe.php .

Weber, Eugen. Peasants into Frenchmen : *The Modernization of Rural France 1870–1914*. Palo Alto, CA: Stanford University Press, 1976.

Wickes, George. *Americans in Paris 1903–1939*. New York: Doubleday, 1969.

Ziesche, Philipp. *Cosmopolitan Patriots: Americans in Paris in the Age of Revolution*. Charlottesville: University of Virginia Press, 2010.

ONE

Emerson in Paris

C. R. Resetarits

Ralph Waldo Emerson visited Paris three times over the course of his life: June 20–July 18, 1833; May 7–June 2, 1848; and March 16–April 3, 1873. While his visits to England have received significant critical attention,[1] each one had a corresponding visit to Paris—and to a certain degree, the importance of these Paris stopovers, particularly his third and final stay in the city, has been overlooked by scholars. When Emerson spoke of England or London in essay or lecture, he often also spoke of Paris, in comparison or contrast, in measured admiration or sweeping judgment, and nearly always in contradiction. Emerson's famous line "Consistency is the hobgoblin of little minds"[2] holds particular relevance for his relationship with Paris. This essay, then, will examine Emerson's three visits to Paris as a narrative arc and observe how the visits figure alone and as a whole. In consideration of each visit, I rely on Emerson's journal entries and letters to garner the most immediate reaction to his experience.

In order to orient Emerson's reactions to Paris, this approach will make note of his emotional and physical state each time he left for Europe. There was a common thread: turmoil of some variety preceded each of Emerson's trips abroad. He was rarely a casual traveler and seemed often to be searching for the next insight, synthesis, or contradiction that he could use in essay or lecture. After each of the first two trips to Europe, he spent years naming and renaming, defining and redefining, the observations he had collected, weaving them into his larger American experience. Emerson's third and last trip, however, was different. For his two previous trips, he had traveled alone and picked up companions along the way. In 1873, he was accompanied by his daughter Ellen, and this final trip was, like the first, about resurrecting his fallen spirit—to keep him afloat and connected in the present.

I. JUNE 20–JULY 18, 1833

There are three aspects to Emerson's first experience of Paris that interconnect with the other two: his "revelation" at the Jardin des Plantes, his constant reference in his journals to his traveler/observer/privileged outsider status, and his pendulating feelings toward the city and his experience of it. These three experiences (or modes of comprehension)—revelation/solution, observer/privileged outsider, and ambiguity/ambivalence—became interwoven components of his Parisian experience: they informed not only his subsequent thinking about the city, but also his emotional outlook thereafter. The catalytic combination of revelatory insight, privileged observer/individual, and ambivalence that often seems at work in the best of Emerson's writing was clearly at play during Emerson's first trip to Paris and continued to inform the next two visits in surprising ways.

When Emerson arrived in Paris on May 29, 1833, he was a twenty-nine-year-old widower; his twenty-year-old wife, Ellen, had succumbed to tuberculosis only the year before. In 1829 he had graduated from the Harvard Divinity School, accepted a job as Unitarian pastor at the Second Church in Boston, and married. He was admired for his sermons at the Second Church but almost from the beginning chaffed under the burden of his ministerial duties. After Ellen died in 1831, he began to express serious doubts about some church doctrine (like communion), but even before her death he was not entirely comfortable with the mundane aspects of pastoral care, and so in 1832 he resigned from these duties.

A letter from Emerson's brother Charles to their Aunt Mary provides a salient image of Ralph Waldo in this period; on November 26, 1832, Charles writes: "Waldo is sick. His spirits droop. . . . I never saw him so disheartened" (Cabot 1887, 173). And on December 10: "Waldo is meditating a departure for Italy. . . . He is a little better. But appears to need a setting-up, which a voyage will give him. . . . Foreign skies cannot change him; yet it almost always breaks up the life of quiet progress, and transforms one's ways of thinking and behaving" (174). In a letter to his brother William, Ralph Waldo Emerson acknowledges his state and reveals that the man who replaced him at the church recommends travel and change of environment: "My malady has proved so obstinate and comes back as often as it goes away, that I am now bent on taking Dr. Ware's advice and seeing if I cannot prevent these ruinous relapses by a sea voyage" (175).

Emerson lands in Malta on February 2, 1833, and begins to work his way north through Italy, spending several months in Rome, Florence, and Venice before heading to Switzerland and then Paris. His travelling companion for much of this part of the journey is the New England artist William Allen Wall, and he visits or travels with several notable American and British travelers. In Paris it is much the same. His journals speak of "My companions, who have been in the *belle ville* before," of meeting up with his cousin Ralph Emerson, and of celebrating July 4th by dining at Lointier's "with General Lafayette and nearly one hundred Americans" (Emerson 1910, 3:155, 156, 158). Included in that "nearly one hundred Americans" are the polymath Oliver Wendell Holmes, Sr., the poet James Russell Lowell, and the artist and wit Thomas Appleton—all friends of Emerson's and part of his Harvard and Boston roots. Oliver Wendell Holmes (who was studying medicine in Paris) writes in a letter to his parents on June 29, 1833, "The more I see of French character, the more I am delighted with it. I have hardly heard an—As I was writing this, Waldo Emerson came up to see me. He had been sitting some time when I heard another knock, and in walked—James Russell!" (Morse 1896, 104).

Emerson's companions and potential companions are important counterpoises to note in this foreign context, as several of Emerson's journal entries express negativity over his status of being alone, foreign, or an observer. Admittedly, Emerson complains about Italy throughout his journals, too, but in Paris he seemed more ambiguous about his own complaints. Emerson was not just "outside" in the city, he was agitated, swinging between attraction and retreat. On first arriving in Paris, he writes in his journal, "France, France. It is not only a change of name: the cities, the language, the faces, the manners have undergone a wonderful change in three or four days. The running fight we have kept up so long with the *fierté* of postillions and padroni in Italy is over, and all men are complaisant" (Emerson 1910, 3:154). A day or two later he is feeling quite differently: "I was sorry to find that in leaving Italy I had left forever the air of antiquity and history which her towns possess, and in coming hither had come to a loud, modern New York of a place" (3:156).

There are constant references to his stranger/observer/foreigner status, sometimes a source of discomfort but often a source of wonderment:

> It were very ungrateful in a stranger to be discontented with Paris, for it is the most hospitable of cities. The foreigner has only to present his passport at any public institution and the doors are thrown wide to him. (3:156)

> If I had companions in the City, it would be something better to live in the Café and Restaurant. (3:165–66)

> [T]he evening need never hang heavy on the stranger's hands, such ample provision is made here for what the newspapers call "*nos besoins recreatifs.*" (3:167)

> [S]o many dazzling shops full of most costly articles of luxury. Indeed,
> it is very hard for a stranger to walk with eyes forward ten yards in any
> part of the city. [3:168]

While visiting "Frascati's, long the most noted of the gambling houses or hells of Paris, and which a gentleman had promised to show me" (3:169), Emerson notes, "many of the company seemed to be mere spectators like ourselves." Three further journal entries from this period are of particular interest due to their timing (just days before his revelatory experience in the Jardin des Plantes) and because of their mixed first-person/third-person tense.

From July 9: "How does everybody live on the outside of the world! All young persons thirst for a *real* existence for an object—for something great and good which they shall do with all their heart. Meantime they all pack gloves, or keep books, or travel, or draw indentures, or cajole old women" (3:159).

From July 11: "Does any man render written account to himself of himself? I think not. . . . Thus, shall I write memoirs? A man who was no courtier, but loved men, went to Rome—and there lived with boys. He came to France, and in Paris lives alone, and in Paris seldom speaks. If he do not see Carlyle in Edinburgh, he may go to America without saying anything in earnest" (3:159).

And, finally, from July 12: "Be cheerful. What an insane habit is this of groping always into the past months, and scraping together every little pitiful instance of awkwardness and misfortune, and keeping my nervous system ever on the rack. It is the disease of a man who is at the same time too idle, and respectful to the opinion of others. *Il tient son affaire*" (3:161).

There are a number of fascinating details in these three entries. One of the most obvious is their chronology in the scope of his trip; after three weeks in Paris and six months in Europe, Emerson seems ready for a turning point and agitated in pondering his true calling and future. His entry of July 9 is part indictment, part pledge, part lament. It begins with sweeping generalities: "How does everybody live on the outside of the world! All young persons thirst for a *real* existence . . . something great and good which they shall do with all their heart," and then collapses into the details of *his* current condition "pack gloves, or keep books, or travel," which he still ascribes to the objectifying and communal "All young persons."

Two days later he asks in first person if he should write a memoir and then, switching to third person, ponders "a man" who might have nothing to say in earnest. Emerson also signals a change in having lived previously in Rome with boys, in living at the moment in Paris alone, and contemplates his future travel stop in Edinburgh for a talk with Carlyle.

There is a near-mythic, man-in-formation element in each of these passages, but his singular and silent persona is particularly evocative and deliberate, suggesting that Emerson is looking for and, to a limited degree, finding, his voice.

The following day he opens his journal entry with an imperative second-person: "Be cheerful." He then proceeds to employ both first- and third-person perspectives in the next two sentences. This point-of-view switching within the same thought suggests a mind engaged at multiple levels, swinging between a variety of perspectives and moods. He asks to be more cheerful but in the next two sentences berates himself for "groping," "scraping," and keeping his nerves "ever on the rack," for being too idle and too "respectful to the opinion of others." His subsequent harsh self-judgments quickly dampen the hopeful possibilities of the initial, "Be cheerful," and lend to it a sardonic echo. The final *"Il tient son affaire"* repeats his desired hopefulness and has often been passed over by commentators. The phrase is from the poet and songwriter Pierre-Jean de Béranger, who was immensely popular and influential during his lifetime (1780–1857) but then largely faded into obscurity. Emerson would very likely have been reading him at the time. An 1833 anonymous review of Béranger's *Chansons Nouvelles et Dernières* offers a clear summary of the poetic and revelatory potential of the phrase:

> The moral sentiment or purpose which is to be developed, the image under which that sentiment is to be illustrated . . . the mechanical engine by which the scattered portions of the image are to be manufactured into a single figure, all become present to the intellect at one glance. The whole future picture is there, in smaller dimensions, like the natural objects seen through a *camera lucida*. Then the poet . . . may go to sleep again; in the expressive language of Béranger himself *"il tient son affaire."* Time and occupation cannot rob him of his idea, for it made its appearance at once, like Minerva from the brain of Jupiter, perfect and armed at all points. ("Review" 1833, 40–41)

In effect, Emerson had written an entry in which he proclaims a desire for cheerfulness, laments his depressive outlook and actions, chides himself for being too idle and too directed by the good opinion of others, and then in wording that is very French and very nearly transcendent, Emerson uses the famous Béranger phrase about openness, acceptance, and poetic inspiration. The phrase reads almost like a secular "thy will be done." It also points back to the beginning "Be cheerful" and redeems it from the irony of the decidedly melancholy admissions that follow. All told, this journal entry reads as a prayer of submission, an act of contrition, absolution, and a zen-like anticipation for inspired intervention.

Two days later, the epiphany takes place in the Muséum d'histoire naturelle (commonly referred to as the Jardin des Plantes). An extended

although condensed, quotation from the journal will illustrate, the import
of the visit and offer some tantalizing observations:

> I carried my ticket from Mr. Warden to the Cabinet of Natural History
> in the Garden of Plants. How much finer things are in composition
> than alone. 'T is wise in man to make cabinets. When I was come into
> the Ornithological Chambers I wished I had come only there. The fan-
> cy-coloured vests of these elegant beings make me as pensive as the
> hues and forms of a cabinet of shells, formerly. It is a beautiful collec-
> tion and makes the visitor as calm and genial as a bridegroom. The
> limits of the possible are enlarged, and the real is stranger than the
> imaginary. . . .
>
> In the other rooms I saw amber containing perfect musquitoes,
> grand blocks of quartz, native gold in all its forms of crystallization. . . .
> Ah! Said I, this is philanthropy, wisdom, taste—to form a cabinet of
> natural history. Many students were there with grammar and note-
> book, and a class of boys with their tutor from some school.
>
> Here we are impressed with the inexhaustible riches of nature. The
> universe is a more amazing puzzle than ever, as you glance along with
> bewildering series of animated forms. . . . Not a form so grotesque, so
> savage, not so beautiful but is an expression of some property inherent
> in man the observer—an occult relation between the very scorpions
> and man. I feel the centipede in me—cayman, carp, eagle, and fox. I am
> moved by strange sympathies; I say continually "I will be a naturalist."
>
> The Garden itself is admirably arranged. They have attempted to
> classify all the plants . . . on Jussieu's system.
>
> Walk down the alleys of this flower-garden, and you come to the
> enclosures of the animals where almost all that Adam named or Noah
> preserved are represented. . . . all manner of four-footed things in air
> and sunshine, in the shades of a pleasant garden, where all people,
> French and English, may come and see without money. . . . It is very
> pleasant to walk in this garden.
>
> As I went out, I noticed a placard posted on the gate giving notice
> that M. Jussieu would next Sunday give a public herborisation . . . and
> inviting all and sundry to accompany him. (Emerson 1910, 3:161–64)

When quoting from this passage in the journal, many critics end at "I will
be a naturalist." This line does read as the pivotal point of the entry and
goes almost verbatim into the first of the four "Natural History" lectures
Emerson gives when he returns to the States. Yet there are other considerations in this entry that have been overlooked. One concerns the com-
pleteness of the entry arc: beginning, climactic middle, exit. There is a
folksy quality to the beginning, as Emerson enters the museum, ticket in
hand, a ticket given to him by a man named Mr. Warden. In the Garden,
inside a variety of cabinets, Emerson finds new levels of classification
that lead to new levels of understanding and new ways of viewing.
Again, these are man-made cabinets, classifications, and observations.
This is a man-made Garden, and yet Emerson brings into his experience

of it the old Edenic naming of Adam and the old preservation of Noah in a typological way that places his Garden experience of the new naming via classification and new preservation via cabinets as a natural heir to that ancient, primordial Garden.

Emerson still claims his visitor/observer status, but this time the status is calming and genial, and his bridegroom metaphor suggests not only a personal reflection back to his old bridegroom/widower self, but also a new order, a new union, and movement forward. The second time he acknowledges his observer mode is as significant as the visitor/bridegroom passage because he names the union—the "occult relation between" and "strange sympathies"—of his observer mode: "Not a form [in Nature, in the Garden, in the Cabinets] so grotesque, so savage, not so beautiful but is an expression of some property inherent in man the observer. . . . I feel the centipede in me." Emerson has become a bridegroom of Nature, the Garden, the Cabinets. He "will be a naturalist," but his naturalist quest will not be the same as that of the scientists he reads or whose lectures he attends while in Paris. He will be a naturalist of those "strange sympathies" and "occult relation" rather than a naturalist of flora and fauna.

One additional aspect of this entry is, I think, worth contemplating. The first half of the entry is loaded with fabulous birds, scientific names, "animated forms," "occult relation," "strange sympathies," and then the declaration, "I will be a naturalist." After that there is a return to the perspective of a man with an appreciation of the Garden as an example *par excellence* of the classification system of M. Jussieu. Then a paragraph mentions Adam and Noah, the French and the English, and the openness of the free gardens for all to see. The paragraph ends with the minimalist, and by this time clearly understated, "It is very pleasant to walk in this garden." It is a curious passage in an entry that otherwise seems to be firmly rooted in the Jardin des Plantes, for Emerson's exuberance here spills out into the larger world, into the theological histories of another Garden and another collection of animals, in collections of "all people," or more specifically, the "French and English." This is a preview of the Emersonian circling and connecting that will be one of the hallmarks of both his form and content.

As I noted before, he ends the entry with a proper exit, "As I went out," again a rather colloquial completion of the arc. He reintroduces M. Jussieu as guide (a common folktale, mythic device) out of the old Biblical Garden and into this new world/way, this new Emersonian garden view with its new orders and connections, new ways of seeing, new beginnings.

Interestingly, there is no mention of Emerson's revelatory garden experience of July 13 in any extant letters from Paris around that time. He does, however, mention walking in the Jardin des Plantes in a letter dated June 29 to his brother William. And of more interest, perhaps, is this passage from a letter to his friends Samuel and Sarah Ripley dated July 9 — the same date as the first of the contemplative and pendulating entries fronting the July 13 Garden visit:

> If he [the poorest Frenchman] may go to this last place [the Garden of Plants] & find not-quite-all plants growing up together in their scientifick classes: then by a public placard, Jussieu gives notice that next Sunday he goes out on a botanical excursion & invites all & sundry to go with him naming the village of the rendezvous. But if the Frenchman prefer natural history of animals he has only to turn down a green land of this garden of Eden, & he shall find all manner of lions bisons elephants & hyenas the giraffe 17 feet high and all other things that are in the dictionary but he did not know were in the world. (Emerson 1939, 1:390)

On the entry from the ninth, we find material recrafted and used as "an event" four days later on the thirteenth — this journal text underscores the creation-myth crafting of the latter passage and Emerson's awareness from the start that he wasn't interested as much in science as science but in science as a subject and process for the writer. And it is Emerson the writer rather than Emerson the naturalist that uses the journal entry of July 13 as grist for his opening series of lectures on *The Uses of Natural History* upon returning to the States.

In his biography, *Emerson: The Mind on Fire*, Robert D. Richardson Jr. concludes that "Above all for Emerson on this trip, Paris meant science" (Richardson 1995, 139). To that point, then, we might ask what did *science* mean for Emerson at this time. David Robinson addresses this concern in his essay, "Emerson's Natural Theology and the Paris Naturalists," a text that began a reevaluation of Emerson's time in Paris. Robinson discusses Emerson and science in Paris in 1833:

> But the literature of classification he now sees as a second-hand substitution for the actual plants arranged in the garden. . . . It was not the idea of scientific classification itself which was so impressive to Emerson, but the physical evidence of its power to reflect truth, that truth being the unity and dynamism of nature. (Robinson 1980, 78–79)

This truth in the unity and dynamism of nature that Emerson recognized in Paris would take him a while — a writerly while — to fully work out, "his most eloquent testimony to its impact on him comes in his first public lecture after his return from Europe in November 1833" (Robinson 1980, 69). As early as the first lecture, however, he is moving toward his real interest in and use of science: its moral, transcendent, visionary, and correspondent possibilities. Discussing Emerson's first lecture back from Europe, Robinson finds "two major emphases of the lecture: his portrayal of the scientific pursuit in heroic terms, and his insistence that such a pursuit will indeed have moral implications" (81). The heroic terms are there in the ending arc of his July 13 Jardin des Plantes entry, just as the moral implications are referenced in his mention of Adam and Noah. As Stephen E. Whicher and Robert E. Spiller, the editors of his early lectures, note, "To a considerable extent, as *Nature* (1836) makes evident, his interest in science was absorbed into his interest in moral philosophy and by 1836 no longer served a special function in his thought" (Emerson 1961, 3). Or as Robinson would so eloquently put it, "the story of Emerson's experience in Paris and his emergence from that experience, explains why an Orphic poet, and not a naturalist scientist, is the hero of *Nature*" (Robinson 1980, 88).

Reviewing the journal entries of the time, we might note Béranger as well as Jussieu. This, more or less, is the focus of Lee Rust Brown in his essay (and subsequent book) on "The Emerson Museum." Rust examines the writerly method and forms that Emerson extracted from his considerations of the cabinets of natural history in the Jardin des Plantes: "Classification, as it appeared in the Muséum, was a technical form that converted everything, not only biological individuals but also the texts that represented them, into new instances of itself" (Brown 1992, 71). What Emerson and the French naturalists share with the Muséum is a "preoccupation with the hieroglyphic aspects of nature" (62). And so, if Paris meant science in 1833, and the meaning of science had evolved into something else by 1836, what might Paris mean for Emerson after that evolution? That question might best be addressed by his trip, a spontaneous and even compulsive trip, to Paris over a decade later in 1848.

II. MAY 7–JUNE 2, 1848

Between November 2, 1847, and February 24, 1848, Emerson delivered sixty-four lectures in twenty-five cities and towns in England and Scotland. Attendance was good at all the lectures and on the whole the press positive, but there were, as well, some controversies.[3] These were, on the whole, minor bumps in a generally positive tour, one that increased Emerson's prestige both in England and back home—but the tour had a wearisome schedule. After the tour, Emerson would spend the next two months in London working on a new series of lectures and being entertained by the elite—savants, artists, aristocracy, and politicos. By early April, he was already contemplating a visit to Paris in letters to his wife, Lidian: "Whether to go to France or not, I have not quite determined: I suppose I must, in all prudence; though I have no money, nor any plain way of obtaining any" (Cabot 1887, 532). The "I must" might appear somewhat out of place in this context: perhaps he felt he should visit Paris because of recent events in February when the Orleans monarchy had been overthrown and the Second French Republic created. Perhaps he was looking to expand his own view of political events beyond the British version. Or perhaps he was feeling the need for inspiration as he continued to work away on the next lecture series, feeling the need to regain more of his distinctly American stance, aware that he had been too long among the London elite and their, perhaps limiting, views. Emerson had, in fact, been advised by a good-humored Tennyson at one soiree to accompany him to Italy rather than think of going to Paris because he would "never come back alive from France" (Cabot 1887, 541). In August 1847, when he was first considering the lecture series planned for that fall, he wrote in his journal "We go to Europe to see aristocratic society with as few abatements as possible. We go to be Americanized, to import what we can" (Emerson 1910, 7:326). He had been thinking for some time about a "real" or natural aristocracy, a by-product of his ideas about "great" representative men. He had also been thinking about Fourier and his "French phalanstery." "Individualism," Emerson offered, "has never been tried" and "all that is valuable in the phalanstery comes of individualism" (7:323). Perhaps he went to Paris most of all in search of that "real aristocracy," to see what this French Republic redux might offer and to meet the very French republicans and intellectuals who had been inspired by his own writings on self-reliance and the individual.

In the 1840s, the Collège de France had developed something of a penchant for Emerson, starting with Adam Mickiewicz (the Polish poet, political writer, and Collège professor) who introduced Edgar Quinet (fellow professor, writer, and ardent republican) to Emerson's work by lending him a copy of *Nature*. By 1844, if not earlier, Quinet was making reference to Emerson in his lectures and discussing him with colleagues. Quinet compared Emerson favorably to Blaise Pascal, while French critic and intellectual Jean-Baptiste Joseph Émile Montégut referred to him as "the American Montaigne," and Mickiewicz named him "the American Socrates" (Chazin 1933, 156, 162).[4] Two French studies of Emerson came out of this enthusiasm, one by "Daniel Stern," the pen name of the infamous Comtesse d'Agoult (Franz Liszt's mistress and the mother of his children) in 1846 and the other by Montégut in 1847 (Reynolds, 25). This then might offer yet another inducement for Emerson to visit Paris and meet his French admirers. Interestingly, Emerson does not mention meeting or wanting to meet any of the individuals named above in his journals but only in letters. The first mention is in a letter to Margaret Fuller on May 31, two days before his return to London:

> I have spoiled my visit here very much by bringing my portfolio of papers to prepare lectures for London, which I go back tomorrow to read, the first on 6th June. The six will take three weeks. Then I shall be ready to go home unless I have courage enough to come back here a little while & complete my visit. I have seen almost no private society. Except De Tocqueville's family & the Comtesse d'Agout who particularly desires to see you on your return. I have heard Lamartine speak on Poland I have heard the orators of the Clubs, seen Rachel three

times on the stage But I am now just ready to begin my visit, &, according to the lost of humanity, it is time to go. (Emerson 1939, 4:78–79)

Fuller and Mickiewicz were great friends, and it may well have been Fuller who first alerted Emerson to the French reception of his work. The second mention is in a letter to his wife, Lidian, after he had returned to London: "I had one very pleasant hour with Madame d'Agout . . . and I was to see Quinet, Lamennais, and others, but I turned my back and came to London. Still, Paris is much the more attractive to me of the two; in great part, no doubt, because it yields itself up entirely to serve us" (Emerson 1939, 4: 80).

Emerson seemed to exercise meticulous attention to his association with the French republicans in his journals. Perhaps it means nothing, or perhaps he was not keen to appear to be particularly engaged. To his wife he sums up the possible attention to Quinet and others as: "but I turned my back," while to Margaret Fuller—who was already actively engaged with the revolution in Italy—he writes, "unless I have courage enough to come back here [Paris] a little while & complete my visit." Perhaps he was hoping to be one sort of man to Margaret and resigned to being a different sort with Lidian. Both letters reveal that he had been interested in meeting with his French enthusiasts but the times, and perhaps his own equivocating heart, made that difficult. These two letters, which he writes at the end of his second trip to Paris, also clearly state the affection he has for the city because "it yields itself up entirely to serve us." In 1833, his time in Paris had helped him find the portal into his new life as lecturer and natural philosopher, if not an actual naturalist. In 1848, Paris seemed to have yielded new insights to him again. To understand better what those insights were we might do well to look again at his journals.

Some of the differences between this visit and the last are striking. Perhaps the clearest of these differences is simply Emerson's attitude: he is happy to be in Paris. He has, in effect, run away to Paris. There is none of the indifferent posings or grumblings of the first trip. If he is less inclined toward the sort of big revelation of 1833, it is only because he is open and ready for a variety of revelations, readjustments, revisions. That is the raison d'être for this Paris visit. The feeling of outsider/observer, so frequent during his first visit, is greatly modified. And when he does mention "a foreigner" he seems by his very act of notice to imply a different stance for himself. Take, for example, this entry:

> It is impossible in a French *table d'hôte* to guess the social rank or the employment of the various guests. The military manners universal in young Frenchmen, their stately bow and salutation through their beards, are like their beards, a screen, which a foreigner cannot penetrate. (Emerson 1910, 7:456)

Emerson sounds more like a tour guide than a tourist here. His very act of notice and explication is indicative of a seasoned sensibility. The pas-

sage is also illustrative of another characteristic of the journal during this
Paris visit: it is full of descriptions of Emerson's view of the essence of
Frenchness, often as part of a comparison and contrast with Englishness;
and the city of Paris is compared again and again with London and found
preferable if not always practically so. The third regular element of Emerson's first visit—his pendulating feelings and doubts about his place in
the world—are transformed this visit. There is doubt but not self doubt.
Emerson is earnestly trying to perfect his understanding of London/Eng-
land/Englishness and Paris/France/Frenchness as well as his ideas about
revolt and reticence, part and wholes, individuals and communities, living amid and living above, and finally issues of language, words, and
artistry. It might seem a great many considerations for a month's worth
of Parisian impressions, but Emerson had come with a clear intent: he
was there to readjust his attitude and facilitate his writing on the series of
lectures, "Mind and Manners in the Nineteenth Century," that he would
begin upon his return to London. He was also working through the realities of the self-reliant poet/seer/lecturer/oracle, needing to live in and yet
above the world. The swings between bother and placidity, between
wanting to be separate and wanting to be integrated, were not just the
anchors of his writing but of his personality. During his second visit to
Paris, Emerson's openness to revision, his authorial voice, and the balancing act of innovative conservatism—which were to be the hallmark of the
second half of his career—cohabited productively.

Keeping these touchstone elements in mind, we might find evocative
a sample of Emerson's journal observations during his second trip to
Paris:

> I covet that which the vilest of the people possesses. . . . Madame de
> Tocqueville, who is English, tells me that the French is so beautiful a
> language, so near, concise, and lucid, that she can never bear to speak
> English. . . . Every blouse in the street speaks like an academician;
> which is not possible in England. (7:451)

> The boulevards have lost their fine trees, which were all cut down for
> barricades in February. At the end of a year we shall take account, and
> see if the Revolution was worth the trees. In Paris, the number of beg-
> gars does not compare with that in London, or in Manchester even. The
> architecture of Paris compares most favorably with that of London.
> (7:452)

> I find the French all soldiers, all speakers. . . . I find the French intensely
> masculine. I find them expressive, not reticent. (7:452–53)

> The most important word the Age has given to the vocabulary is
> Blouse. It has not yet got into the Dictionary, and even in America for a

year or two it has been of doubtful sound. . . . But, at last, the French Revolution has decided forever its euphony. (7:454)

In coming to the city, and seeing in it no men of information, you remain on the outside. . . . But all this Paris seems to me a continuation of the theatre, when I come out of the theatre, or of a *limonade gazeuse* when I come out of the restaurant. This is the famous lotus which the mariners ate and forgot their home. I pinch myself to remember mine. (7:464)

The French have greatly more influence in Europe than the English. What influence the English have is by brute force of wealth; that of the French, by affinity and talent. (7:465)

It is doubtful whether London, whether Paris, can answer the questions which now rise in the minds. 7:467)

I have been exaggerating the English merits all winter, and disparaging the French. Now I am correcting my judgment of both, and the French have risen very fast. . . . But I see that both nations promise more than they perform. They do not culminate. (7:468)

We [Emerson and A. H. Clough] now dine daily at a *table d'hôte* . . . where five hundred French *habitués* usually dine at one franc sixty centimes. Of course it is an excellent place for French grammar. Nouns, verbs, adverbs, and interjections furnished gratuitously. (7:470)

The final Paris entry for this visit is a particularly long one. At times, Emerson sounds like a travel guide, at other times like a patronizing culture critic: "The manners of the people, and probably their inferiority as individuals, make it as easy to live with them as with so many shopkeepers whose feelings and convenience are nowise to be consulted" (7:471) and "The manners of the people are full of entertainment, so spirited, chatty, and coquettish, as lively as monkeys" (7:472). There is also a final flurry of comparisons to England/London:

Paris has great merits as a city. Its river is made the greatest pleasure to the eye by the quays and bridges; its fountains are noble and copious; its gardens or parks far more available to the pleasure of the people than those of London. . . . [T]hen what a luxury is it to have a cheap wine for the national beverage as uniformly supplied as beer in England. . . . [T]he social decorum seems to have here the same rigors as in England, with a little variety in the application. . . . A special advantage which Paris has is in the freedom from aristocratic pride manifest in the tone of the society. It is quite easy for any young man of liberal tastes to enter on a good footing the best houses. It is not easy in England. (7:472)

In nearly all of his comparisons of England/London and France/Paris while in Paris, Emerson seems to favor Paris, or at least readjusts to a neutral stance. This is important to note because that stance changes once he returns to the States. In his final reflections, Emerson reveals a hint at the inner turmoil beneath his famous outer reticence: "So that on the whole I am thankful for Paris, as I am for the discovery of ether and chloroform; I like to know that, if I should need an amputation, there is this balm; and if hard should come to hard, and I should be driven to seek some refuge of solitude and independency, why, here is Paris" (7:473). Ether, amputation, driven, hard to hard, refuge—these are night-marish elements, indicative of his anxieties over the upcoming lecture series in London and, perhaps, the works and pressures he would find on returning home again. Add this "here is Paris" statement with the two contemporary passages from letters to wife Lidian and friend Margaret Fuller that started this section, and it seems clear that Emerson had come to look at Paris as a refuge, a personal refuge.

Larry J. Reynolds's study, *European Revolutions and the American Liter-ary Renaissance*, provides one of the few extended looks at Emerson dur-ing this time in Paris. Reynolds focuses on Emerson's interaction with the Republican movement, his initial sympathy with the socialists, his even-tually (and perhaps habitual) drifting above the on-the-ground details of the evolving turmoil, and how this led to the take-away message of the series of lectures he would deliver in London: "which returned to the visionary themes of his early addresses and glorified the inspired indi-vidual, aloof from the political strife of the times" (Reynolds 1988, 25). Reynolds's study also helps explain Emerson's severe turning away from his clear affection and sympathy with Paris, France, and the Second Re-public movement due to his perceptions of the Bloody June Days of 1848. The bloodshed that began on June 23 would be greatly exaggerated by the establishment London *Times* (which, as intended, dampened the fo-cus and hopes of England's own socialist proponents), and the American press would rely on the *Times* for their own view of the turmoil in France. When Emerson returned home, he would find a decidedly negative atmosphere toward French political radicalism.

Now we can return to earlier connections I noted between Emersonian thought and the French republicans and see how Emerson's aloof recom-mendations, his reluctance to be too enthusiastic about any political change, his equivocating process of deliberation might, after all, have been wise advice. As an added irony, once the conservatives regained power in France, some of them turned to Emerson's writings "to counter the enthusiasm for socialism among the people" (Reynolds 1988, 50). The affection that Emerson so clearly displays in his journal during his 1848 visit would not be revisited for nearly twenty-five years. In subsequent essays and lectures back home, Emerson would become more firmly con-vinced of the superficiality of the French Second Republic and of his own initial attraction to it. He turned his attention and focus to England and often used France only as a foil for comparisons. "In *English Traits*, he treats the French in passing even more harshly, claiming at one point that 'in France "Fraternity," "equality," and "indivisible unity" are names for assassination'" (Reynolds 1988, 43). The harshness of this change in view provides insight into Emerson as private, self-reliant person and public representative man. As private man Emerson seems to truly and honestly enjoy his visit to Paris, and he certainly seems more comfortable and connected in Paris in 1848 than he had been in 1833. As a public figure, however, he was evaluating and reevaluating his experience as means for expansion of his transcendental themes, his lecture and writing career, his audience, critics, and his place in the larger world of thinkers and representative men. When the totality of this second Paris visit is contemplated, when we consider how he experienced Paris as a haven for his psyche and yet felt the need to disparage it as an idea/ideal/entity for his public persona, we get a better measure of what Lawrence Buell once identified in his biography of Emerson as "the limit, but also the greatness, of Emersonian Self-Reliance" (Buell 2003, 106).

III. MARCH 16–APRIL 3, 1873

In the years following his 1848 lecture tour in Great Britain and visit to Paris, Emerson would come to be the most famous man of letters in America, lecturing coast to coast. As early as 1871, however, Emerson began to suffer from aphasia and memory loss. When a fire destroyed his Concord home on July 24, 1872, his sense of loss coupled with his thinking and speaking issues effectively put an end to his lecturing career. The Emersons' friends and admirers rallied around the family after the fire, donated money to help them rebuild, and convinced Emerson to take an extended vacation to Europe and Egypt, with his daughter Ellen, while his house was being rebuilt.

Emerson and Ellen stayed a few weeks in Paris on their way to Egypt in late fall of 1872, but the couple would stay longer upon their return from Egypt. The second stay figures—if only briefly—in the journals and letters. Emerson seems to be only a tourist in Paris: he is not searching for new careers or new views. And so for Emerson and Paris, the third time around was all charm and comfort. As his daughter Ellen Tucker Emerson would write in letters to her mother, "Father is in the full tide of dinners and calls, busy every moment, and likes it better than usual" (E. T. Emerson 1983, 72), or to her sister Edith, "We are both very happy in Paris" (73). And to her brother Edward, she writes of names that must have echoed rather wonderfully in her father's not always reliable memory: "Now we are starting for the Jardin des Plantes. Charles took Father there the other day and was pleased with his pleasure, and Father has gone alone several times since" (72). Emerson doesn't write very much in his journal about this Paris visit, only three little entries, but when he does write the echoes are everywhere and he seems quite content, at last, to simply be in Paris, to let it pick him up and bring him out one last time:

> In Paris, your mere passport admits you to the vast and costly public galleries. . . . Your health mends every day. Every word spoken to you is a wonderful and agreeable riddle which it is a pleasure to solve—a pleasure and a pride. Every experience of the day is important, and furnishes conversation to you who were so silent at home. (Emerson 1910, 10:414)

In each of the three visits Emerson made to Paris, he found rich sources of complaint, composure, and point of view. Each time he visited, he seemed to be looking for something, and each time the City of Light delivered; it was perhaps not what he expected, but perplexingly, even transcendentally, Paris seemed always to offer Emerson just that something he needed.

NOTES

1. See, for example, Ireland (1882). This work came out the same year that Emerson died.

2. A fuller rendition is "A foolish consistency is the hobgoblin of little minds, adored by little statesmen and philosophers and divines. With consistency a great soul has simply nothing to do." (Emerson 1983, 265).

3. For more on this, see Scudder (1935, 171–72).

4. See also Howard (1937); Howard provides a translation of the original article by "Daniel Stern," which she was able to procure from the Bibliothèque Nationale.

REFERENCES

Brown, Lee Rust. "The Emerson Museum." *Representations* 40, special issue: Seeing Science (Autumn 1992): 57–80.

Brown, Lee Rust. *The Emerson Museum: Practical Romanticism and the Pursuit of the Whole.* Cambridge, MA: Harvard University Press, 1997.

Buell, Lawrence. *Emerson.* Cambridge, MA: The Belknap Press of Harvard University Press, 2003.

Cabot, James Eliot. *A Memoir of Ralph Waldo Emerson.* Vol. 1. Boston: Houghton Mifflin and Co., 1887.

Chazin, Maurice. "Quinet as Early Discoverer of Emerson." *PMLA* 48, no. 1 (March 1933): 147–63.

Dant, Elizabeth A. "Composing the World: Emerson and the Cabinet of Natural History." *Nineteenth-Century Literature* 44, no. 1 (June 1989): 18–44.

Emerson, Ellen Tucker. *The Letters of Ellen Tucker Emerson.* Vol. 2. Ed. Edith E. W. Gregg. Kent, OH: Kent State University Press, 1983.

Emerson, Ralph Waldo. "Self-Reliance." In *Emerson: Essays and Lectures.* New York: Library of America, 1983, 257–82.

———. *The Early Lectures of Ralph Waldo Emerson.* Vol. 1 (1833–1836). Ed. Stephen E. Whicher and Robert E. Spiller. Cambridge, MA: Harvard University Press, 1961.

————. *Journals.* 10 vols. Ed. Edward Waldo Emerson and Waldo Emerson Forbes. Boston: Houghton Mifflin Co., 1910.

————. *The Letters of Ralph Waldo Emerson.* 6 vols. Ed. Ralph L. Rusk. New York: Columbia University Press, 1939.

Howard, Besse D. "The First French Estimate of Emerson." *New England Quarterly* 10, no. 3 (September 1937): 447–63.

Ireland, Alexander. *In Memoriam, Ralph Waldo Emerson: Recollections of His Visits to England in 1833, 1847–8, 1872–3, and Extracts from Unpublished Letters.* London: Simpkin, Marshall, 1882.

Morse, John T. Jr., ed. *Life and Letters of Oliver Wendell Holmes.* Vol. 1. Boston: Houghton Mifflin and Co., 1896.

"Review of *Chansons Nouvelles et Dernières* by P. J. de Béranger (Paris, 1833)." *Foreign Quarterly Review* 12 (1833): 28–49.

Reynolds, Larry J. *European Revolutions and the American Literary Renaissance.* New Haven, CT: Yale University Press, 1988.

Richardson, Robert D. Jr. *Emerson: The Mind on Fire.* Berkeley: University of California Press, 1995.

Robinson, David. "Emerson's Natural Theology and the Paris Naturalists: Toward a Theory of Animated Nature." *Journal of the History of Ideas* 41, no. 1 (January–March 1980): 69–88.

Scudder, Townsend III. "Emerson's British Lecture Tour, 1847–1848, Part II: Emerson as a Lecturer in Britain and the Reception of the Lectures." *American Literature* 7, no. 2 (May 1935): 166–80.

TWO

Je l'ai dans mon sang!

Paris in Edith Wharton's Madame de Treymes

Marta Miquel-Baldellou

Edith Wharton was scarcely six years of age when her family moved to Europe, where they would spend four years (two of which in Paris), in an attempt to compensate for the depreciation of American currency at the close of the Civil War. According to her biographer R. W. B. Lewis, while Edith could not share her parents' fondness for the French capital, she would later associate Paris with the first stirrings of her creativity. It was early on during her stay in Paris that she began storytelling, a habit she called "making up," which soon became a passion and likely the roots of her later vocation. In the autobiography Edith Wharton was to write in 1933, *A Backward Glance,* she recalled two particular episodes that stood out in the memories of her childhood in Paris: one was dining every Sunday with Henry Bedlow, an old Rhode Island friend and neighbor of the family, who would tell her fairytales and about mythology. As she described in her autobiography:

> The imagining of tales (about grown-up people, "real people," I called them—children always seemed to me incompletely realized) had gone on in me since my first conscious moments; I cannot remember the time when I did not want to "make up" stories. But it was in Paris that I found the necessary formula. Oddly enough, I had no desire to write my stories down (even had I known how to write, and I couldn't yet form a letter); but from the first I had to have a book in my hand to "make up" with. (Wharton 1933, 33)

Edith Wharton would afterward draw from these early events in Paris, when the impulse to "make up" urged her to take a book that was in reach, turn the pages and evoke whatever fancies she chose to create, adding to the illusion the fact that she could not even read yet. Later on, she would notice there was something ritualistic in this performance that came regularly and imperiously, and no matter how she tried to struggle against it, she often felt compelled to abandon the playmates that had been kindly invited to spend the day, rush to her mother and ask her to entertain them because she could not possibly skip her imperious need to "make up." Edith Wharton's father, George Frederic Jones, soon became aware of Edith's precocious tendency to turn the pages of books and thus decided to teach her how to read while in Paris; she shortly acquired the skill with remarkable ease. However, it was during the course of the following year, when the family went home to New York, that Edith's fondness for books would gain depth as soon as she discovered her father's library.

Despite the fact that Edith Wharton and her family returned to America in the summer of 1872, when she was ten years old, she had become well acquainted with France, and her early memories of Paris would significantly contribute to developing her creativity as a writer. She appeared to hint at a reason when, years later, in an essay about short fiction entitled "Telling a Short Story" (1925), she went as far as to claim that "like the modern novel, the modern short story seems to have originated—or at least received its present stamp—in France" (qtd. in White 1991, 128). From a more personal perspective, in a letter addressed to her friend Sara Norton, when Edith was to leave America for Paris again some thirty years later, she referred to her childhood stay in Paris, pointing at "the curse of having been brought up there," and as a result of this early connection having it "ineradicably in one's blood" (qtd. in Lewis 1985, 161).

At that stage, Edith Wharton had already developed a sort of intimate relationship with Paris, which would always be associated with literature and social manners, as her stay in Paris at such a young age not only initiated her into the world of letters but also granted her a great capacity for observation. Even though for the most part Wharton's childhood and adolescence would remain associated with New York and Newport, between her fifth and twenty-first birthdays she spent eight years in Europe, staying in Paris for an important part of this period. Having experienced these formative years abroad, she had insights into a great variety of manners in Europe, and correspondingly, had also acquired a sharp eye to observe the ways of her own American society when she returned from the old continent.

After these years away from her native country, Wharton confessed in her autobiography that she "had felt the nobility and harmony of the great European cities till our steamer was docked at New York" (Wharton 1933, 44), thus implying the sense of beauty she claimed to have acquired in Europe received a shock, a reaction which Carol Singley describes as "a powerful reaction to the ugliness of the city" (21). With a child's eyes, she contrasted the squalor of the New York docks in the 1870s with the glories of Rome and the architectural majesty of Paris that she had contemplated for years. In this respect, as Sarah Bird Wright (1997) argues, in the unpublished autobiography entitled "Life and I," which Edith wrote when she was only ten years old, she insisted that, at that time, she felt herself an exile in America, and often dreamed her family would eventually return to Europe. Hence, it can be argued that what Elizabeth Ammons claims to be "Edith Wharton's argument with America" began at an early age, as the writer would gradually distance herself from America through her frequent transatlantic journeys and long stays in Paris.

From her infancy, Edith Wharton had grown accustomed to New Yorkers who either arrived from abroad or embarked on a European tour, thus she assumed that New Yorkers generally remained in close and constant contact with the land of their ancestors. However, when she married Edward Robbins Wharton and moved to Boston, she became acquainted with a community of wealthy and sedentary citizens who surprisingly showed no desire to cross the Atlantic and retain their roots. In these new surroundings, Wharton became progressively aware of the social change that was taking place in the United States, since, as Janet Beer Goodwyn claims, the community of old New York families from which Edith Wharton came was doomed to disappear under the weight of a capitalistic society. As happens with Lily Bart in *The House of Mirth*, Edith Wharton began to feel like a product of her heredity and the historical moment which would eventually give rise to American materialism and the ensuing waste of human and spiritual resources.

Between the years 1885 and 1905, Edith Wharton's bicontinental habitation strengthened her concepts of native and foreign mind-sets. She was frustrated at the sharp contrast between both civilizations and noticed how the disadvantages of each nation highlighted the positive points of the other. In a letter to her friend Sara Norton, she said that she would gladly give up all that fine civilization, meaning Paris, for the spring flowers of Lenox (Lewis 1985, 146). In 1905, the same year as the letter, Edith Wharton's highly acclaimed and eminently American novel, *The House of Mirth*, came to light. While the action is entirely set in New York, the characterization of the heroine, Lily Bart, is an individual in conflict with her environment. In this respect, Blake Nevius (1976) described *The House of Mirth* as a naturalist representation of the victimizing effect that an environment may have on the individual, to the extent of comparing Lily Bart's conflict with her native environment with that of the heroine in Gustave Flaubert's *Madame Bovary*, whom Nevius identifies as "the spiritual godmother of Lily Bart" (1976, 56), thus identifying a French heroine as Lily Bart's most blatant precedent.

Critics like R. W. B. Lewis and Sarah Bird Wright claim that the years immediately following the publication of *The House of Mirth* were decisive for Wharton's final expatriation from her native country. In 1907, Edith Wharton and her husband moved into the Louis XIV hotel—the Paris apartment of the Vanderbilt's—at 58 Rue de Varenne, in the elite Parisian Faubourg of Saint Germain. Her exile, however, was not complete until she departed from the New York Mount for the last time in 1911. Her journeys to New York from Paris from 1907 to 1911 were mainly characterized by ambivalent feelings. After many months in Paris, the Mount and her American friends, especially Henry James, reconciled her to her native country, but simultaneously, she was also beginning to consider the possibility of a divorce from her husband. The subsequent sale of her American home moved her toward settling down in Paris for good. Once the Mount had been sold and she proceeded with the divorce, Paris became her permanent home, as she would only return to America on two more occasions: in 1913, for the wedding of her niece Beatrice Jones, and in 1923, to receive an honorary degree from Yale University.

Edith Wharton was still hesitant to make her expatriation permanent. According to Percy Lubbock, Wharton went to live in Paris not as an exile, but in order to enjoy France. There she became acquainted with the best society—and she also found intellectual liberty (Lubbock 1947, 50). Nonetheless, as R. W. B. Lewis claims, Wharton remained quintessentially American for the most part, as she never seemed to adopt the manners and the identity of Europeans. During her youth in France, Edith Wharton had become fluent in French and had succumbed to the intellectual stimulation of France, to the extent that, according to Sarah Bird Wright, she embraced France so passionately that she thought it a perverse component of destiny that she had not been born French. Benedict Anderson refers to the "anomaly of nationalism," regarding nationality as a cultural artifact that gathers an imagined political community, commands profound emotional legitimacy, and ultimately turns chance into destiny. And yet, unlike her close friend and compatriot Henry James, she never entertained the idea of relinquishing her American nationality. Edith Wharton's vast knowledge of the French culture entitled her to assimilate into France, but she also refused to be an exile of that inclination. In this respect, Sarah Bird Wright claims that Edith Wharton belonged to an imagined community in America, displaced to France, whose cultural hegemony transcended the borders of geography and nationhood (Wright 1997, 33). Wharton envisioned the United States as the country that held absolute sovereignty over her, even if her infatuation with Paris and her immersion in the French society was to last for a lifetime.

In 1907, when she settled in the Parisian quarter of Saint Germain, Wharton was in her forties. The author had become a popular name in this Parisian quarter, and her French friend Paul Bourget soon introduced her to the social and intellectual circles so that she could obtain her first glimpses of the social, artistic and intellectual milieu of the time. During this first period, according to R. W. B. Lewis, Wharton projected the image of a woman with unusual self-control, even displaying a remarkable air of restraint and repression in Paris that she seemed to lack in The Mount; thus implying Paris had brought about these subtle changes in behavior. Wharton confessed her awkward feelings, though, celebrating her birthday in a place she considered to be her new home, despite the fact it was inevitably foreign. Likewise, she would soon make new acquaintances among Parisians while she also caught up with the old friends she had made during her previous but shorter stays in Paris. Wharton gradually began to feel that the city of Paris, and particularly the Faubourg Saint Germain, might be the place to which she belonged, since her initial aversion vanished. She also became aware that the Parisian Faubourg of Saint Germain, rather than merely a geographical setting, was also the seat of the most distinguished French nobility and aristocracy, a set who welcomed intellectuals and important artists.

Paris was at the time in the midst of the so-called belle epoque, which would last until the outbreak of the Great War in 1914. This period was characterized by social stability and a special concern for preserving class distinctions. Edith Wharton believed the Saint Germain Faubourg was a suitable combination of privacy and easy access to intellectual and social life. From her room at the Rue de Varenne, she could easily feel part of this milieu, while she also noticed that, as a foreigner, she was necessarily removed from certain circles. We see similar feelings of belonging and detachment in her portrait of Fanny de Malrive, an American-born marquise in her novella *Madame de Treymes*, which was the first literary output resulting from her initiation into the Parisian society. Together with her friend Henry James, Wharton became particularly interested in literary works which analyzed transatlantic relations; in Millicent Bell's view, her interest in Franco-American cultural comparisons was even more objective than that of James, as hers responded to "the precise observation of real manners" (Bell 1995, 5).

In *Madame de Treymes*, Fanny Frisbee, who bears some resemblances to Edith Wharton herself, appears to be lively and dashing during her youth in New York, when she meets her suitor, John Durham. Nonetheless, when she marries a French nobleman and moves to live in Paris as Fanny de Malrive, she begins to feel repressed due to the contradictory forces of Faubourg society. Even though Fanny de Malrive has been enriched by her perceived refinement, she has also been damaged by these influences—as John Durham, her former American suitor, who visits her in Paris, notes that there is "some vast impersonal power, controlling and regulating her [Fanny's] life in ways he could not guess" (Wharton 1995, 4). R. W. B. Lewis has noted that Fanny de Malrive represents Edith Wharton's Paris experience, as she, like the character, had escaped New York to be imprisoned within a devastating marriage from which she desperately strives to be released. In an attempt to gain freedom and marry her American suitor John Durham, she asks her powerful sister-in-law, Madame de Treymes, for help, only to discover that such freedom has a fatal cost.

John Durham finds himself caught between "his own lamentable New York" (Wharton 1995, 1) and the radiance of Paris, which he describes as what might be "the most beautiful city in the world" (2). Likewise, he also makes it clear that his attraction to or repulsion from Paris is entirely dependent on his courtship of Fanny de Malrive. Durham made the acquaintance of Fanny Frisbee in New York, but it is precisely in Paris, in the midst of this foreign environment, that he becomes aware of the changes she has undergone. He begins to realize it is precisely her foreign quality, the sense of difference that Fanny Frisbee has acquired as Fanny de Malrive, which draws him toward her. From the beginning, John Durham identifies Paris with Fanny de Malrive, and his progressive appreciation of the city develops on the basis of their relationship. Through the lens of cultural dislocation, everything seems to acquire a specific significance that he could not possibly perceive in his own country. As a case in point, he considers his walk with Fanny along the streets of Paris particularly meaningful, whereas he admits it would be regarded as a fairly unimportant event in New York.

Conversely, Fanny de Malrive feels attracted toward John Durham and his family precisely because of their Americanism. After spending an important period in Paris detached from her compatriots, Fanny rejoices in the possibility of taking tea with the Durhams—she even considers it an important event, as it grants her the opportunity to be with "dear, good, sweet, simple, real Americans again" (5). Fanny declares she feels safe with them, while John Durham progressively gains insight into the charms of a sophisticated society, its complicated beauty, and its double-faced possibilities. Despite having spent fifteen years away from her native country, Fanny states she becomes a better American every day even from afar, although she never considers the possibility of going back, especially after the separation from her husband, as it is agreed she must live in France on account of her son.

Even if Durham has recently arrived in Paris and Fanny de Malrive has lived in the French capital for fifteen years, they necessarily both perceive the city from a foreign perspective. Durham is thrilled to unravel the complexities of a new, strange society, while Fanny is required to imbibe the conventions and regulations put upon her through a close-knit Parisian social circle because she married a French marquis. Consequently, even though they are both Americans in Paris, their respective degree of commitment to the Parisian society, as well as their level of cultural dislocation in a foreign environment, differs to a remarkable extent. As a more gifted connoisseur of French ways, Fanny de Malrive often initiates Durham into French society, especially when he unveils his intention to marry her once she obtains the divorce. Although Fanny seems to hold on to the illusion of "being once more American among Americans" (17), when Durham proposes to her, she is also well aware of the fact she has undergone an important change, acknowledging she is no longer Fanny Frisbee. During the time she has spent living in Paris, she has been shaped by her experiences, thus becoming somehow Frenchified. In her encounters with John Durham, Fanny de Malrive admits she is now part of this new circle, acknowledging she belongs to them. As such, she is well aware of the mysterious solidarity of this new social group, and she soon draws Durham's attention to this, knowing it would surely puzzle him as an American:

> That is what I meant when I said you could never understand! There is nothing in your experience—in any American experience—to correspond with that far-reaching family organization, which is itself a part of the larger system, and which encloses a young man of my son's position in a network of accepted prejudices and opinions. Everything is prepared in advance—his political and religious convictions, his judgements of people, his sense of honour, his ideas of women, his whole view of life. (11)

The important role that the family as an institution plays in the French society is perceived as the major deterrent to Fanny's divorce. It would ultimately deprive her of her son. Aware of the intricate machinations exerting control over all the members of this community, Fanny hopes to keep her son away from what she perceives to be a terrible influence, as she knows his adherence to her French relatives would surely determine her son's fate for life. Fanny's confession to her French relatives (regarding her son) baffles Durham, because, as an American, he judges the influence of Fannie's French relatives as an inconceivable reason not to follow one's individual desires. Durham is well aware that the French laws sanction divorce, and looking into the issue from an outsider, he is unable to perceive the problematic situation his potential wife is facing.

Fanny de Malrive's French society is reminiscent of the kind of culture Edith Wharton encountered when she lived in the Parisian quarter of Saint Germain. In her autobiography, Wharton stated that, as a stranger and a newcomer, she "enjoyed a freedom not possible in those days to the native-born" (Wharton 1933, 258), although she also admitted it took her some time to acquire the rudiments of a so-called "unwritten law" she perceived to be at work in all their social gatherings. Consequently, as a non-native, at first she was not required to follow these social conventions, but later she gradually felt the need to acknowledge them so as to fit within the French society.

In *Madame de Treymes*, Paris is presented as a city of ordered beauty. The place seems to embody the European experience, as a homage to history and culture. John Durham gets acquainted with Paris through Fanny de Malrive's eyes, and he soon establishes a sort of symbiotic relationship between the city of Paris and Fanny; he perceives Paris and its society entirely through Fanny's response and the prospects of their future union. Durham's growing attraction to her arises as a result of her European experience. He perceives Fanny to be mature and accomplished, having acquired the complexities and intricacies that characterize French society. Fanny thus displays qualities she appeared to lack when she resided in her native country, and these render her more attractive from Durham's American perspective.

Janet Beer Goodwyn has argued that language arises as a recurrent metaphor in the text, as the lexical uses—mainly those of the law and the church—are constantly applied and misapplied, and there seems to be neither any room for individual use or interpretation, nor any possibility for translation or even understanding on the part of the foreigner or the outsider. Gaining insight into the common ways of communication pertaining to the Parisian society may grant outsiders access, even if no sort of intimacy, within the Faubourg Saint Germain. In the course of his interactions with Fanny de Malrive, and especially, with members of the Parisian society, John Durham is exposed to some details of social conduct, and the frequent and unproblematic use of silence—or lack of language—arises as one of its most striking features. Durham acknowledges Fanny must have learned the ways and the meanings of silence during her long stay in Europe, thus admitting "it was a part of her long European discipline that she had learned to manage pauses with ease" (Wharton 1995, 4). Durham thus realizes Fanny Frisbee has undergone a clear transformation, which can be perceived as a sort of transculturation. She even seems to acquire a different personality as Fanny de Malrive; she has become a refined product of the foreign society as a result of her marriage. Durham's sister also notices Fanny looks significantly different, and ultimately admits she "never saw anything so French!" (21). Likewise, even Durham gains awareness into Fanny de Malrive's "exotic enjoyment of Americanism" (22), which proves her gradual detachment from her native culture as well as her cultural adoption into the foreign community.

As a result of her immersion in French culture, Fanny de Malrive introduces Durham into her social circles, and thus, plays the role of a social and cultural mediator. In relation to language, Fanny advises Durham to give importance to silence in the Faubourg society, encouraging him to "look for the truth always in what they don't say" (56). From an outsider's perspective, the Parisian society is often perceived as impenetrable, complex, and even oppressive owing to its intricate rules and unspoken statements, and Durham's impotence is finally voiced when he exclaims "your French justice takes a grammar and dictionary to understand" (80). An American is thus perceived as unable to unravel the complexities and idiosyncrasies of the Parisian community.

The aura of mystery to French society is ratified by the complex system of communication they use but also by the effective metaphor of light and darkness in relation to both American and French citizens. As Janet Beer Goodwyn argues, the social gatherings of Parisians are often described in shades of darkness and take place in stifling, though luxurious, enclosures, whereas when Americans interact, they are generally surrounded by a metaphorical dazzling light in the open air. In this respect, when Durham approaches the Hôtel de Malrive, located beyond the Seine, his attention is first drawn to the "shutters closed to the silence of the high-walled court" (Wharton 1995, 71), thus associating the hotel with an antique order of things, old national prejudices, and even a past period of feudalism. Conversely, when Fanny de Malrive visits the Durhams, she feels safe again among her compatriots, stating that Durham's mother takes her back into "that clear American air where there are no obscurities, no mysteries" (14). The effective and recurrent use of this metaphor emphasizes, on the one hand, how complex and impenetrable the Parisian society can become for outsiders, and on the other hand, the nostalgic emotions awakening when American compatriots living far from their native country get together.

In addition to Fanny de Malrive, John Durham also holds frequent interviews with his cousins, the Boykins, a married American couple who have lived in Paris for twenty-five years. The Boykins are described as exiled Americans who clearly state their reluctance to thrust themselves into French society. Even if they have lived in Paris for an extended period of time, they hold on to their Americanism, giving shape to a sort of American colony in Paris:

> In the isolation of their exile they had created about them a kind of phantom America, where the national prejudices continued to flourish unchecked by the national progressiveness: a little world sparsely peopled by compatriots in the same attitude of chronic opposition toward a society chronically unaware of them. (27)

The Boykins are well aware that, even if they are granted access to the Faubourg society, they will never belong. As opposed to John Durham's mother, who keeps a tourist's view of the European continent and frequently regards it as a vast museum, the Boykins have been exposed to the French society, and thus, have acclimated to Faubourg ways. Conscious of how Parisians perceive foreigners, the Boykins reiterate their will to remain apart from this social circle, arguing Parisians only take them into consideration to give money in their charity bazaars. This apparent exclusion contributes to strengthening their sense of Americanism as well as reinforces their skepticism toward Parisians. Both communities often interact with each other, and the Boykins are also welcome to take part in some social gatherings, while surmounting their difference with respect to the rest of the Faubourg community.

In Edith Wharton's novella, John Durham has so far gained insight into two different ways of coping with expatriation. The Boykins acknowledge their lack of integration into the Parisian community; giving shape to a sort of isolated American colony detached from the French and resorting to their own American values while living in France. Conversely, Fanny de Malrive has literally and metaphorically married into the Parisian society, having sworn allegiance to her newly acquired French identity, and thus becoming part of the social circle of the Faubourg Saint Germain. Having acquired a privileged position within the French society as the wife of a marquis, Fanny de Malrive has gained insight into the complexities underlying the French community, and as an American well-acquainted with the French culture, she initiates her puzzled compatriot John Durham into the intricacies of the French ways. As a connoisseur, Fanny is well aware that her French family would never consent to a divorce since, even though the French laws allow legal separations, their Catholicism makes divorce an impossibility. Moreover, having acquired the principles regulating the French community, Fanny knows she may risk her right to keep her son if she dares divorce her husband. Precisely because of the importance attached to the family in the Faubourg society, Fanny believes only her sister-in-law, Madame de Treymes, may intercede for her as a mediator to reach an agreement with her French relatives and thus be permitted to divorce.

Despite the fact Madame de Treymes is not the actual heroine in Edith Wharton's novella, her latent presence becomes paramount as she personifies the French community, and by extension, the city of Paris itself. Madame de Treymes embodies a pervasive social power and influence that extends everywhere. She is genuinely French, and thus, John Durham admits that, in her presence, the Frenchified Fanny de Malrive becomes the American Fanny Frisbee again, as her newly acquired French ways are necessarily overshadowed by Madame de Treymes's genuine Parisian manners. Being a native Parisian, she approaches the community of Americans living in Paris with caution and with "the unblinking attention of a civilized spectator observing an encampment of aborigines" (Wharton 1995, 23). Admitting that the Durhams are the first actual Americans she has ever become acquainted with, she feels curious and even inquisitive to learn of their ways as an entirely different race, thus approaching a sort of contact zone, to use Mary Louise Pratt's term. When Durham requests her help in getting consent for Fanny's divorce, Madame de Treymes declares herself to be Fanny's friend, and correspondingly, she feels glad to offer her help and thus aid Durham in his purpose. Nonetheless, the interviews held between John Durham and Madame de Treymes underlie a series of misunderstandings as Durham takes Madame de Treymes' words at face value, and is unable to gain insight into their real meaning, and especially the meaning of her continuous lapses into silence, and what is ultimately left unsaid.

Durham's bafflement becomes evident as he comprehends his failure to understand Madame de Treymes's reasoning and behavior, precisely because he perceives them as very different from his own. Making use of her habitual undertones, she offers Durham the possibility of persuading her family into a divorce, provided that he pays off the debts her lover, Prince d'Armillac, has incurred. Consequently, for the most part, Madame de Treymes is mainly characterized through ambivalence. She appears as an obliging and highly respected woman, eager to assist Durham and Fanny in their endeavors but, as a Parisian as well as a privileged member of the Faubourg, she is also profoundly committed to the rules and conventions underlying her community, which she believes take precedence over any individual will. In this respect, Durham would eventually know Madame de Treymes's overt consent to a divorce truly responds to her ultimate pledge to safeguard the interests of the community.

Knowing about the Parisian ways ruling the Faubourg, Fanny's skepticism with respect to Christiane's initial acceptance of her divorce seems understandable and even justified. However, encouraged by Durham's American confidence and her renewed exposure to her long-forgotten Americanism, she feels exultant at apparently having regained her freedom, along with her own native perspective and way of thinking. In this sense, hopeful that she may easily obtain the divorce, Fanny also feels free to release herself from the French community to which she has belonged for the past several years, admitting "her coming liberation had already freed her from the garb of a mental slavery" (Wharton 1995, 69). Despite Fanny's exultation, Durham admits his perplexity at Madame de Treymes's consent to the divorce, since he finally refused to accept her request. It is not until their last encounter that Christiane unveils that she finally agreed to the divorce. She is well aware that if Fanny was to remarry, they may easily claim custody over Fanny's son and raise him according to their French values. Consequently, Madame de Treymes's ultimate confession immediately leads Durham to view his marriage to Fanny as implausible, knowing Fanny would never remarry at the cost of being deprived of her son. Christiane de Treymes thus tries to convince Durham to remain silent, marry Fanny, and never let her know about it, hence enticing him to use silence in her own French way, which Durham, being American, necessarily condemns and abjures.

Despite her apparent nonchalance, in the course of the interactions with John Durham, Madame de Treymes gradually reveals her vulnerability and weaknesses. She confesses her adultery and also gives vent to her misery when she is informed that her lover, Prince d'Armillac, has been obliged to leave France to escape arrest for his gambling debts. Although Madame de Treymes personifies social power and influence, and she is committed to the welfare of the community, she also appears as a victim of the same regulations she supports and defends. During the last encounter with Durham, she reveals her machinations and intrigues, and even allows Durham to know about the consequences that may arise as a result of Fanny's divorce. In this sense, as a result of her acquaintance and social intercourse with Americans, Madame de Treymes is able to gain insight into a different perspective and approach to the world, focusing on the will of the individual rather than the welfare of the community, and ultimately acquiring a more humanized appearance—becoming in the process Christiane instead of Madame de Treymes. Consequently, Madame de Treymes arises as an eminently tragic character, since Durham ultimately seems to understand her motivations and even feel some sort of sympathy for her.

These series of complex interactions, misunderstandings, and attempts at reaching a balance between both communities reflect, as Janet Beer Goodwyn admits, the complicated beauty of Paris as a mirror image of the attitudes and beliefs of a whole community, mainly characterized by solidarity and tradition. This framework embodies a network that pervades all aspects of social life. John Durham thus feels entrapped in a labyrinth of social intrigue, moving smoothly from attraction to deception, and finally conforming to a principle that is taken for granted within the French community. This ultimate renunciation, in David Holbrook's words, makes him an example of Edith Wharton's "unsatisfactory" men. Hence, from the perspective of an outsider, John Durham learns that coming to terms with the Parisian community involves either faithful allegiance or utter exclusion. Once the individual has become part of the community and has acknowledged its regulations, it becomes nearly impossible to forsake his commitment to the group. In this respect, Fanny de Malrive's marriage sanctions her alliance with the Faubourg group, and the implausibility of a divorce excludes Durham from the intricacies and complexities of the Parisian set that had initially drawn him to Fanny.

According to Katherine Joslin, Edith Wharton's novels from *The House of Mirth* to *The Age of Innocence* mostly stress the bonds demanded from the individual by the social group, inasmuch as protagonists from Lily Bart to Newland Archer must learn the coded meanings and values of a culture in order to be able to exert any sort of control over their own destinies. Nonetheless, it is often the case that these heroes and heroines are often unable or unwilling to read and interpret these coded meanings, and therefore, Edith Wharton's novels often focus on the lives of those individuals that find themselves at odds with the larger community. In this sense, as Katherine Joslin claims, feeling expatriate everywhere, in a foreign community and in one's native culture, arises as the most frightening fate for the individual. In *Madame de Treymes*, Fanny de Malrive is caught between her native Americanism and her newly acquired alliance with the Parisian Faubourg as a result of her marriage. She faces the dilemma of choosing between marrying Durham, that is to say, going back to her roots as an American, or rather keeping her son, thus symbolizing her apparently unbreakable union to the French community. Fanny de Malrive is thus caught between two cultures, and her crucible seems to reflect Edith Wharton's complex position in relation to her native New York and the city of Paris, which began to gain depth and complexity at the time she published this novella.

Living abroad and being a foreigner—but brought up in Paris and having it in her blood, as she would say—Edith Wharton may have shared the feelings of most of the characters featured in her novella. Like the Boykins, even if she would always consider herself American and never relinquish her nationality, she necessarily began to lose touch with her native country, especially after her divorce from her husband in 1913 and the outbreak of World War I. She therefore held on to the old New York of her childhood and her youth. Likewise, Edith Wharton's initial self-restraint in the Faubourg Saint Germain and her process of adaptation are also reminiscent of those of John Durham, being at odds to gain true insight into the ways of the French and, necessarily, feeling excluded from certain circles as a foreigner. Nonetheless, Fanny de Malrive's situation is certainly most remindful of that of Edith Wharton, as being brought up in Paris, she would spend the rest of her life in the French capital, feeling it was truly the place she belonged, even if she would never renounce her American roots.

As Edith Wharton would mention in her autobiography years later, despite any evident social conventions underlying the Parisian Faubourg Saint Germain, as a stranger as well as a newcomer, she enjoyed a liberty that seemed unattainable to the native-born Parisians. Likewise, she immediately felt widely accepted as a writer, stating that there lay precisely one of the most obvious distinctions between the social worlds of New York and Paris, claiming that "in Paris no one could live without literature, and the fact that I was a professional writer, instead of frightening my fashionable friends, interested them" (Wharton 1933, 261). In Paris, Edith Wharton enjoyed a privileged position within French society in addition to an important sense of freedom she appeared to lack in her native country. In this respect, even though she had met the American journalist and Paris correspondent to the London *Times* Morton Fullerton in the United States through her dear friend Sara Norton, it was precisely in Paris that their affair gained depth and was consummated, as Edith Wharton declared to be in love for the first time there when she was in her mid-forties. Conversely, Edith Wharton's husband gradually realized he was unable to fit in Paris, and due to his continuous health problems, mainly nervous depression, he often went back to his native country, unable to compete with his wife's fondness of French society and her success in adapting to French ways.

As a writer as well as an attentive observer of her new reality, Edith Wharton was able to perceive in what ways the French social order differed from that she had known in America. Her perspective as an outsider enabled her to gain insight into the Parisian ways, feeling able to perceive the foreign culture with a certain degree of objectivity. In this respect, when she had lived for more than ten years in Paris, Edith Wharton wrote a series of articles about French society so as to instruct Americans in French culture. These essays were collected in a volume entitled *French Ways and Their Meaning* (1919) whereby, in addition to showing her knowledge about France and the French, she also presented her ideas about her own native culture in comparison. In the preface to these articles, Edith Wharton declared there were two ways of judging a foreign nation, which were mainly either at first sight, in the manner of a passing traveler, or soberly and advisedly, after having resided for some time in that nation. Since she would identify herself with the second judgment, her reflections must be taken as those of a connoisseur, to the extent that critics like Adam Gopnik have argued in relation to Edith Wharton that "no American writer ever grasped quite so well the dynamics of French society" (Gopnik 2004, 211). In this sense, owing to this knowledge, in addition to *French Ways and Their Meaning* (1919), Edith Wharton also published two more nonfiction works having France and the French as a main point of focus: *A Motor-Flight through France* (1908), which was her first French travel book, and *Fighting France, from Dunkerque to Belfort* (1915), arising from her experience during World War I in France.

As a result of her everlasting connection with Paris, Edith Wharton not only gained insight into the differences and similarities between both nations, but as a woman writer, she also paid close attention to the differences arising between women in both countries. As a case in point, in a chapter within *French Ways and Their Meaning* focusing on the New French woman, Wharton firmly establishes a difference between French women and her compatriots in relation to their social roles before and after marriage. In Edith Wharton's view, in America, an unmarried girl is granted complete freedom and is enabled to interact with boys of her age, whereas once she is married, and thus she acquires her own responsibilities, she is completely "withdrawn from circulation" (Wharton 1919, 115). Conversely, in France, young girls are often kept under restriction, but after their marriage, not only are they granted social freedom, but their opinion is well considered by their husbands as well as highly esteemed in society. In this respect, Edith Wharton concluded that "the French woman is distinctly more grown up than her American sister" (120). In this respect, as an American as well as a foreigner well-acquainted with French culture, Edith Wharton gained insight into the freedom and power French women often enjoyed as opposed to their American counterparts in the New York of her youth. In her early novella depicting French society once she had already settled in Paris, Edith Wharton's portrait of Madame de Treymes illustrates the social influence and power this character is able to exert as a married French woman, while her American counterpart, Fanny de Malrive, is left at the mercy of her French relatives. As Katherine Joslin argues, Edith Wharton thus moved to Paris to flee the restrictions placed on women and attach herself to a new community of thinkers and writers where, even if she was to remain an expatriate, she was also permitted to give free vent to her creativity and gain a deeper insight not only into Parisian culture as well as into her native nation, but also into her own creativity as a writer.

REFERENCES

Ammons, Elizabeth. *Edith Wharton's Argument with America*. Athens: University of Georgia Press, 1980.

Anderson, Benedict. *Imagined Communities: Reflections on the Origin and Spread of Nationalism*. London: Verso, 1991.

Bell, Millicent, ed. *The Cambridge Companion to Edith Wharton*. Cambridge: Cambridge University Press, 1995.

Goodwyn, Janet Beer. *Edith Wharton: Traveller in the Land of Letters*. New York: St. Martin's Press, 1990.

———. *Kate Chopin, Edith Wharton and Charlotte Perkins Gilman: Studies in Short Fiction*. Houndmills, UK: Palgrave Macmillan, 2005.

Gopnik, Adam, ed. *Americans in Paris: A Literary Anthology*. New York: The Library of America, 2004.

Holbrook, David. *Edith Wharton and the Unsatisfactory Man*. London: St. Martin's Press, 1991.

Joslin, Katherine. *Edith Wharton*. London: Macmillan, 1991.

Lewis, R. W. B. *Edith Wharton: A Biography*. New York: Fromm International, 1985.

Lubbock, Percy. *Portrait of Edith Wharton*. New York: Appleton-Century, 1947.

Nevius, Blake. *Edith Wharton: A Study of Her Fiction*. London: The University of California Press, 1976.

Pratt, Mary Louise. *Imperial Eyes: Travel Writing and Transculturation*. London: Routledge, 2009.

Singley, Carol J., ed. *A Historical Guide to Edith Wharton*. Oxford: Oxford University Press, 203.

Wharton, Edith. *Fighting France, from Dunkerque to Belfort*. New York: Scribner's Sons, 1915.

———. *French Ways and Their Meaning*. New York: Appleton, 1919.

———. *A Backward Glance*. 1933. Reprint, New York: Charles Scribner's Sons, 1964.

———. *The Age of Innocence*. 1920. Reprint, New York: Macmillan, 1987.

———. *The House of Mirth*. 1905. Reprint, New York: Vintage, 1990.

———. *A Motor-Flight through France*. 1908. Ed. Mary Suzanne Schriber. Reprint, DeKalb: Northern Illinois University Press, 1991.

———. *Madame de Treymes*. 1907. Reprint, London: Penguin Books, 1995.

White, Barbara A. *Edith Wharton: A Study of the Short Fiction*. New York: Twayne, 1991.

Wright, Sarah Bird. *Edith Wharton's Travel Writing: The Making of a Connoisseur*. London: Macmillan, 1997.

THREE

Forget Paris

*Sherwood Anderson and the
American Expatriate Grotesque*

Carl Miller

Sherwood Anderson generally merits brief mention in biographical studies of the American expatriate literature in Paris, with his inclusion being
as predictable as his marginalization. The year of Anderson's first trip to
Paris—1921—stands as perhaps the pinnacle of his literary career. The
critical success of *Winesburg, Ohio* (1919) and *Poor White* (1920) had recently solidified his literary reputation within both American and European artistic circles, with H. L. Mencken writing that Anderson's writing
"embodies some of the most remarkable writing done in America in our
time. . . . Nothing quite like it is to be found in our literature" (Anderson
1919, 163). Later that year, Anderson was named the initial winner of the
prestigious Dial Award,[1] and his own critical talents were soon validated
in his early championing of the two most transcendent American expatriate writers in Paris: Gertrude Stein and Ernest Hemingway.

At the same time, though, Anderson was forty-five years old when he
first arrived in Paris—largely disqualifying him from a place among the
so-called Lost Generation—and had already produced the most critically
acclaimed works of his career. While his time in Paris was highly memor-
able, he spent only a few months there in his lifetime and, by the time of
his second—and final—trip there in 1927, his writing would come to be
overshadowed by that of his Parisian acquaintances and protégés. By
1951, Irving Howe would write that "no one can deny that our present
world is closer to Hemingway than to Anderson" (Howe 1951, 256), and

35

this statement holds all the more true today. As a result, it is easy to dismiss Anderson as a compulsory footnote in the American expatriate movement of the 1920s.[2]

In spite of this, Anderson's contribution to American literature in Paris is both highly significant and subtly complex, with his practice marked simultaneously by artistic indirection and critical clarity. Anderson was a driving force behind the rise of American literature in Paris, while Paris was a driving force behind Anderson's precipitous decline within American literature. His expatriate experience constitutes an extended struggle with his seminal concept of the grotesque, and an understanding of his time abroad necessitates an understanding of his domestic experience before, in between, and after Paris.

THE MOVEMENT BEFORE THE MOVEMENT

To begin with, Anderson's Paris trips were not the first time he had thoroughly engaged in an extralocal literary scene. In what he would romanticize as the defining event of his life, Anderson had walked away from his job as president of Anderson Manufacturing in Elyria, Ohio, and moved to Chicago in 1913,[3] where he became a vital part of the Chicago Literary Renaissance of the 1910s. This movement—whose unofficial membership included Theodore Dreiser, Carl Sandburg, Floyd Dell, and Edgar Lee Masters—would come to define American literature in the period immediately preceding the Parisian expatriates of the 1920s. While Chicago was admittedly still an American city, it represented an overtly cosmopolitan change from the small-town life that Anderson had renounced, and the setting would bear a decided impact on Anderson's work from 1913 to 1921. Although Anderson's writing rarely offers a direct depiction of Chicago (in contrast to Sandburg's Chicago poems and Dreiser's *The Titan*), the city nevertheless provided the ideal objective, intellectual, and unfamiliar setting in which to render a definitive portrait of small-town American life.

While Anderson's masterpiece—*Winesburg, Ohio*—is set in late-1800s small-town Ohio, it was almost exclusively written in 1915 and 1916 in a plain room in a Chicago boarding house among an ambitious set of young musicians, writers, painters, and actors. Its original title—"The Book of the Grotesque"—would become the first story in the work, in which an old writer looks down from a window above the town and gains the advantage of objective detachment. As such, the character comes to understand—better than any of the town's other residents—the true nature of both art and existence. "In the beginning," he explains, "when the world was young there were a great many thoughts but no such thing as a truth. Man made the truths himself and each truth was a composite of a great many vague thoughts. All about in the world were the truths and they were all beautiful" (Anderson 1919, 6). However, while truths do exist, Anderson characterizes them as both plural and situational; no truth is the same for everyone, and even individual conceptions of the truth are decidedly temporary and piecemeal. The writer in the story goes on to explain that "the moment one of the people took one of the truths to himself, called it his truth, and tried to live his life by it, he became a grotesque and the truth he embraced became a falsehood" (7).

On the eve of his first trip to Paris, Anderson appeared wary of such an impending grotesque obscuring his own progression as an artist. In a March 1921 letter to Paul Rosenfeld, Anderson admits that "neither Poor White [n]or Winesburg were selling much until W. L. George and later Sinclair Lewis began talking about me. Now they do sell . . . surprisingly well for me. In other words, I find people taking these two fellows' words on me as an artist. The gods must be amused" (Anderson 1953, 72). Such popular recognition and critical expectations threatened to align Anderson with a particular style and a singular artistic identity—possibilities he outrightly detested. Anderson observed an increasingly codified style among the writers of the Chicago Renaissance, and he yearned to gravitate instead to a scene that resisted any such formal expectations. In the same letter to Rosenfeld, Anderson emphatically states, "I can accept no standard I have ever seen as to form. What I want is to be always an experimenter, an adventurer. If America could have the foolish thing sometimes spoken of as 'Artistic Maturity' through me, then America could go to the devil" (72). Anderson's humorous statement highlights his tired frustration with American culture at that moment as much as it does his desire for artistic freedom. It would assume ironic significance when he was awarded the inaugural Dial Award that October for his contributions to American literature, as the award's formal statement said that its mission was to provide "the leisure through which at least one artist may serve God (or go to the devil)."

Anderson's original reasons for traveling to Paris are largely the result of this overriding philosophy of perpetual reinvention. In a December 1920 letter to Rosenfeld, Anderson writes, "It will be very hard for the men of this generation to escape weariness. . . . Someday, with me, it will take the form of having to escape out of these Middle-Western towns for good. In the back of my mind I am always vaguely planning on that" (69–70). While Anderson had briefly left Chicago to live in New York in the fall of 1918, he would come to wonder if he had "come to New York, half wanting to go on to Europe and not quite daring" (Anderson 1968, 304). Now, a little over two years later, he looked to move past the site of his greatest triumphs in search of a new standard of aesthetic and literary truth.

PARIS IN SPRING

On January 20, 1921, this opportunity presented itself in the form of a telegram from Rosenfeld asking: "Will you go to Europe on May seventeenth? Will pay your passage both ways. Have reserved berth for you and me. Wire by Sunday" (Fanning 1976, 1). Anderson responded affirmatively to Rosenfeld, expressing how happy the news had made him and restating the melancholy that the Midwest had presently brought upon him. While Rosenfeld did not stipulate where they were to travel in Europe, Anderson wrote, "I suppose of course you'll want to go to Paris" (Fanning 1976, 1). The destination of Paris was rather obvious, as in the wake of World War I it had very quickly become the hub of expatriate literary and artistic culture in Europe. However, it was still a literary scene in embryonic transition, and thereby offered a significant opportunity to both exert his influence on it and have it exert its influence on him. On May 14, 1921, Anderson and Rosenfeld set sail for Paris on the *Rochambeau* along with Anderson's second wife, Tennessee Mitchell, in spite of the fact that the couple's marriage was already on its way to collapse. Mitchell would appear in very few of Anderson's correspondences and journal entries during the trip, and her presence—at least in the artistic sense—may be considered largely negligible.

The three would spend the next two months in Paris and its environs, with the city leaving an indelible first impression on Anderson. On June 6, Anderson wrote: "We came right up to Paris and have been on the go ever since. I find myself loving Paris wholeheartedly and without reservation" (Fanning 1976, 7). Indeed, Rosenfeld later recalled that "Sherwood was overwrought on our first day in Paris. Crossing the court of the Tuileries . . . [he said through] tears, 'I have never thought anything on earth could be so beautiful'" (8). Much like Chicago had for the previous decade, Paris offered Anderson a fresh and objective canvas on which to cast his artistic talents; unlike Chicago, though, Anderson saw in this latter setting an elevated sophistication and global recognition, as the Louvre, Sainte-Chapelle, Notre Dame, and Chartes Cathedral provided him with a series of historic and inspirational subjects the likes of which did not exist in America.

Not surprisingly, Anderson's observations of France largely developed into an extended comparison of French and American cultures. In the Paris Notebook that he would keep on the trip, Anderson notes that the American impulse is to rise to heights of greatness, even at the abandonment of one's original identity. He explains that "the American is afraid he will . . . not quite conform to the accepted standards"; meanwhile, he continues, "with the Frenchman it is not so. It is his passion to be an individual sharply defined, to stand forth among men"[4] (Fanning 1976, 25). This French willingness to stand out was evident in everything from the everyday fashion of Parisian residents to an usher scolding

Anderson for an insufficient tip, and even extended to a barber's willingness to cut Anderson's hair in an unconventional manner, with Anderson subsequently depicting the barber as a contemplative and open-minded artist.

Anderson's trip to Chartres Cathedral with Rosenfeld bore particular significance, as Rex Burbank describes it as the moment when Anderson "found at last the symbol of imaginative fulfillment of love and art" (121). This experience would serve as the basis for the epiphanic climax of Anderson's *A Story Teller's Story* (1924) and Fanning observes that Anderson "immediately began to incorporate their message of sacred craftsmanship into his private aims as an American writer" (20).

Anderson would further praise the fact that Paris and France offered a simpler life. He lamented that "the philosophy of America, that every citizen may hope to rise to the highest estate has had a dreadful effect upon those who do not rise" (Fanning 1976, 34). In France, meanwhile, he witnessed a heightened sense of honor and comfort in one's established lot. "The waiter not being ashamed of his place in life" subsequently meant that he would "not [be] contemptious [*sic*] of you because you are not rich" (34). As a result, Anderson felt that France offered a scene in which "everything is more intimate" (28).

Anderson also noted that "in Paris there are as many bookstores as there were saloons in Chicago before prohibition" (34), and he readily embraced these literary havens, much as he did the café and garden lifestyle of the city. His journal records random walks and a fascination with the local characters that he encountered, with his immersion into Parisian culture driven by the shift from American transience to French permanence. In *A Story Teller's Story* Anderson wrote, "Often I have asked myself whether, in America, anyone lived anywhere at all. . . . Are people only staying in [places] for the time being? . . . I ask the question because I am myself typically an American and I have not accepted my own place yet" (Anderson 1968, 295). By contrast, Anderson was struck by the "sense of ownership of France in the French" (Fanning 1976, 33), which showed in everything from cuisine to architecture to historical preservation.

This sense of ownership of France by its native citizens would prevent Anderson from fully integrating himself among the locals; instead, his social success in Paris was largely the result of his distinct Americanism. Lewis Galantière, a Parisian journalist who had first met Anderson during his time in Chicago, would comment that "Sherwood was so happy in France, and the reason was somewhat that the French liked him so much. . . . He carried with him, wherever he went, the authentic American culture, and he made America appear to be what at its best it is" (Fanning 1976, 22). In this case, Anderson's relatively unrefined habits and interests were an advantage. He willingly flouted convention at local eateries, spoke French poorly, and openly criticized individuals as he saw fit; even in upper-class French homes, Anderson was at ease talking of Ty Cobb, Babe Ruth, and the other stars of American baseball. While he had been warned of potential anti-American sentiment in Paris prior to his departure, there are no such instances evident in his journal. At the time of his departure in July 1921, Anderson wrote, "As for the French People—they have been fine and have done everything possible to give us a good time" (Fanning 1976, 21).

ANDERSON AND THE LITERATI

Anderson's temporary move to Paris offered him an artistic environment that was distinct from his American residences, with the added bonus of an exceptionally talented group of writers who had come to Paris for much the same reason. J. Gerald Kennedy explains that "exile affords the opportunity for change, growth, and insight as well as the possibility of alienation, confusion, and corruption" and, among the American expatriates of the 1920s, "their representations of Paris enable us to trace the implications of each writer's attachment to the city of exile" (Kennedy 1993, 37). Anderson's limited time in France would not qualify him as a proper expatriate, but it would provide him with a utopian sense of growth and artistic possibility. More significant than the writing that Anderson did in Paris were the relationships that he developed with many of the expatriate figures of the Parisian literary scene. If Anderson did not set out to establish himself as a power broker in the literary community, he at least wished to serve as an effective arbiter of taste and to move among the inner circle of the Parisian literati.

Upon arrival in Paris, Anderson was quickly introduced to Ezra Pound, James Joyce, and Sylvia Beach—and came away with a distinct impression of each of them. Although Anderson described Pound tepidly as "an empty man without fire" (Fanning 1976, 12), he felt an innate affinity with and respect for Joyce. Anderson had never heard of Joyce at the time that he wrote *Winesburg*,[5] but had made up for lost time by embracing Joyce's work and using it as a model for artistic integrity and innovation. Joyce seemed to him "a long, somewhat gloomy, handsome man with beautiful hands. Everyone liked him at once" (27–28). At the time, Joyce was attempting to finish *Ulysses*, although the book had already been banned in both America and Britain. In his Paris Notebook, Anderson astutely acknowledged that "among all modern writers [Joyce's] lot has perhaps been the hardest and it may well be that his Ulysses is the most important book that will be published in this generation" (28).

Anderson also became friends with the Baltimore-born Sylvia Beach, whose Shakespeare and Company bookstore would gain international fame the next year as the original publisher of *Ulysses*. Anderson was originally attracted to her bookshop upon seeing a copy of *Winesburg* in the window, remarking to Beach that it was the only store in Paris where he had seen his book. Indeed, Beach told him that when she had inquired about Anderson's work at other Paris bookstores, she was told that they carried only his fairy tales. Beach was equally impressed with Anderson in the flesh, as in her memoirs she describes him as "a man of great charm . . . a mixture of poet and evangelist (without the preaching), with perhaps a touch of the actor" (Beach 1959, 31).

It was Beach who arranged the most significant introduction of Anderson's time in Paris—an appointment with Gertrude Stein at 27 rue de Fleurus, which Beach would describe as "something of an event" (Beach 1959, 32). Meeting Stein was the highlight of Anderson's trip, and it fostered an affinity between them that carried through to Anderson's death in 1941. The relationship between Anderson and Stein seems highly unlikely, given Anderson's relatively uncultured, Midwestern business background in relation to Stein's highly cosmopolitan and avant-garde leanings. In addition, at the time of their meeting Stein had already lived in Paris for eighteen years, and would continue to reside there for the rest of her life. Lacking any hyperbole, she would ultimately state, "America is my country, but Paris is my hometown."

In spite of these inherent obstacles, Stein would come to represent Anderson's greatest critical triumph. He had first come across Stein's work by reading *Tender Buttons* (1914) while in Chicago, and had felt that—with respect to her earlier work—"a great revolution in the art of words had begun and was passed over with a laugh" (Fanning 1976, 52). Although Stein was actually two years older than Anderson, her literary reputation paled in comparison to his and her career seemed at a relative impasse when the two first met. Of his first seeing Stein, Anderson writes:

> Imagine a strong woman with legs like stone pillars sitting in a room hung thick with Picassos. . . . The woman is the very symbol of health and strength. She laughs, she smokes cigarettes. She tells stories with an American shrewdness in getting the tang and the kick into the telling. (51–52)

Stein, in *The Autobiography of Alice B. Toklas* (1933), has Alice's character describe the initial meeting in a more emotional sense:

> Gertrude Stein was moved and pleased as she had very rarely been. Gertrude Stein was in those days a little bitter, all her unpublished manuscripts, and no hope of publication or serious recognition. Sherwood Anderson came and quite simply and directly as is his way told her what he thought of her work and what it had meant to him in his development. . . . Gertrude Stein and Sherwood Anderson have always been the best of friends, but I do not believe even he realizes how much his visit meant to her. (132)

The relationship between the two writers would manifest itself in a number of public critical affirmations over the next few years, beginning with Anderson's notable introduction to Stein's *Geography and Plays* in 1922. In it, he sought to put aside the "America[n] impression of Miss Stein's personality, not at all true and foolishly romantic" (Anderson 1922, 6); in Stein, instead, he had found a figure whose substance sufficiently overrode her eccentricities. He professed to her having "a discrimination in the arts such as I have found in no other American born man or woman" (6), and who had accordingly "forgone the privilege of writing the great American novel" out of fidelity to artistic originality[6] (8). This is a crucial point, as Stein represented a commitment to genuine originality and artistic purity, as opposed to fixation on a grotesque form (in this case, the great American novel). In a 1923 letter to Stein, Anderson stated that he considered her advice "the most clear-headed criticism I've had" (White, 34).

Almost as famous as his relationship with Stein was Anderson's role in the Parisian development of Ernest Hemingway. Anderson first met Hemingway in Chicago in 1920, when the younger writer moved to Chicago, and it was Anderson who first encouraged Hemingway to go to Paris, after Anderson had returned from his initial summer in France. He told Hemingway, "the place to go was Paris, where pleasant rooms and good wine were cheap, the cathedrals beautifully crafted stone on stone, and the lovers all along the Seine kissing unashamedly. . . . He was able to write in his notebook; story ideas flowed, American stories that he saw clearly in that city of bridges" (Reynolds 1986, 252–53). Hemingway left for Paris a little over a month after that, and Anderson would provide him with crucial letters of introduction to Gertrude Stein, Sylvia Beach, and Ezra Pound.

In Hemingway, Anderson saw an authentic protégé who he felt embodied his own best qualities as a writer. In his December 1921 letter to Stein introducing her to Hemingway, Anderson called him "an American writer instinctively in touch with everything worth-while going on here" (Anderson 1953, 85). In 1925, Anderson would again write to Stein that he liked Hemingway's stories ("all of them"), and provided the jacket commentary for Hemingway's short story collection, *In Our Time*, that same year, in which he wrote, "Mr. Hemingway is young, strong, full of laughter, and he can write . . . the clear putting down of which has always made good writing so good."

However, the two writers were inherently divided in their regard for the established literary hierarchy. In spite of his massive ego, Anderson saw literary development as a collective project that relied on mutual cooperation and goodwill. Hemingway, on the other hand, saw literature as a veritable prizefight—both an expression of machismo and a competitive field that necessitated the conquest of former champions. In 1925, Hemingway wrote *The Torrents of Spring*, a novel frantically written in ten days with the ostensible purposes of criticizing the established writers of Chicago and Paris and relieving him of his contract with Boni and Liveright (for whom Anderson was also writing at that time). Stylistically and thematically, the work is primarily a parody of Anderson's *Dark Laughter* (1925), a book that Anderson had conceptualized during his time in Paris. Howe observes that, to Anderson, Hemingway's gesture was both "a blow from his friend and . . . a sign of the shifting critical attitude to his work" (Howe 1951, 202). Although Hemingway's text received poor critical reviews, it stands as the lone forgettable work among his first five novels,[7] while Anderson would not write another notable novel in his lifetime.[8]

In order to leave no doubt as to his intent, Hemingway sent Anderson what the latter called "certainly the most self-conscious and probably the most patronizing letter ever written," in which Hemingway explained that *The Torrents of Spring* would be a "fatal" book for Anderson which "was intended to bring to an end, once and for all, the notion that there was any worth in [Anderson's] work" (Anderson 1942, 475). Anderson dismissed Hemingway's book as a work that "might have been humorous had Max Beerbohm condensed it into twelve pages," and likewise considered Hemingway's letter "so raw, so pretentious, [and] so patronizing that in a repellant way it was amusing" (475). But Hemingway's outright malice clearly struck a nerve in his mentor; the letter he wrote to Hemingway in response, Anderson would remember, "was something to the effect that I thought it foolish that we writers should devote our time to the attempt to kill each other off. . . . Speaking of the knockout blow he had given to me, . . . I think I did say that I had always thought of myself as a pretty good middleweight and I doubted *his* ever being able to make the heavyweight class" (475).

Stein would rally to Anderson's defense, and would use her initial bestseller—*The Autobiography of Alice B. Toklas*—as a platform to glorify Anderson and to undercut Hemingway. In the book, Toklas's character explains that "Gertrude Stein and Sherwood Anderson are very funny on the subject of Hemingway. . . . Hemingway had been formed by the two of them and they were both a little proud and a little ashamed of the work of their minds" (Stein 1933, 215). Hemingway, she further states, was "yellow" for having publicly mocked and betrayed his literary mentor (215–16). When Anderson returned to Paris in 1927, Toklas claims that Hemingway was predictably nervous about Anderson coming to Paris (he had, after all, been the one who first taught Hemingway shadow boxing), while explaining that Anderson had no intentions for revenge.[9]

Indeed, in spite of his response to Hemingway's letter, Anderson maintained an admirably evenhanded approach to Hemingway's work for the rest of his life. While he disliked Hemingway's *Green Hills of Africa* (1936)—calling it "a really lousy book" (Anderson 1953, 345)—he was complimentary of most of Hemingway's other post-1926 works, such as describing *A Farewell to Arms* (1929) as "a fine novel" (205). Writing to book publisher Henry Schuman in 1938, Anderson spoke against the calls to censor Hemingway's *To Have and Have Not*, on the grounds that "Mr. Hemingway is a great writer" and that "nothing he writes will hurt anyone" (397). Most revealingly, in a 1933 letter to Stein, he writes that her *Autobiography* made him "a bit sorry and sad . . . when you took such big patches of skin off Hemmy with your delicately held knife" (295). To the end of his life, Anderson would look upon his two most prominent Parisian associations with respect, objectively holding their art above any personal affinity or animosity he had for them.

BEYOND PARIS

Anderson returned from Paris reenergized and eager to experience other unfamiliar cultural settings; at the very least, Howe explains, "it was inconceivable to Anderson that, after Paris, he could return to advertising copy and Chicago" (Howe 1951, 133). Between his visits to Paris, he lived at times in New York, Reno, New Orleans, and Berkeley, while returning to Chicago only briefly. It is also little coincidence that, living in New Orleans in February 1922, Anderson wrote to Stein that "the old French Creole Quarter [is] the most civilized place I've found in America" (Anderson 1953, 87), in part because it reminded him so much of Paris. In the majority of his other letters to Stein over the next six years, Anderson expressed his desire to return to France, with his writing in that time taking a direct cue from his Parisian experience. After the publication of *Many Marriages* (1923)—a morally cynical and rhetorically rambling novel that received mixed critical reviews[10]—Paris would provide the philosophical foundation for Anderson's next two novels: *A Story's Teller's Story* (1924) and *Dark Laughter* (1925).

Anderson originally intended *A Story Teller's Story* to be titled *A Modernist Notebook*, and to provide a veritable blueprint for innovative writing in the 1920s. In format, the book would resemble Anderson's Paris Notebook, with both its autobiographical vignettes and its artistic contemplation on seemingly mundane subjects. There are also multiple instances where the works mirror one another in their critique of American culture and naïve fascination with Europe.

However, Fanning warns that "the reader who overemphasizes Anderson's anti-Americanism may well miss what is really the book's main theme: the confrontation between fancy and fact" (Fanning 1976, 75). This had already been evident in select passages from his Paris Notebook, with Anderson admitting that he saw France as a nation with "no sense of growing" and no new ideas; in America, by contrast, "we have a constant inflow of new people and impulses" (24, 45). The advantage of historical precedent and permanence made it exceedingly difficult for the contemporary French to be original, and in this respect Anderson felt a decided edge for himself as an American artist. Furthermore, Anderson stresses in his journal that "one of the mistakes being made by the French is that they seem to take it for granted that all the rest of us, who come so gladly to France and Paris come to see and admire them. . . . [Instead,] what attracts us to this place is old France" (23). He concludes definitively, "If Paris is beautiful present day Frenchmen did not make it so" (25).

While Parisian/French scenes constitute only a small portion of *A Story Teller's Story*, they offer a continuation of these observations. In the epiphanic climax of the book, Anderson marvels at the artistry and craftsmanship of Chartres Cathedral while equally cognizant of the ugly contemporary sheds that face it. Just as tellingly, upon catching his first breathtaking glimpse of the cathedral, Anderson's thoughts returned to home soil:

> At that moment I was very far away from that land, the background of my tales, the Middle West of America. . . . As I sat there nearly all of the reality of me was still living in the Middle West of America, in mining towns, factory towns, in sweet stretches of Ohio [and Illinois] countryside, in great smoke-hung cities, in the midst of that strange, still-forming muddle of people that is America. (Anderson 1968, 308)

For all his romanticization of Paris, it is clear that Anderson knew it would always be a foreign canvas to him. In a letter to Rosenfeld upon returning to America, Anderson explained that, "in [his] own way," he was "trying to live in the old tradition of the [French] artists" (Fanning 1976, 94), at least in the sense of artistic originality and integrity. Rather than re-creating the exotic scenes of Parisian culture he had witnessed, Anderson emphasized, "I want to write beautifully, create beautifully, not outside but in this thing in which I am born, in this place where in the midst of ugly towns, cities, Fords, moving pictures, I have always lived, must always live" (94). In the midst of the epiphanic scene at Chartres, Anderson stresses that "for all one might say about American life it had been good to me . . . and had poured itself out richly enough" (Anderson 1968, 313).

While Anderson's expatriate experience had helped him make peace with his American existence, it had not provided him with a definitive artistic direction to pursue. This fact would become readily evident in his subsequent epic project, *Dark Laughter*, a work that is perhaps most evident of Anderson's time in Paris. With respect to subject, the work offers an unprecedented (for Anderson) emphasis on African American culture, and it was while visiting Konrad Bercovici in France that Anderson "spoke of the American negro and [his] hope that some day an American artist would see the beauty of their caracters [sic] and persons" (Fanning 1967, 35). His status as an outsider in France also made him extensively consider the outsider status that African Americans were afforded in America.

With respect to form, *Dark Laughter* would easily surpass any of his previous works in linguistic sophistication and structural complexity. Anderson would write to George H. Daugherty in 1925: "I think as a matter of prose experiment you will sense what Joyce was driving at [in *Ulysses*] when you read *Dark Laughter*. As I think I told you when you were here, I very frankly took his experiment as a starting point for the prose rhythm of the book" (Anderson 1953, 148). And in terms of scope, Anderson intended for *Dark Laughter* to be the great synthesis of all his previous experiences, with Paris providing the crucial foreign setting. In a letter to Otto Liveright, Anderson described *Dark Laughter* as a book whose "setting embraces the Middle West, the Ohio River Valley, the Mississippi River, and New Orleans. In it there are lazy, dancing Negroes, a description of the Quat'z' Arts Ball in Paris shortly after the Armistice, and an intense love story. . . . It is going to be by far the best novel I have ever written" [11] (142).

With regard to popular sales, Anderson proved correct; whereas works like *Winesburg* and *Poor White* had sold moderately, *Dark Laughter* would become Anderson's only bestseller in his lifetime, selling 50,000 copies in its first year. The all-encompassing nature of this mega-project, though, indicates a definitive lack of theme or direction, ultimately relegating this book below a relatively self-contained work like *Winesburg*. While it is unfair to wholly affix the blame for Anderson's sophisticated shift to his Parisian experience and influences—Anderson was already thoroughly exposed to cosmopolitanism from his time in Chicago—*Dark Laughter* represents an exponential leap in complexity, and may be seen as a conscientious attempt by Anderson to match the erudition and scope of Joyce, Pound, and Stein. These elements are perhaps most evident in the Parisian scenes of the book, with Jean Méral emphasizing *Dark Laughter's* "explorations of Freudian themes" in which Paris is portrayed as a "city [that] is markedly Dionysian" (Méral 1989, 178). Méral continues that "this episode introduces the idea that Paris offers an opportunity for debauchery and nocturnal revelry leading to a state of emotional violence that is the psychological equivalent of the physical violence of war" (141–42).

Such complexity strips much of the raw energy that characterized Anderson's best work. From *Winesburg* ("You will have to know life . . . [and] stop fooling with words" [Anderson 1919, 89]) to his Paris Notebook ("The great are great because of simplicity" [Fanning 1976, 29]), Anderson's prior work is littered with warnings against the kind of work that *Dark Laughter* had become. Fanning contends that "Anderson's sensibilities were simply not attuned to either receive or dispense this type of beauty. When he tried to make his work intellectual, thesis-directed, it usually collapsed into the drab and mediocre" (87). While *Dark Laughter* was an initial economic success, it was a decided critical failure. With respect to style, theme, language, and political correctness, Howe calls *Dark Laughter* "a book which belonged to a rejected past" (Howe 1951, 220).

Compared with small-town Ohio and the developing Midwest, Anderson was relatively unfamiliar with much of the material of *Dark Laughter*.[12] As a result, he had essentially failed to take his own advice, and had fallen into the high modernist ambition of expatriate literary culture. Anderson could not wholly dedicate himself to cosmopolitan life, nor distinguish his experience and observations in Paris from those of any number of other expressive tourists. Paris, in short, had given him a literary standard to aspire to, but had led him astray of the authentic material that had fueled his literary rise to that point.

PARIS REDUX

With his literary career at an impasse, and fueled by the nostalgic recollection of his earlier trip to Paris, Anderson set sail for Europe on the S.S. *Roosevelt* in December 1926, a trip that was to last until March 4, 1927. His tempered anticipation upon arrival—along with his ever-increasing struggle with alcohol—is evident in a December 1926 letter to Stein: "I was so happy to be in Paris—after London. I drank too much. This morning my hands shake but I am still happy to be here" (White, 57). In comparison with his first trip, decidedly little was recorded by Anderson on this second trip, as it lacked the novice enthusiasm and overriding positivity of his initial visit.

After his letter to Stein, what correspondence he did provide displays an increasingly cynical attitude. In a January 1927 letter to Paul Rosenfeld, Anderson writes, "Got to Paris and [had] the flu. Was in bed 10 days. . . . The Americans in Paris are terrible. Such a shuffling lot. I am to see Joyce this afternoon. Perhaps he will be alive. I am none too alive myself. No sweet, new impulses" (Anderson 1953, 165). The relative dearth of journalism by Anderson on this trip speaks to his difficulty writing anything at that moment. In that same letter to Rosenfeld, he explains, "Everything I have written seems dead stuff. God knows what I am in. I am all right physically, but for the time being am no judge of anything. . . . My fancy tosses and jumps constantly. I work on a novel for a week, then throw it away. I write a short story. It seems nothing" (165) Having spent his last six years in artistic and physical transience, Anderson had not accumulated an effective store of personal experiences or established a distinct artistic objective, and his time in France did little to remedy either of these issues. In an April 1927 letter to John Anderson upon returning to America, Sherwood calls his trip to Paris "a dead blank time" and admits that although he had tried to write "for days, weeks, and months now I can't do it." (166).

By this time, Anderson was over fifty years old and had become increasingly wary of the expatriate writers in Paris who had come seeking inspiration from the city now considered the hub of literary modernism. On his first trip there he had noted that "in France the art movements fall naturally into groups. . . . The individual artist being doubtful or afraid gives himself to a group hoping to gain strength there" (Fanning 1967, 24), a statement that proved decidedly more evident on his second trip there. The now-fashionable trend of Parisian expatriatism had spawned a culture in which artistic debate and theory were paramount, while effective literary production was undervalued. In such a way, the artist had been given priority over the art.

Ironically, Anderson's earlier work again foretells this plight, with the character of Enoch Robinson in *Winesburg* ("Loneliness") offering an autobiographical model of Anderson. Enoch was twenty-one years old when he went to New York City and proceeded to be "a city man for fifteen years. . . . In his own mind he planned to go to Paris and to finish his art education among the masters there, but that never turned out" (Anderson 1919, 92). Similar to Enoch, Anderson was twenty-three when he ventured to an American metropolis (Chicago instead of New York), but—unlike Enoch—Anderson would make it to Paris to engage with the great masters of his artistic craft. Within Enoch's avant-garde circle, "there was nothing particularly striking about them except that they were artists of the kind that talk. . . . They talk of art and are passionately, almost feverishly, in earnest about it. They think it matters much more than it does" (92–93). By the time of his second trip to Paris, Anderson had effectively become Enoch Robinson—frustrated with the contemporary state of art, unable to make a wholly original contribution himself, and thoroughly disgusted with the self-importance attached to individual artists.

Such disillusion is evident in a May 1927 letter to Rosenfeld upon his return from Europe, when Anderson confessed that "it made me pretty sick seeing Hemingway this winter. What seems to me to have happened to Joyce made me ill" (Anderson 1953, 173). While Anderson bore no grudge against Hemingway's writing, he now found his pupil's personality to be insufferable, and felt that celebrity had done much the same to Joyce. Nor did he reserve this condemnation solely for others, as his own popularity had become a source of embarrassment. In a letter to Rosenfeld the previous month, he stated: "I went to Paris and found myself close to famous. That's just plain sickening. God knows, I hope you escape it. It's sheer nonsense without a spark of meaning" (170). In an April 1927 letter to Roger Sergel, Anderson would explain this commentary in greater detail:

I went over to Paris, had a success of a sort there.
You haven't come to that yet. I mean feeling yourself established. You
get what is called fame.
Sherwood Anderson—
A man's name . . .
I get you too making a figure of me, and it hurts.
The world is full and full of that nonsense.
Hemingway made a damn fool by it; Joyce, too. I saw it popping in
them both.
I am Joyce.
I am Hemingway.
Christ!
Is there nothing more important than that kind of absurd importance,
in me and others?
If the arts make men like that, damn and God damn the arts.
(Anderson 1953, 168–69)

By this point, the ironic humor of Anderson's earlier commentary on
American art ("America could go to the devil") had been replaced by a
deeply cynical condemnation of the Parisian literary scene, which he felt
had assumed the form of a grotesque. In August 1922, Anderson had said
of Stein, "I do not think her too important," but rather that she simply
"had an important thing to do" (88–89). Anderson had always believed
that artistic success was reliant on the contributions of a large body of
predecessors, with the writer serving only as the fortunate synthesizer of
the work and ideas of others. His seemingly inert comment about Stein
may therefore be seen as the ultimate compliment, much as he had once
praised her for abandoning popular fame in favor of artistic integrity in
Paris. Now, he witnessed a generation of writers increasingly using Paris
as a vehicle for standardized inspiration and self-importance. Anderson
left Paris at the beginning of March 1927, and—despite his continued
affinity for Stein—never expressed the desire to return there again.

LITTLE PYRAMIDS OF TRUTH

When Stein and Toklas moved out of their longtime Paris apartment in
1938, Anderson wrote to them that "it seems strange to think of the two
of you in any place other than the beautiful rooms in the rue de Fleurus"
(Kennedy 1993, 76–77). By contrast, in many ways it seems strange to
think of Anderson in Paris to begin with, instead of Chicago or rural
Ohio. Anderson's finest literature is strikingly American and isolationist.
While the best work of Stein and Hemingway is quintessentially international, Anderson's forays into these settings and subjects are generally
awkward, limited, and relicary. The movement that would make canoni-
cal heroes out of Stein, Hemingway, and Joyce would dismiss Anderson

as an old hand who had been unable to match the challenge of high modernism.

Ultimately, it was not the dynamic literary and intellectual environment of Paris that Anderson sought and valued; it was instead the city's nostalgic element of a simpler art and the assurance of historical permanence. In a 1927 letter to John Anderson, Sherwood warned: "Don't be carried off your feet by anything because it is modern, the latest thing" (Anderson 1953, 165). As a result, Anderson's ultimate rejection of the literary culture of 1920s Paris seems predictable; he saw his own writing diminish under its cutting-edge approach, and he dismissed it accordingly.

On the other hand, Anderson's rejection of American literature in Paris can just as surely be viewed as a more complex and original reaction to the movement—and as a rejection of an impending artistic grotesque. During his respective times in Chicago and Paris, Anderson found himself at the center of the foremost American literary movements of both the 1910s and the 1920s, and he would eventually abandon each one in his never ending search for artistic independence and growth.[13] A final example from *Winesburg* is testament to this inevitable process in the character of Dr. Reefy ("Paper Pills"), who erected "little pyramids of truth . . . and after erecting knocked them down again that he might have the truths to erect other pyramids" (Anderson 1919, 14). In much the same way that the Chicago Renaissance did not offer Anderson a final artistic solution, so too had the Parisian expatriate circle run its useful course. For Anderson, authenticity could only be accomplished through abandonment, an act that would render his undeniable influence on American literature in Paris effectively obscured.

NOTES

1. The eight winners of the Dial Award represent a literary tour de force of the 1920s. In addition to Anderson, winners included T. S. Eliot (1922), Van Wyck Brooks (1923), Marianne Moore (1924), E. E. Cummings (1925), William Carlos Williams (1926), Ezra Pound (1927), and Kenneth Burke (1928). It says a great deal that Anderson was the initial winner, much the same as it does that his work appeared in six of the first seven issues of the most influential literary journal in American modernism.

2. Even Anderson publicly stated in his final years: "For all my egotism, I know I am but a minor figure" (Howe 1951, 243)—a statement that is more a reflection of the critical mood of that moment than an objective assessment of his career accomplishments.

3. While this was the first time Anderson had gone to Chicago with a definitive artistic purpose, it was in fact the third time he had lived there. He first moved there briefly to stay with his brother, Karl, and work as a manual laborer shortly before the turn of the century. After joining the Army for the Spanish-American War and enrolling for a time at Wittenberg University in Springfield, Ohio, he returned to Chicago in 1900 to work as an advertising copywriter, and would remain employed there until 1906.

4. Fanning faithfully transcribes the complete text of Anderson's Paris Notebook, a seventy-four-page notebook written in longhand that is housed in Chicago's Newberry Library. Any grammatical errors are the result of Anderson's epistolary style; as Fanning notes, Anderson "was neither a good speller nor a good punctuator; he was just a good writer" (Fanning 1976, 23).

5. A decided irony, given that *Winesburg* has often been compared to Joyce's *Dubliners* (1914) in both form and subject.

6. Anderson ended this enthusiastic introduction for Stein by declaring: "Would it not be a lovely and charmingly ironic gesture of the gods if, in the end, the work of this artist were to prove the most lasting and most important of all the word slingers of our generation!" (Anderson 1922, 8). This is a highly ironic statement, given that it was made at the very moment that Joyce's *Ulysses* was being published in Paris; however, given Anderson's familiarity with and affinity for Joyce, it also emphasizes the unmatched respect he had for Stein's art.

7. On the heels of *The Torrents of Spring*, Hemingway would write *The Sun Also Rises* (1926), *A Farewell to Arms* (1929), *To Have and Have Not* (1937), and *For Whom the Bell Tolls* (1940). His contract with Boni & Liveright broken by their refusal to publish his first work, all of his subsequent books would be published by Scribner's.

8. From 1926 onward, Anderson's remaining novels would be *Tar: A Midwest Childhood* (1926), *Alice and the Lost Novel* (1929), *Beyond Desire* (1932), and *Kit Brandon: A Portrait* (1936).

9. Anderson and Hemingway would finally meet on Anderson's final day in Paris as he was packing to depart, in a somewhat awkward exchange of (to Anderson) dubious intent. Hemingway offered to have a drink with him at the bar across the street from the hotel, and—upon both individuals deciding on a beer—Anderson writes that Hemingway declared "Here's how," and then "turned and walked rapidly away. He had, I dare say, proved his sportsmanship to himself" (Anderson 1942, 476).

10. A notable champion of the work was F. Scott Fitzgerald—one of the most influential critical voices of the decade and a fellow American in Paris—who considered *Many Marriages* to be Anderson's best book.

11. The Parisian roots of this novel are also evident in the fact that Anderson sent the first six copies of *Dark Laughter* to Stein, Hemingway, Rosenfeld, Bercovici, Otto Liveright, and Margaret Gay (his French translator).

12. Not surprisingly, as a follow-up to *Dark Laughter* Anderson returned to a familiar format with the semi-autobiographical novel *Tar: A Midwest Childhood* (1926).

13. After returning to America in 1927, Anderson moved around the country incessantly, particularly across the Southern and Southwestern regions. He only made two more trips abroad: to Amsterdam in 1932 and to South America in 1941, on which he died of peritonitis on the way there in Panama.

REFERENCES

Anderson, Sherwood. *Dark Laughter*. New York: Boni & Liveright, 1925.
Anderson, Sherwood, Gertrude Stein, and Ray Lewis White. *Sherwood Anderson/Gertrude Stein: Correspondence and Personal Essays*. Chapel Hill: University of North Carolina Press, 1972.
———. *Letters of Sherwood Anderson*. Edited by. Howard Mumford Jones and Walter B. Rideout. Boston: Little, Brown, and Company, 1953.
———. *Sherwood Anderson's Memoirs*. New York: Harcourt, Brace and Company, 1942.
———. *A Story Teller's Story*. Edited by Ray Lewis White. Cleveland: Case Western University Press, 1968.
———. *Winesburg, Ohio*. Edited by. Charles E. Modlin and Ray Lewis White. New York: W. W. Norton, 1996.
———. "The Work of Gertrude Stein." In *Geography and Plays*. By Gertrude Stein. 5–8. Boston: The Four Seas Company, 1922.

Beach, Sylvia. *Shakespeare and Company*. New York: Harcourt, Brace, and Company, 1959.

Burbank, Rex. *Sherwood Anderson*. New York: Twayne, 1964.

Fanning, Michael. *France and Sherwood Anderson: Paris Notebook, 1921*. Baton Rouge: Louisiana State University Press, 1976.

Hemingway, Ernest. *In Our Time*. New York: Boni & Liveright, 1925.

Howe, Irving. *Sherwood Anderson*. New York: Sloane, 1951.

Kennedy, J. Gerald. *Imagining Paris: Exile, Writing, and American Identity*. New Haven, CT: Yale University Press, 1993.

Méral, Jean. *Paris in American Literature*. Translated by Laurette Long. Chapel Hill: University of North Carolina Press, 1989.

Reynolds, Michael. *The Young Hemingway*. New York: Basil Blackwell, 1986.

Stein, Gertrude. *The Autobiography of Alice B. Toklas*. New York: Harcourt, Brace, and Company, 1933.

FOUR

From Dada to Nada

*The Dadaist Influence on Hemingway's Works
between 1922 and 1926*

Jonathan A. Austad

Dadaism expressed the resentment and mistrust that permeated society following World War I, and, in particular, it was a movement that captured the social milieu in Paris. Firmly embedded both within the Parisian artistic and literary circles, it strongly influenced Hemingway's early poems and short stories between 1922 and 1926. Arriving in Paris in late 1921, his artistic and literary associations helped his writings transform to a style that resembles Dadaism and maintains their philosophical vision. His works during his first period in Paris (December 1921–August 1923) are more aesthetically aligned with Dadaism, showing a more radical and abstract style and were published in artistic journals such as *Double Dealer*, *transatlantic*, and *Querschnitt*. Although these works were well received by fellow expatriates in Paris who were more receptive to modern art, Hemingway sought notoriety in America, which was not as open to radical literary approaches. Works during his second period in Paris (January 1924–February 1926) are more moderate to accommodate an American audience but contain residual elements of Dadaism. This research will show Hemingway's experimentations with Dadaism as he develops his unique style for which he gained international fame, and, in so doing, it will pay particular attention to his first collection of short stories: *In Our Time* (1925), where he successfully balances between radical and conventional aesthetics. Although Hemingway was not a Dadaist and bitterly denounced the movement on a number of occasions, it provided him a conduit to channel his frustrations living in a postwar society that he found to be void of political, social, and religious values and sharpened his antagonisms and criticisms.

Other research that examines artistic influences on Hemingway focuses on his connection to either Cézanne or Cubism. Lisa Narbeshuber, for instance, claims that Hemingway's *In Our Time* resembles Cubist aesthetics because of its disintegration of the world that Narbeshuber finds to be analogous to Cubism's search to destroy the picture plane to create a new visual reality (Narbeshuber 2006, 9). However, she admits that Hemingway's negation does not correspond to Cubist idealism. Cubism seeks to destroy visual reality to create new meaning and push for new ideals. Hemingway only destroys the world that he depicts and does not provide an alternative system to replace the ones that he criticizes; hence, he rejects Cubist's "utopian spirit" (13). This research will argue that Hemingway's aesthetics in his early works, and in particular *In Our Time*, closely resembles Dadaism. Rather than abstracting the picture plane, Dadaism abstracts ideas. It also does not share Cubism's utopian ideals because it does not create an alternate system. Hemingway's early short stories similarly focus on the abstraction of ideas without utopian values. To this end, rather than Cubist fragmentation, *In Our Time* more closely resembles Dadaist collages that juxtapose random images of the modern world to produce feelings of spontaneity, absurdity, and negation. Importantly, Hemingway does not consider himself a Dadaist and does not exhibit all elements of Dadaism. Dadaist criticisms are playful, whereas Hemingway's works are seldom playful and often have a harsh, bitter tone. However, Dadaism played a key role in the Parisian mind-set after World War I and became one of the leading artistic voices, and, due to their direct and indirect influence on Hemingway, he appropriates the movement's nihilist sentiments, which constitute the philosophic lens that dominates his early works.

Dadaism emerged in Switzerland in 1916 with *The Cabaret Voltaire*: one of the first politically charged Dadaist publications. The magazine protested the war and criticized nationalist sentiments. It expressed mistrust and disillusionment toward social institutions and attacked human reason, which they believed lead to the chaos of World War I. Tristan Tzara's explanation of the origins of the group's name in *Dadaist Manifesto* (1918) demonstrates their attitude toward reason: "We see by the papers that the Kru Negroes call the tail of a holy cow Dada. The cube and the mother in a certain district of Italy are called: Dada. A hobby horse, a nurse both in Russian and Romanian: Dada" (Motherwell 1951, 77). The name has various connotations in diverse languages, but there is no relationship between them. In each language the word is obscure and unrelated, and this highlights their desire to remove meaning from art. Tzara advises "don't waste your time on a word that means nothing" (77). There is no meaning to their name because meanings impose order. With the advent of the war, they found no solutions through political, social, or religious means to cure society from the atrocities that the war created. These systems readily embraced the war at its outbreak, and, once the war lost meaning, such systems could not offer viable explanations for it. A purposeless war made life seem absurd, and Dadaist art reflects this. Tzara's explanation on how to create a poem exemplifies their absurdity. His explanation shows that a Dadaist poem has a pattern and purpose: the poet should follow these directions explicitly with the intent of creating a poem. However, the product is obscure. Words have no logical thought because of the random order in which they are drawn from the bag. Dadaism argues that "logic is an inorganic disease which is imprisoned by the senses and proves the impotence of our minds" (Kristiansen 1968, 458). A Dadaist poem refuses to capture human emotions, inspire, or delight human sentiments. It does not capture beauty, imagination, emotion, sentiment, thoughts, or ideals. It merely is a string of random words with the label "poetry." Tzara's critique delves deeper than denouncing reason; he additionally removes the poet's influence and questions the role of a poet to achieve what Peter Bürger calls system-immanent criticism. System-immanent criticism is the tearing down of all aspects of society, even itself.[1] Duchamp's *L.H.O.O.Q.* (1917) similarly achieves this by questioning art's definition. He uses a postcard of *Mona Lisa* and adds a mustache and goatee to eliminate artistic technique and remove traditional notions of beauty. Duchamp undercuts the importance of the artist's abilities to create art by altering a mass-produced object. Tzara likewise removes poetry's importance by concluding that anything can be considered poetry and anyone can be a poet. Tzara's advice to "copy conscientiously" random words mocks a traditional poet's concentrated use of words to evoke images or thoughts. His endowment of this newly created poet with poetic "sensibility" and ability to be "infinitely original" further dismantles the poet's shroud. Creating a poem from a series of words from a newspaper article is original but equating this to the creative process of a poet is Tzara's playful criticism against the poet and poetry.

Richard Huelsenbeck's "End of the World" (1916) further captures Dadaist abstraction of ideas through random images, and it illustrates their frustration with the war through the poem's impulsive language and obscure allusions. Fragmented images comprise the poem: a cockatoo "sings" at the "headquarters" while the cannons "lament all day"; Herr Mayer reflects on the loss of his eye, while others shout: "God save the king"; Father Homer writes about "peace" and "war"; and nobody knows whether there will be a "tomorrow" (Motherwell 1951, 226). More careful examination reveals that the war ties together these seemingly dichotomous images to illustrate the disorder of war. Nothing escapes its impact: the cockatoo, Herr Mayer, and Father Homer all experience the devastation of the war. The cannons drowned out the cockatoo's song,

Herr Mayer looses an eye, and Father Homer confronts difficult theological questions pertaining to peace and war. The seemingly unrelated and ambiguous images are a focused attack to mock the futility of war.

Donna Kristiansen asserts that Dadaism shares three main elements: absurdity, spontaneity, and negation. Kristiansen defines Dadaist absurdity as contradiction and opposition of harmony. Paul Éluard's "Les Fleurs" illustrates this with its contradiction of ideas. The second stanza contradicts the first. Dadaists use opposing thoughts and ideas to negate meaning. They use impulsive language, discourse, actions, thoughts, behaviors, etc. to capture absurdity. There is no meaning to their art and searching for meaning is absurd. Dadaism counters its own values, believing all ideas are meaningless. André Breton clarifies in "Three Manifestos": "We are incapable of treating seriously any subject whatsoever, let alone this subject: ourselves" (203). Dadaist spontaneity comes in two forms: simultaneity and bruitism. Simultaneity is multiple noises that occur at the same time, and bruitism is noises from diverse elements such as typewriters, hammers, pipes, etc. Tzara's "Dance Soiree with Programme" (1916) comprises three poems that are read simultaneously in three different languages (German, English, and French) to capture the multiple noises of simultaneity. A rattle, whistle, and drum randomly interject the poems to demonstrate the various sounds of bruitism. The confusion of the simultaneous narratives and disorienting noises eliminate rationality and produce the feeling of impulsiveness. Dadaist negation is the destruction of all ideas. Tzara exclaims in a section called "Dadaist Disgust" in his 1918 *Dadaist Manifesto*:

> Every product of disgust capable of becoming a negation of the family is Dada; a protest with the fists of its whole being engaged in destructive action: *Dada; knowledge of all the means of rejected up until now by the shamefaced sex of comfortable compromise and good manners: Dada; abolition of logic, which is the dance of those who are impotent to create: Dada; of every social hierarchy and equation set up for the sake of values by our valets: Dada; every object, sentiments, obscurities, apparitions and the precise clash of parallel lines are weapons for the fight: Dada; abolition of memory: Dada; the abolition of archaeology: Dada; abolition of prophets: Dada; abolition of the future: Dada; absolute and unquestionable faith in every god that is the immediate product of spontaneity*: Dada; elegant and unprejudiced leap from a harmony to the other sphere; trajectory of a word tossed like a screeching phonograph record; to respect all individualities in their folly of the moment: whether it be serious, fearful, timid, ardent, vigorous, determined, enthusiastic; to divest one's church of every useless and cumbersome accessory; to spit out disagreeable or amorous ideas like a luminous waterfall, or coddle them—with extreme satisfaction that does not matter in the least—with the same intensity in the thicket of one's soul—pure of insects for blood well-born, and gilded with bodies of archangels. Freedom: Dada Dada Dada, a roaring of tense colors,

and interlacing of opposites and of all contradictions, grotesques, in-
consistencies: LIFE (Tzara 1918 quoted in Motherwell 1951, 81–82).

Tzara indicates "disgust" in all things. Negation destroys logic, memory,
sentiment, future, and so on. Dadaists further destroy all social components. Tzara elaborates in his lecture on Dadaism: "I know that you have
come here today to hear explanations. Well, don't expect to hear any
explanations about Dadaism. You explain to me why you exist" (Tzara
1918, 247). He refuses to explain Dadaism's meaning or aim because this
would refute their purpose. Kristiansen explains that Dadaism "leads to
total negation. Man is nothing; everything is of equal unimportance.
Everything is irrelevant; nothing is relevant. The combination of the infinity of ideas and arbitrariness which governs our existence causes the
Dadaists to see absurdity in life" (Kristiansen, 400). All ideas are equally
and simultaneously important and unimportant. Man Ray's sculpture
Compass (1920) juxtaposes a magnet with a gun. No logical correlation
exists between the magnet and gun; each is equally irrelevant and absurd. His *Dadaphoto* comes to a similar conclusion by equating a sculpture
(a stand, metal pole, and cut out of a head and shoulders) with the arms
of a live woman: both are equally important and trivial.

By the end of the war, with millions of people losing their lives and no
clear objectives gained, society felt abandoned by political ideals and
identified with Dadaism's critique. George Hugnet indicates that Dadaism captured a culmination of social sentiment that stemmed from the
nineteenth century but was not fully realized until after World War I
(Hugnet quoted in Motherwell 1951, 167). Other movements such as Fu-
turism, Cubism, and Vorticism promoted faith in ideals, but the war
shattered people's trust in humanity. Dadaism attacked institutions that
promised higher meaning and order but brought destruction and chaos.
People identified with its mistrust of ideals, and it gained popularity in
New York, Barcelona, Berlin, Hannover, Cologne, and Paris.

In Paris it penetrated beyond the artistic circles and infiltrated into the
literary realm, beginning with a periodical entitled *Litterature*, which
sought to breakdown "contemporary thought" as a means of solving
"pending problems" (Motherwell 1951, 65). The focus of the movement
in Paris was "revolt at any price." Comprised of Louis Argon, André
Breton, Philippe Soupault, Guillaume Apollinaire, and Man Ray, they
attacked past aesthetics by removing beauty, emotion, pleasure, and artistic expression from art. One technique they added in Paris was capturing random unconscious desires, which Apollinaire described as surrealism. The movement captured the disillusionment that people felt and
attracted large public interest at the Dadaist exhibition at the Palais des
Fêtes on January 23, 1920.

Paris was a common gathering place for expatriate writers such as
Sherwood Anderson, John Dos Passos, Ford Madox Ford, Hilda Doolit-

tle, James Joyce, Ezra Pound, F. Scott Fitzgerald, and Ernest Hemingway. Prior to the 1920s American writers in Paris were concerned with Poe, Emerson, Thoreau, Whitman, Hawthorne, and Melville (Fitch 1983, 162), but this changed after the war with an influx of new writers who shifted literary aesthetics. Aragon, Picabia, Tzara, and other Dadaists were "highly visible in Montparnasse cafés and cinemas" (200) and had a particular influence on these writers, who identified with the movement's critique of the war and extreme skepticism. Literary expatriates in Paris gravitated toward Dadaism's social critique and innovative aesthetics. The movement had particular influence on Gertrude Stein and Sherwood Anderson, both of whom became Hemingway's key mentors. Stein identified with Dadaism's critique of World War I, feeling that it "irreparably changed human consciousness" (Bay-Cheng 2005, 52). Her "Composition as Explanation" argues that the war created an audience more receptive to modern aesthetics by unifying artists with their audience in a collective experience (Stein 1946, 460). Stein asserts that modern art is not widely accepted until long after its creation; however, World War I advanced the appreciation of modern aesthetics into the contemporary moment:

> This then the contemporary recognition, because of the academic thing known as war having been forced to become contemporary made every one not only contemporary in act not only contemporary in thought but contemporary in self-consciousness made every one contemporary with the modern composition. And so the art creation of the contemporary composition which would have been outlawed normally outlawed several generations more behind even than war, war having been brought so to speak up to date art so to speak was allowed not completely to be up to date, but nearly up to date, in other words we who created the expression of the modern composition were to be recognized before we were dead some of us even quite a long time before we were dead. And so war may be said to have advanced a general recognition of the expression of the contemporary composition by almost thirty years (460).

War gave Stein's works more focus, but, more importantly, it created in Paris an audience more receptive of new artistic techniques. Conventional methods no longer seemed relevant to people who experienced the war and no movement attacked the war and its effects better than Dadaism. Stein frequently entertained Dadaist artists such as Aragon, Man Ray, Breton, and Soupault. She, like the Dadaists, believed that the war had changed human reason, and she adopted their negation of family, future, memory, authority, and sexual mores (Bay-Cheng 2005, 11). Stein employed Dadaist techniques like surrealism and automatism to remove beauty, emotion, and sentiment and attack logic. Bay-Cheng in *Mama Dada* notes that Stein also adopted fragmentation, collage, automatic speech, and repetition (53), which mechanize Stein's art. Bay Cheng indicates that Stein's inconsistent verb use in *Four Saints* creates the impression of several images occurring simultaneously, whereby a portrait gives sequential events a single moment (57). Stein's poem "If I Had Told Him: A Completed Portrait of Picasso" achieves Dadaist spontaneity, absurdity, and negation. Its repetition of words captures Dadaist automatism and mechanization to give it a feeling of impulsiveness. It also expresses Dadaist simultaneity by synchronically capturing multiple fragmented moments. Analogous to Tzara's "Dance Soiree with Programme" with its use of simultaneity and bruitism, words in Stein's poem serve as oratory sounds comparable to that of the repeated noises of a machine. Stein negates reason through words that are void of metaphor, illustration, and analogy. Comparable to Huelsenbeck's "End of the World," she juxtaposes words that have little or no correlation, such as "Would he like it," "Shifting shutters," and "So and so and also" (Stein 1998, 506). Words are void of analogy, emotions, or pleasure, making them equally meaningful and meaningless.

Dennis Ryan examines the influence of Dadaism on Anderson and estimates that he advised Hemingway upon Hemingway's departure to Paris "to look at the work of Picabia, Duchamp, Hartley, and other Dadaists" (Ryan 1996, 2). "A Divine Gesture," written in July, 1921, is unique to the Hemingway canon and often problematic for critics. Ryan indicates that the story parodies Anderson, who he notes was "indebted to Gertrude Stein's experimental method[s] . . . [and] had learned Stein's Cubist/Dadaist techniques, including automatic writing" (2). Like Stein, Anderson had contact with several Dadaists, and Ryan concludes about the pervasiveness of Dadaism:

> Nevertheless, Dada spirit and technique continued to flourish in the works of Anderson, Stein, Ezra Pound, T. S. Eliot, and other modernists. In fact, during the same month that Hemingway composed "A Divine Gesture," Eliot was in the midst of composing *The Waste Land*, wherein the sounds "DA/Da . . . DA/Da . . . DA/Da" are accompanied by a host of strange utterances ("Drip drop drip drop drop drop drop," "Co co rico co co rico," "Weialala leia/ Wallala leialala") signaling Dada's effect upon the artist and the poem. Eliot was not the least of the many artists Dada affected over the period 1915–1921. Hemingway, just coming into his own, also learned from Dada, but mocked it and adherents like Sherwood Anderson who had taken the movement too seriously (6–7).

Dadaist aesthetics influenced several writers, particularly in Paris. Ryan may be correct in his conclusion that Hemingway mocks Anderson and Dadaism in "A Divine Gesture"; however, the story, written before Hemingway's arrival in Paris, demonstrates his awareness of their aesthetics and perhaps foreshadows Dadaism's influence on his later style. "A Divine Gesture" contains Dadaist irrational thought, absurdity, and spontaneity. God searches for Adam and Eve in a garden but only finds bathtubs, bootjacks, and broken flowerpots. Questions, posed to find meaning and truth, are answered. The bootjacks inquire why they cannot squirm, and God responds: "I'm busy" (Hemingway 1922, 267). An absurd response answers a spontaneous question, as there is no rational correlation between the bootjacks' question and God's answer. Impulsive language in the story captures Dadaist randomness and absurdity. God demands the bootjacks to stop squirming and one responds: "We mustn't squirm today. We mustn't squirm to-day. Hy ya ta did eeyay. We mustn't squirm today" (267). Hemingway abandons logical thought with nonsensical words that serve as oratory sounds.

The war initially altered Hemingway's style, giving it more focus and criticism. His early poems before and after the war reveal a gradual shift: prior to the war his poems center on sports, school, and summer, but his poetry between 1918 and 1919 emphasize battles, death, and loss of ideals. However, as Michael Reynolds points out, these writings were "still grounded in nineteenth century technique" (Reynolds 1986, 159). In Paris, expatriate writers and artists helped him to find new artistic direction. Paris gave Hemingway connections to a wide array of artists, writers, and thinkers seeking to expand conventional aesthetics. Hemingway struggled with his war experiences and found in Paris people equally scarred by the war. With Dadaism's critique and apathetic attitude toward the war and political ideals, he identified with their exposition. Sylvia Beach's Shakespeare and Co. gave Hemingway access to Dadaist artists such as Aragon, Breton, Soupault, and Man Ray for him to expand his literary and artistic horizons. He became familiar with Dadaist techniques through Anderson and Stein. Stein, in particular, gave him literary tools such as automatic writing, repetition, and tearing down conventional literary barriers to voice his disillusionment.[2]

"My Old Man" and "Fifty Grand," written in 1922 and his first stories in Paris, are more conventional in composition (i.e., phrasing, dialogue, linear structure, character development, etc.) than "A Divine Gesture." However, by 1923 with his associations with Stein, Pound, Joyce, and others, Hemingway changes his style, desiring to write more like other avant-garde writers on the Left Bank. "Up in Michigan" (1923) shows the beginnings of this transformation with Hemingway successfully balancing between avant-garde works like "A Divine Gesture" and mainstream stories like "My Old Man." He appropriates Stein's repetition in "Up in Michigan" to achieve authorial distance. For example, the third paragraph reiterates Liz's interest in Jim:

> Liz *liked* Jim very much. She *liked* it the way he walked over from the shop and often went to the kitchen door to watch for him to start down the road. She *liked* it about his mustache. She *liked* it about how white his teeth were when he smiled. She *liked* it very much that he didn't look like a blacksmith. She *liked* it how much D.J. Smith and Mrs. Smith liked Jim. One day she found that she *liked* it the way his hair was black on his arms and how white they were above the tanned line when he

washed up in the washbasin outside the house. *Liking* that made her feel funny. (emphasis added, Hemingway 1987, 59)

Repeating Liz's "like" for Jim creates a mechanized narration void of authorial sentiment. Unlike Dadaism and Stein, the story is not entirely void of human emotions, sentiments, or ideas; however, Hemingway removes himself from the narrative and does not impose his ideas onto the reader. He does not tell the reader what to think about Liz's crush on Jim or Jim's eventual violation of Liz. This is not to say that the reader does not have an emotional attachment to the characters or an opinion on their subsequent relationship, but, comparable to "A Divine Gesture," the story exists without authorial bias in a manner analogous to Dadaism. Hemingway continued his experimentation with authorial detachment in March 1923, when he was writing the vignette that later would be Chapter VI in *In Our Time*. Reynolds notes that Hemingway initially wrote the story in the first person but then changed it to the third person to make it more impersonal (Reynolds 1989, 124–25).

"The Soul of Spain with McAlmon and Bird the Publishers" (1923) shows Hemingway's experimentation with Dadaist aesthetics in poetry with his use of assonance to repeat the "ain" sound. Comparable to Stein's "If I Had Told Him: A Completed Portrait of Picasso," Hemingway conveys mechanical repetition through sounds that are less literary and more auditory. Logic and narrative are secondary, making the poem appear random. It also employs Dadaist negation by attacking political ideals, family, home, science, literature, art, sports, etc., and it especially attacks ideals and reason. As with Tzara's attack on poetry, Hemingway turns his attack to art and literature by referring to Menken, Waldo Frank, Ezra Pound, and Dadaism as "shit" as well. The poem exemplifies Dadaist disgust and negates all ideals, even influential ones. Hemingway's denouncement of Dadaism could be interpreted that he was opposed to the movement or did not take it seriously. He uses the same word to describe Tzara and the movement in a 1924 letter to Pound: "Tzara and such was *shit* in France" (emphasis added, Hemingway 2002, 116). However, it would be wrong to suggest that such criticism undermines Dadaism's influence on Hemingway or uncovers his true feelings, as few artists or writers escape Hemingway's censure. Furthermore, such criticism does not explain why in "The Soul of Spain with McAlmon and Bird the Publishers" he uses the same word to criticize Pound, when Hemingway repeatedly admits Pound's influence on his writings: "Ezra Pound taught me to write more than anyone else alive" (Sandison 1999, 60). Using the same phrase for his mentor and Dadaism equates the two. "The Soul of Spain with McAlmon and Bird the Publishers" is Hemingway's subtle homage to both Dadaism and Stein with its repetition and negation.

A later poem, "Portrait of a Lady" (1926), again utilizes Dadaist techniques and pays tribute to Stein by mimicking her style. He employs Stein's repetition with the phrase "a poem." to achieve mechanical narration. As with Tzara's critique on poetry, Hemingway's poem lacks emotion and sentiment and random words and images attain Dadaist negation. Hemingway asserts that a poem, rather than providing instruction or meaning, merely is a poem. He undercuts its value by asserting that it is "not good," "can be laughed away," is "cheap," is "not worth writing," "states something that everybody knows," is "insignificant," and he finally questions whether the poem is really a poem (Hemingway 1983, 90). Analogous to Tzara's conclusion of poetry that expands its definition, Hemingway questions the purpose of a poet and poetry.

By August 1923, Hemingway was burgeoning as a young writer. He successfully published *Ten Poems* and *In Our Time*, but his success was confined to Europe where he found a more favorable audience for his style. By 1924 he moves from being a virtually unknown avant-garde writer to a more conventional but successful writer. He struggled with American publications for his innovative techniques and difficult themes. After a brief period in Toronto, he returned to Paris on July 10, 1924, with more confidence and poise. Using automatic writing techniques that he learned from Anderson and Stein, and, notably, that Anderson and Stein learned from Dadaists, he began working on the short stories what would complete *In Our Time*. Stories written during his second period in Paris have a more mature style, more successfully balancing a conventional style with Dadaist absurdity, spontaneity, and negation.

As previously noted, Dadaist absurdity is contradiction and opposition. Dadaists contradict images to negate meaning. Hemingway employs this in his stories. An emergency cesarean section disrupts Nick's and his father's camping trip in "Indian Camp." Hemingway juxtaposes Nick's and his father's joyous fishing trip with the trauma of a woman who has been in labor for two days and a father who is in the upper bunk with an injured foot. Hemingway opposes Dr. Adams's callous statement that the Native American mother's screams are not important with the father rolling over against the wall to contrast Dr. Adams's desire to perform the surgery with the Native American father's desire to help his wife or at least no longer hear her screams. Hemingway also contrasts the birth of the infant with the death of the father. Finding the Native American with his throat cut from ear to ear undercuts Dr. Adams's elation over a successful surgery. "Soldier's Home" opposes Krebs's desire to be recognized for his sacrifices during the war with society's desire to forget it. The story opposes Krebs' need to truthfully talk about his experiences with people's desire to be thrilled by exaggeration. It places in opposition Krebs' desire to live a life without consequences with his parents urging him to "settle down to work" and make something of himself (Hemingway 2003, 75). "Mr. and Mrs. Elliot" shows a contradiction of desires: Hubert's desire to keep himself "pure" versus his disappointment with the wedding night, and his desires to have a baby versus Cornelia's desire not to have intercourse. Hemingway maintains the authorial distance that permeated his first stories in Paris, but his stories during his second period in Paris reveal a much more sophisticated style, able to contrast complex themes with precision. Collectively, *In Our Time* employs contradiction and opposition: happiness versus sadness, suffering versus joy, war versus peace, life versus death, friendship versus betrayal, morality versus immorality, legality versus illegality, passivity versus violence, innocuousness versus ominousness, bravery versus cowardice, and so on.

His stories between 1924 and 1926 also capture Dadaist spontaneity. Similar to Tzara's "Dance Soiree with Programme" that captures multiple sounds from various noises, Hemingway employs spontaneity in *In Our Time*, which collectively embodies the aesthetic properties of simultaneity and bruitism. As Reynolds claims birth, death, violence, war, wounds, water, love, and irony unite the volume (Reynolds 1989, 234). Multiple voices and perspectives comprise a cacophony of sounds and images ranging from fathers, sons, husbands, wives, Native Americans, African Americans, doctors, laborers, thieves, boxers, enlisted soldiers, officers, refugees, immigrants, expatriates, revolutionaries, and deposed kings. Much like Man Ray's photomontage *Tristan Tzara*, which forms complex images that represent diverse themes relevant to the 1920s (i.e., violence, sexuality, morality, love, immediacy, etc.), *In Our Time* collectively forms complex images of the modern world with themes of life, death, violence, sexuality, war, love, honor, bravery, camaraderie, family, sports, etc. The volume comprises a collage of random images, in a manner analogous to Huelsenbeck's "End of the World," that together examine the absurdity of a modern world that is void of meaning.

Negation is perhaps the best correlation between Hemingway and Dadaism. *In Our Time* captures the irrelevancy of ideals and criticizes the failures of systems. It demonstrates Tzara's exclamation: "I am against all systems, the most acceptable system on principle is to have none" (Motherwell 1951, 79). *In Our Time* agrees with Tzara's belief that all systems are problematic because they attempt to find meaning and order in a meaningless and chaotic world. The title evokes *The Book of Common Prayer*'s exclamation "Give us peace in our time, O Lord" to illustrate what each character seeks. They search for peace but fail to find it through conventional means. Characters turn to religion, government, political ideals, science, family, friends, love, etc. but fail to find it through these avenues. The soldier in Chapter VII turns to Jesus for deliverance and promises to tell the whole world about Jesus if he is saved but ends up not even telling the girl at the Villa Rossa about his experience. Harold Krebs entirely loses his religious feelings in "Soldier's Home," once attending a Methodist college and then losing his faith during the war. His mother pressures him with religion, but "Krebs [feels] embarrassed and resentful" about religious matters (Hemingway 2003, 75). Political ideals also fail. Nick finds comfort with his "separate peace" in Chapter VI. No longer is he concerned about the war. Happiness derives from being sent home due to his wound. Officers Drevitts and Boyle show the abuse of power by killing two Hungarians robbing a cigar store in Chapter VIII. Chapter XV emphasizes the indifference of the executioners and the priest with the execution of Sam Cardinella. Rather than discussing Cardinella's crimes to make the execution an act of justice, Hemingway stresses Cardinella's emotional suffering to shift the focus to the loss of life. Authority figures are indifferent to suffering and only are concerned with their own interests. Home and family also fail in *In Our Time*. Dr. Adams's home is no sanctuary in "The Doctor and the Doctor's Wife." His wife is a Christian Scientist who interrogates him after a difficult day. Hubert exhibits traditional ideals of love, marriage, and family in "Mr. and Mrs. Elliot," but, in the end, he abandons these aspirations to focus on writing. The husband in "Cat in the Rain" is indifferent to his wife's desire to have a child and her yearning goes unfulfilled.

In Our Time collectively argues that ideals are meaningless and irrelevant. Those who commit or sacrifice to ideals become frustrated, and their goals are unattained. The soldier gives up drinking and his friends in "A Very Short Story" so that he can get a job and be married; however, Luz breaks off the marriage when she falls in love with an Italian major. The revolutionist sacrifices himself for political ideals in "The Revolutionist," but his aspirations are never realized. Hemingway equates selfishness to selflessness: both are equally irrelevant.

Hemingway slightly deviates from Dadaist negation in *In Our Time*. It exhibits antagonism toward past and present institutions, but complete Dadaist negation is never fully achieved. *In Our Time* negates the importance of social institutions but never entirely destroys them. The end of "Indian Camp" returns to the initial imagery of Nick and his father in the boat with Nick's father in control. The military men that executed the cabinet ministers are still in power at the end of Chapter V, and Drevitts and Boyle are not reprimanded for their behavior in Chapter VIII. The struggle with Hubert and Cornelia in "Mr. and Mrs. Elliot" and the husband and wife in "Cat in the Rain" continues, and the desires within each relationship are still unfulfilled. Thus, *In Our Time* criticizes the past and current authority, but, unlike the Dadaists, it does not entirely deviate from it or show the complete removal of social, political, or religious institutions. It merely stresses the problems that such institutions and ideals create. Dissimilar to the Dadaists, it asserts that the Dadaist ideal of negation can never be fully achieved. The current system is destructive and thereby needs to be altered, but *In Our Time* never explicitly calls for the destruction of such systems or shows how this destruction can be achieved. Instead, *In Our Time* asserts that, with the inability to attain complete destruction of social systems, individuals must rely upon themselves. This can be seen in "The Revolutionist" where a young idealist seeks a world revolution through socialist communism; however, his search results in his being impoverished, tortured, and imprisoned. He foolishly tries to change the world, believing success in Italy "will be the starting point of everything" (Hemingway 2003, 81). Hemingway treats the revolutionist with pity, clinging to his values in the face of opposition and failure. Political systems lead to suffering (i.e., torture and imprisonment). The revolutionist places ideals above his needs and thereby suffers. Individuals cannot trust ideals; so, one solely must rely on oneself. "L'Envoi," where a revolutionary committee overthrows the existing king and forces him to stay within the palace grounds, emphasizes "[T]he great thing in this sort of an affair is not to be shot oneself!" (157). Hemingway's negation asserts complete failure of social institutions and their ideals and necessitates that a person turn to himself or herself.

"A Clean Well-Lighted Place" is perhaps the best representation of Dadaist negation. Originally written in 1926, the story represents more clearly Hemingway's philosophic vision that he was developing in *In Our Time* and connects more strongly to the nihilist sentiments embedded within Dadaism with greater focus on the meaninglessness of life that the characters confront. An old man comes into the café to find momentary solace from the futility of life. To cope, he previously attempted suicide, which two waiters discuss to better understand.

> "Last week he tried to commit suicide," one waiter said.
> "Why?"
> "He was in despair."
> "What about?"
> "Nothing" (Hemingway 1987, 288).

The old man struggles with emptiness but can find no solace. Although the waiter's response is a cavalier dismissal of the old man's anxiety by stating that his problems are based on nothing, the waiter's prophetic assertion is accurate to the old man's dilemma, who struggles with the nothingness that surrounds him. He discovers no meaning to life. He uncovers no purpose. Analogous to Dadaism, the old man feels frustrated and disappointed that there is no method to find order or meaning. Institutions and ideals do not help him. He is left in despair and seeking to end the meaninglessness of his life. He now enters the café to deaden his frustrations with alcohol.

Hemingway's connection to Dadaist negation becomes clearer with the juxtaposition of words and ideas in *Dadaist Manifesto* and "A Clean Well-Lighted Place" and further demonstrates the influence of Dadaist principles on Hemingway. Tzara illustrates the meaninglessness of finding purpose by stating that logic, science, religion, history, music, and art are inept. All these institutions attempt to discover meaning, but none offer valid explanations. Tzara's repetition is also significant. After each ideal he uses the word Dada. He uses a term with ambiguous meaning to argue that these ideals are just as ambiguous and meaningless. "A Clean Well-Lighted Place" echoes the tone and tenor and repetition of "Dadaist Disgust" found in *Dadaist Manifesto* as the older waiter reflects upon his fears:

> What did he fear? It was not fear or dread. It was *nothing* he knew too well. It was all a *nothing* and a man was *nothing* too. It was only that and light was all it needed and a certain cleanness and order. Some lived in it and never felt it but knew it all was *nada* y pues *nada* y *nada* y pues *nada*. Our *nada* who art in *nada*, *nada* be thy name thy kingdom *nada* thy will be *nada* thy *nada* in *nada* as it is in *nada*. Give us this *nada* our daily *nada* and *nada* us from *nada* as we *nada* our *nadas* and *nada* us not into *nada* but deliver us from *nada*, pues *nada*. Hail *nothing* full of *nothing*, *nothing* is with thee (emphasis added, Hemingway 1987, 291).

Hemingway's repetition of "nada" offers the same meaning of Tzara's use of the word "Dada." As previously mentioned, the word "dada" is ambiguous; in essence, it means nothing. The word "nada" literally means nothing. Both words comment on the emptiness and absurdity of life that is void of meaning. As the waiter reflects on the meaning of life, he is prompted to pray; however, he prays to nada. He no longer turns to religion; he no longer seeks political ideals; he no longer searches for scientific explanation. All these institutions, promising higher understanding and order, have failed. Being weary by his constant search, he becomes frustrated, and, much like the Dadaists, he withdraws to a state of nothingness. This story more boldly asserts the inability to find purpose through conventional means, and it demonstrates a more determined nihilistic approach of Hemingway that is analogous to Dadaist negation.

"A Clean, Well Lighted Place's" denouncement of reason and ideals exhibits similar criticisms that Hemingway made in "A Divine Gesture," "Portrait of a Lady," and "The Soul of Spain with McAlmon and Bird the Publishers." However, unlike "A Divine Gesture," "A Clean Well-Lighted Place" is not a parody. Hemingway clearly is not mocking Dadaism, Anderson, or Stein but illustrates the difficulties of living in a post-war society void of meaning or values. Hemingway's purposeful imitation of *Dadaist Manifesto* pays tribute to Tzara's and Dadaism's influence. Hemingway's tone, though not as lighthearted as Tzara, captures Dadaist disgust in all things. He no longer teases or disregards Dadaism as he did prior to living in Paris, but his imitation of Tzara's repetition shows the sincerest form of flattery. Hemingway finds value in the movement as a way to convey his frustrations. Dadaist criticism established itself as the prevailing voice that shaped social and artistic thought during the early 1920s (becoming the zeitgeist of postwar Europe), and Hemingway borrows its criticism of social and political ideals at the beginning of his career to hone his emerging literary voice.

NOTES

1. Bürger describes system-immanent criticism as the attack on an institution from within (Bürger 1984, 21). Dadaism differs from other art movements because it does not criticize art's past, but it attacks the institution of art in its methods of production and distribution.

2. Michael Reynolds mentions that one technique that Hemingway learned from Stein was surrealism. Reynolds notes that in 1923, Stein did not "understand why [Hemingway] was laboring over the manuscripts" and advised Hemingway to use automatic writing to help him focus (Reynolds 1989, 38).

REFERENCES

Bürger, Peter. *Theory of the Avant-Garde*. Trans. from the German by Michael Shaw. Theory and History of Literature #4. Minneapolis: University of Minnesota Press, 1984.

Bay-Cheng, Sarah. *Mama Dada: Gertrude Stein's Avant-Garde Theatre*. New York: Routledge, 2005.

Duchamp, Marcel. *L.H.O.O.Q.* 1919. Private collection, Paris.

Fitch, Noel Riley. *Sylvia Beach and the Lost Generation*. New York: W.W. Norton, 1983.

Hemingway, Ernest. *Complete Poems*. New York: Bison Books, 1983.

———. *The Complete Short Stories of Ernest Hemingway*. New York: Scribner, 1987.

———. "A Divine Gesture." *The Double Dealer*. (May 1922), 267–68.

———. *In Our Time*. New York: Scribner, 2003.

———. *Selected Letters 1917–1961*. Edited by Carlos Baker. New York: Scribner, 2002.

Kristiansen, Donna M. "What Is Dada?" *Educational Theatre Journal* 20, no. 3 (October 1968): 457–62.

Man Ray. *Compass*. 1920. The Metropolitan Museum of Art, New York.

———. *Dadaphoto*. 1920. Musée national d'Art moderne, Paris.

Motherwell, Robert, ed. *The Dada Painters and Poets: An Anthology*. New York: Wittenborn, Schultz, Inc., 1951.

Narbeshuber, Lisa. "Hemingway's *In Our Times*: Cubism, Conservation, and the Suspension of Identification. *The Hemingway Review* 25, no. 2 (Spring 2006): 9–28.

Reynolds, Michael. *Hemingway: The Paris Years*. New York: W.W. Norton, 1989.

———. *The Young Hemingway*. Oxford: Basil Blackwell, 1986.

Ryan, Dennis. "'A Divine Gesture': Hemingway's Complex Parody of the Modern. *The Hemingway Review* 16, no. 1 (Fall 1996): 1–17.

Sandison, David. *Ernest Hemingway: An Illustrated Biography*. Chicago: Chicago Review Press, 1999.

Stein, Gertrude. *Selected Writings*. New York: Random House, 1946.

———. *Writings 1903–1932*. New York: Library of America, 1998.

FIVE

The Nightinghouls of Paris

Robert McAlmon's Queer Paternalism and The Twilight of the Expatriate Movement

Chase Dimock

Out of all the famous writers and artists of the Lost Generation, perhaps no one figure has been so influential and central as a figure of the American expatriate movement in Paris and yet rewarded with so little acknowledgment as Robert McAlmon. Aside from two biographies, (the most recent, Sanford J. Smoller's from 1975), only recently has some scholarship been devoted to reclaim McAlmon from the margins of a literary history footnote and properly recognize his contributions to the expatriate literary movement as a writer, publisher, and pillar of the community.[1] McAlmon moved to Paris at the very beginning of the famed expatriate movement in 1921 and grew in reputation and infamy to be one of the elder statesmen of the community by the early '30s when the movement drew to a close. McAlmon was a mercurial figure, known for his sardonic wit, his loud, sometimes-amusing, sometimes-violent outbursts in bars and cafes in Paris; yet he was equally respected for his prodigious literary output and quiet kindness to other writers and artists through his patronage (Smoller 1975, 6). By the golden age of the era, McAlmon became the resident expert of the quarter and young expatriates sought him for making connections with other artists, publishing help, and advice on the cheapest places to drink. McAlmon was the first to publish works by Ernest Hemingway, Djuna Barnes, and Gertrude Stein, among other crucial writers of American modernism. McAlmon's omnipresence in the Montparnasse community placed him in the background of many of the period's significant landmarks. He was also the man who took Hemingway out to the Bullfights in Pamplona, an event which would be immortalized in *The Sun Also Rises*. He typed proofs of James Joyce's monumental novel *Ulysses*, and due to the convoluted system of notes and addendums in Joyce's manuscript, the voice of Molly Bloom that the first generation of readers received was McAlmon's interpretation of the text, until the original manuscript version was published many years later (McAlmon 1992, 118).

While scholars of the aforementioned writers have noted McAlmon's presence behind their works, only recently have scholars and readers had access to McAlmon's own texts. Today, thanks to Edward N. S. Lorusso's publication of three of McAlmon's early works (*Miss Knight and Others*, *Village*, and *Post-Adolescence*) in 1992 and Sanford J. Smoller's discovery and publication of his lost novel *The Nightinghouls of Paris* in 2007, we are now presented with enough material to retrieve McAlmon from the lost and found of the Lost Generation. The rediscovery of McAlmon's work shines a new light on the familiar narratives and mythologies of the expatriate movement in Paris. McAlmon's centrality as a figure within the community gave him an intimate knowledge of the eccentricities and insecurities that circulated behind the iconic visages of our most lionized and beloved artists of the era. McAlmon's stories, along with his memoir *Being Geniuses Together* provide an honest, if not sometimes caustic perspective on Hemingway, F. Scott Fitzgerald (both of whom at one point allegedly punched him for insinuating their homosexuality), Gertrude Stein, Ezra Pound, Ford Maddox Ford, Wyndham Lewis, Djuna Barnes, and several other writers who gathered in the cafes of Montparnasse.

Beyond merely being a historical archive of information on expatriate Paris, McAlmon's work deserves attention for his own distinctly modernist voice and, in particular, his early depictions of queer sexuality and gender identity. Although McAlmon never directly confessed his own bisexuality in his publications, he nonetheless realistically and sympathetically portrayed the complex psychologies of gay, lesbian, and transvestite characters and the gay underground of 1920s Berlin in his collection of short stories *Distinguished Air: Grim Fairy Tales* from 1926 (reprinted as *Miss Knight and Others*). A similar interest arises in the newly discovered semi-autobiographical novel *The Nightinghouls of Paris* in which he depicts his queer relationship with two young Canadian writers, John Glassco and Graeme Taylor (whom he fictionalizes as Sudge Galbraith and Ross Campion) and the drama of Djuna Barnes's (Chloe Andrews in the novel) contentious love affair with Thelma Wood (Steve Rath). Not only does McAlmon's novel satisfy our desire for a new narrative and gossip about this romanticized period of literary history, but the story also illuminates the difficulties of signifying and pursuing queer desires and identities in the era. Although McAlmon never explicitly states his textual alter-ego Kit O'Malley's sexuality in the novel, it is nonetheless clear that McAlmon as Kit becomes a father figure to the Canadian boys, refereeing their queer relationship with one another at the same time as he guides them through their growing pains as writers and members of the expatriate community. In the process, Kit's mentorship in the ways of expatriate living expands the reach of queerness beyond mere same-sex desire, suggesting the inherent queerness of the lifestyles of the expatriates whose presence in Paris eschews the normative, heterosexual imperatives of creating stable, productive, domesticated lives predicated on reproduction and allegiance to a nation. Combining his elder statesmanship of expatriatism with the youth and immaturity of his Canadian arrivals, McAlmon dramatizes the sunset of the golden age of the indulgent expatriate movement against the tenuous sunrise of a new generation of writers whose literary visions had been influenced by the expatriates, yet struggle in rectifying those narratives with the conservative social expectations set for their postwar generation.

ROOTING MCALMON AMONG "THE DERACINATED ONES"

At a young age, Robert McAlmon inherited the nomadic spirit that would compel him to move to Paris among his many migrations throughout his life. Born the youngest of ten children on March 9, 1896, in Clifton, Kansas, McAlmon was the son of a Presbyterian minister who uprooted the family many times during his childhood, moving to several different small towns in the Midwest (Knoll 1957, 5). Despite the difficulty of never permanently situating himself in a particular community as a child, McAlmon always held on to his midwestern identity and as a writer returned to it several times in his work. In his novel *Village* (1990), McAlmon insinuates an adolescent attraction to a young Gene Vidal in Madison, South Dakota, who would later grow up to father famous gay author, Gore Vidal (Vidal 1992, xi). The Midwest as a space of queer nostalgia and melancholy also appears in McAlmon's short story "Miss Knight" about a crass drag-performer in Berlin who maintains a resolutely unsophisticated midwestern persona despite having been cast away from his home due to rampant homophobia. The fact that McAlmon wrote these odes to the Midwest across the Atlantic in Paris places him among other expatriates such as Gertrude Stein with *The Making of Americans* whose alienation from America served to whet their interest and sharpen their insight into American culture and politics. Although he never returned to the Midwest, McAlmon retained it as part of his identity and defended it against what he felt were unfair caricatures, specifically those of Sinclair Lewis in *Babbit* and *Mainstreet*, whom he accused of giving to "the fake-superior pseudo-intellectual, and to the Europeans, a picture of America which they like to believe in order to feel their superiority" (McAlmon 1992, 33).

As with the majority of the members of the Lost Generation, Robert McAlmon's young adult years were profoundly shaped by the shift in social attitudes and values during World War I. While the previous generation of Americans clung to their postindustrialization capitalism, McAlmon's generation sought to criticize and interrogate an American culture that placed unquestioned value in the burgeoning middle-class lifestyle and did little to attend to class, race, and gender disparities in the pre–welfare state era. This generation was particularly influenced by Harold Stearns' 1921 work *America and the Young Intellectual* in which he argues that American culture is particularly antagonistic toward the social criticisms of the emerging generation of artists and intellectuals because "moral idealism is precisely what the institutional life of America today does not want"(Stearns 1921, 21).[2] Stearns work was highly influential on the work of fellow expatriate writer Malcolm Cowley whose chronicle of life among the expatriates in *Exile's Return* has become arguably the most influential investigation of the ideological component of the Lost Generation's expatriation. Cowley's book breaks down the expatriate movement into a standardized narrative of alienation, expatriation, and return that has come to inform many readings of the Lost Generation's work. While McAlmon solidly maintained that his motivations, both personal and ideological for moving to Paris were unique from the romantic vision of "exile" that his compatriots maintained, it is nonetheless enriching to map McAlmon's biography against Cowley's dominant narrative.

Using the royal "we" to describe his experience despite not always specifying which artists from the generation are huddled under its umbrella, Cowley begins the narrative of expatriation with a social awakening in the universities:

> In college, the process of deracination went on remorselessly. We were not being prepared for citizenship in a town, a state, or a nation; we were not being trained for an industry or a profession essential to the common life; instead we were being exhorted to enter the international republic of learning whose traditions are those of Athens, Florence, Paris, Berlin, and Oxford. (Cowley 1994, 28)

While Cowley's narrative of expatriation presupposes college as the origin of their politics of social critique, McAlmon on the other hand found his university experience to be provincial and stifling. After spending a few post–high school years bumming around South Dakota doing manual labor, McAlmon entered the University of Minnesota in 1916 where his brother had been a football star, but found little stimulation or motivation as a student and eventually transferred to USC when the family moved to Los Angeles after his father's death (Smoller 1975, 17). At USC, which was still a small, religious institution, McAlmon's intellectual curiosities and literary aspirations were met with conservative hostility. Unlike

Cowley, McAlmon's interest in modern literature and thought came in spite of the university atmosphere, not because of it.

As a second formative stage in expatriate ideology, Cowley factors the emergence of World War I and the young students' desire to take up the cause of fighting for the romantic fervor of liberty and patriotism even before America had entered the war. In his biography on McAlmon, Sanford J. Smoller writes of McAlmon's lack of interest in the romance of war:

> Unlike Hemingway, Dos Passos, Cummings, and Cowley, who were to rendezvous with him in Montparnasse, McAlmon felt no immediate impulse to see "History's Greatest War" or even to do his bit for suffering humanity. America joined the allies on 6 April 1917, but McAlmon did not enlist until March 1918. Ironically, McAlmon, like F. Scott Fitzgerald, joined the service because he wanted to go to Europe, but he never left the states, except perhaps for off-duty excursions to Tijuana. (Smoller 1975, 19)

While McAlmon shared the desire to wander abroad to Europe, he maintained no high-minded ideals about his participation being a case of putting political conviction into action like Cowley would maintain or Hemingway would document in *A Farewell to Arms*. Additionally, missing duty on the front spared McAlmon from directly confronting the brutality of the war that was irrefutably integral to the Lost Generation's critique of Western ideology.

Once the American idealists returned to their native soil, Cowley's narrative houses them in the bohemian comforts of Greenwich Village, where they enjoyed close proximity to the hub of American publishers and liberal politics. Here, McAlmon's narrative converges with Cowley's as he too migrated from California after his release from the Army to Greenwich Village, where he was integrated into the literary world with the friendship of William Carlos Williams and Marsden Hartley. As McAlmon sought to establish himself among the young modernists, according to Cowley, a growing sense of dissatisfaction with American civilization was kindled among his compatriots. Interpreting Harold Stearns's argument about America's anti-intellectualism as meaning that there was no place for them in America, the soon-to-be expatriates embraced "the idea of salvation by exile." As Cowley sums it up, their mantra was "They do things better in Europe; let's go there" (Cowley 1994, 74). While McAlmon shared many of their criticisms of American culture, he maintained a steadfastly unromantic vision of expatriation and unwillingness to uncritically valorize Europe. Responding to the question "Why do you prefer to live outside America?" posed by Eugene Jolas to several expatriates in a 1928 article in *Transition* on writers abroad, McAlmon responded:

> We deracinated ones, if we are deracinated, may not all have come to
> Europe impelled by some motive of the heart and mind. I came, intend-
> ing to return, or to travel much. I felt in America that Europe was
> finished, decayed, war- and time-worn out. There it seemed that in
> Europe the sense of futility would be too enveloping, However there is
> the rot of ripe fruit, and there is the blight and decay of green fruit.
> (Knoll 1957, 12)

McAlmon's response tempers the expatriate insistence on the "they
do things better there" mantra. As Smoller puts it, "He at least had no
desire to become 'spiritualized' in Europe's crumbling temples" (1975,
50). Despite his lack of mystified reverence for old Europe, McAlmon far
outlasted Malcolm Cowley and those writers grouped under his royal
"we." Disappointed with the war-ravaged continent and the inability of
many to maintain a steady living, Cowley and his exiles' return to America came as they accepted publishing jobs and integration into a mainstream that they had previously detested. Further explaining his motivation for staying in Paris in Jolas's survey, McAlmon responded, "I prefer
Europe, if you mean France, to America because there is less interference
with private life here. There is interference, but to a foreigner, there is
fanciful freedom and grace of life not obtainable elsewhere" (Knoll 1957,
12). McAlmon's preference for France had nothing to do with any fetish-
ized taste for French or European culture, but it was instead based on the
liberties he could enjoy thanks to France's relaxed morals and more socially progressive government. As a bisexual man, McAlmon benefited
from France's lack of a sodomy law and relaxed obscenity laws that
allowed him to publish gay-themed texts like *Distinguished Air*, Djuna
Barnes's *Ladies Almanack*, and Ken Sato's *Quaint Tales of the Samurai* without censorship.

McAlmon's ability to stay in Paris well after many of the ideologues
had left was due to perhaps the least ennobling of all human motivations:
economics. McAlmon's opportunity to go abroad came in 1921 with his
sudden and capricious marriage to the lesbian writer Bryher, who was
the long-term companion of the famed American imagist poet, H.D.
McAlmon's marriage to Bryher was a matter of gossip and controversy
among the members of their artistic milieu, a battle still waged among
scholars of the expatriate era. While many assumed McAlmon married
Bryher as an opportunist interested in her wealth and nicknamed him
"McAlimony" after their divorce, there is considerable evidence in his
correspondences that he was unaware she was Annie Winnifred Ellerman, daughter of shipping magnate John Ellerman, the richest man in
Great Britain (Smoller 1975, 38). Regardless of whether either McAlmon
or Bryher had real interest in one another or they simply desired to ma-
nipulate the marriage for material gain, both benefited financially and
artistically from the arrangement. The marriage afforded McAlmon the
chance to go abroad to England and to eventually settle into Paris with an

allowance that permitted him to concentrate on his writing and start his publishing company.

By contrasting McAlmon's path toward expatriation with Malcolm Cowley's dominant narrative what we uncover is a base antinormative queerness that guided his presence in Paris. McAlmon's exploitation of the heterosexual contract of marriage and the privileges attached to it granted him and his lesbian wife the liberty of economic inheritance that came presupposed under the system of patriarchy and legitimized their queer lifestyles. McAlmon and Bryher had limited contact over the course of their marriage and spent most of their time on their individual artistic pursuits and chasing their own objects of desire, paying little attention to any of the vows they must have taken or to any of the cliché imperatives of domesticity like settling down, reproducing, or working a steady job to ensure their welfare and contribute productive labor to the economy. As his peers such as Cowley left Paris for some or all of the aforementioned comforts of heteronormativity, McAlmon remained in a Montparnasse space filled with drink, dancing, sex, and indolence that catered to all immediate desires without an imperative toward the hallowed responsibility of normative heterosexuality.

LIVING IN THE EXPATRIATE AFTERMATH

The Nightinghouls of Paris reads as an attempt on McAlmon's part in two temporal frames to take stock of what the expatriate movement in Paris had been and what it continues to signify to the literary world and general public. First, as Smoller notes in his introduction, McAlmon wrote the novel well after his time in Paris had come to an end and he was working with family in Arizona in 1945–1947 (Smoller 2007, xxxvii). In this respect, it is more apparent how readily McAlmon would desire to cast himself in a paternal, or at least avuncular, role in the lives of Graeme Taylor and John Glassco seeing as by this time in his life, McAlmon had advanced into middle age and had time to contemplate his legacy and to analyze the influence of the Lost Generation on American culture. Second, as we know from the time frame in which Robert McAlmon lived with Graeme Taylor and John Glassco in real life, the novel takes place roughly between 1928 and 1930. Although McAlmon would be hardly into his mid-thirties by this time, in the transient environment of Paris, McAlmon's nearly decade-long expatriation cast him as one of the older statesmen of the quarter. By this time, McAlmon although usually unsentimental, was already announcing the death of Montparnasse's golden age (Smoller 1975, 188).

While the Quarter may have lost some of its key luminaries and a bit of its mystique for McAlmon and other expatriates, its importance in the American cultural imaginary was beginning to flower. Smoller writes,

"Fancy American-style bars had replaced the crude but direct bistros and *bal musettes* of the early twenties. With the financial boom at its apex, rich American tourists had turned Paris into their private Babylon" (1975, 188). The incursion of American tourists brought into Montparnasse the consumerist hunger for the exotic sanitized for digestible commodification that McAlmon and other expatriates had originally fled from by inhabiting a section of Paris that had previously been a seedy neighborhood.[3] Ironically, the American thirst for Paris can be blamed in part on the expatriates' own success as an artistic movement. By the late 1920s, Hemingway's novels had achieved massive popularity and F. Scott Fitzgerald, who had already achieved fame and celebrity before trying out the expatriate lifestyle, further brought attention to the lives of American artists communing in the bistros of Paris. The romanticism of expatriatism and the "salvation by exile" that Cowley describes had in less than a decade been turned into a popular commodity for the American public.

McAlmon laments the commodification of the expatriate lifestyle in the novel with his depiction of Duff Twysden (fictionalized as "Lady Mart"), who is better known as the elusive object of desire Lady Brett Ashley in Hemingway's *The Sun Also Rises*. Arguing that Hemingway "gave her a romantic glamour she didn't really possess in life," McAlmon portrays Lady Mart as desperate and dependent on her new found celebrity as McAlmon recalls a conversation with her after Hemingway (fictionalized as Forrest Pemberton) had given her 1,000 francs in pity:

> Pemberton's thousand francs were making Mart feel momentarily secure and gay. That was about what it should be. He had claimed to love her, and the story of his romance made thousands of American college boys' hearts quiver. A thousand francs was a reasonable price to pay, if she didn't get him for more. On Mart's side, she would be pointed out to tourists and romantic young men as the heroine of his book. . . . Before I left La Coupole Mart was deep in conversation with three college boys from America. One was thrilled to discover that she was the original of Pemberton's frail heroine. Mart was being gay, feeling capable of making more conquests, and what do boys come to Paris for if not to have romance? (McAlmon 2007, 72)

At this point, Montparnasse had become a Lost Generation theme park, complete with Americanized facsimiles of the bars and cafes that used to exist and Duff Twysden happy to pose for pictures as Lady Brett Ashley like a man in a Mickey Mouse costume. Not only had the fictionalized version of expatriate Paris in Hemingway's work covered up the unfortunate reality of its inhabitants, but also this glorified fiction had come to replace the reality of the community even for those who visited the actual streets.

GUIDING A NEWLY LOST GENERATION

If the work of the expatriate authors had such an impact on the pop culture of young America—that Hemingway's novel had inspired, "hundreds of bright young men from the Middle West" who were "trying to be Hemingway heroes, talking in tough understatements from the sides of their mouths" as Malcolm Cowley claims, then the impact on this young generation of writers was particularly prescient, as they not only imitated the characters, but wanted to imitate the prose sensibilities as well (Cowley 1994, 225). Ushering in this new generation whose tastes and talents had been tailored around Lost Generation prescriptions, McAlmon simultaneously closes the curtains on the golden age of the expatriate movement and initiates a new, uncertain, even doomed generation with the arrival of Canadian youths Sudge and Ross. McAlmon sets the scene for their arrival in a bar in the Quarter as he is engaged in conversation with Hilaria, a noted Cuban *demimondaine* (or "*poule*" as McAlmon terms women of ill-repute in the quarter) on the prowl for young men. McAlmon as Kit O'Malley says to her "You got going strong, didn't you? But hell, with the summer supply of virgins and frustrated old ladies arriving, no man can afford to have his abilities exploited.' (McAlmon 2007, 4). Establishing the bars of Montparnasse as replete with world-wise women looking to prey on younger men, McAlmon sends in the boys:

> I saw them for the first time. They would touch Hilaria's gallivanting heart which had a tincture of the maternal within it. Reticently they approached, shy boyishly eager. Hilaria took Ross's hand to shake and her strong grip threw him off balance. She laughed with tender delight "Drink with Hilaria. I am the education for all leetla boys who wander lonely in Montparnasse, if they are of beauty." (5)

As a potential initiator of the boys into the economy of pleasure in the Quarter, Hilaria is written as both seductress and as a maternal figure, with both facets figured as alluring and threatening. With Hilaria, McAlmon initiates a discourse of cross-generational relationships that combines sexual desire with a parental drive toward mentorship. Ultimately, as the novel progresses, McAlmon crosses both of those desires to the point where they are nearly indistinguishable, suggesting even among same-age relationships, that sexual couplings are always structured by a paternalistic or maternalistic relationship of power.

Having established the elder patrons of the Quarter as capable of both benevolence and exploitation, McAlmon contrasts the world-wise with an innocent vision of Sudge and Ross.

> They were perfect visual examples of Etonesque schoolboys, with gray trousers, pink and white reticence, and grave, palpitating courtesy. Sudge looked fifteen but claimed to be eighteen, and Ross was twenty-

two. With bashful curiosity they admitted not knowing how to get acquainted with people in the quarter. I felt aged and dissipated, sure that Hilaria and I would horrify their ideas of correctness. (5)

At this point, McAlmon places himself as Kit in a similar structural position to Hilaria in so far as he too senses both the desire to corrupt what appears to be immaculate school children. Yet, Kit is partially disabused of this assumption when Sudge explains that he is sick with a social disease. Immediately, Kit takes the place of a wise veteran of the Montparnasse sexual milieu, suggesting the name of a reputable doctor.

"Sound," Sudge said with polite relief. I knew then I had adopted the boys. "I've heard about you," Sudge said. "Somebody pointed you out as you passed the Dome and said you knew everybody. That's why we came down here. Ross and I have festered all spring trying to know Paris." (5)

As Kit agrees to show them around Paris and introduce them to the remaining writers and personalities of note among Montparnasse, McAlmon grants Kit guardianship and responsibility over both the sexual maturation of the boys as well as literary mentorship as a guide through the textual and physical space of the expatriate world. Sexual guidance becomes a prerequisite for living in the Quarter and becoming a writer, thus McAlmon's construction of the space of expatriate Paris does not place sex and sexuality at the margin or a fringe benefit of living there, but as a force already presupposed and integrated in the natural course of artistic production.

From this point, Kit takes the boys under his wing and initiates them in a whirlwind tour of the clubs in the Quarter. McAlmon summarizes his first night with his new mentees:

I got beautifully lit that night and went to Zelli's, and from there to other places in Montmartre. . . . I don't know how I got home, because when I left the jazz gaiety of a Negro cabaret I forgot to remember. When I lifted my head from the pillow in the morning, I saw Ross sleeping in rosy peace beside me. He woke up as I wondered what we had done the night before. He sat up and smiled winningly. "Sound night we had?" he questioned with staunch cheer. (8)

McAlmon's description of the aftermath of a night of drunken carousing purposefully leaves ambiguous how he ended up in bed with the young man and whether or not any sexual activity had occurred. He strategically sets up a defense of plausible deniability where a queer readership can read sexuality in between the lines while McAlmon himself could always claim lack of memory or responsibility in the haze of a drunken night he no longer could recall. Although McAlmon has no discomfort in honestly exploring the queer sexuality of his characters, he always stops short at addressing the full sexuality of his own narrative doppelganger in his works. McAlmon later depicts in careful, sensitive detail the confused and ill-defined love and attraction between the boys, but his own sexual desire for the boys is veiled.

John Glassco's own fictionalized memoirs of his time in Paris, *Memoirs of Montparnasse* retells his first encounter with McAlmon from an opposite perspective and orientation toward closeting. In his memoirs, which McAlmon actually depicts him writing in *The Nightinghouls of Paris*,[4] it is McAlmon who is demonstrably homosexual while he himself never alludes to his own queer feelings.

> I had already noticed his small thin mouth and piercing stare, but it was clear he was far from being the kind of invert whose predilection shapes his whole personality. . . . It soon appeared that his chosen role was to be the fatherly or avuncular, and I began to hope he was more vain of being seen with young men than actually covetous of their favors. This hope was dispelled by a burly, moonfaced man, dressed in baggy tweeds and with his necktie clewed by a gold pin, who came noisily into the bar and greeted our table with a loud "Well, Bob, up to your old tricks again?" (Glassco 1995, 43)

While McAlmon's version of the meeting grants us only enough interiority into the narrator to know that he is compelled to take a fatherly position within the boys' life in the Quarter, Glassco's rendition gives us his full motivation for his generosity. Glassco's early impression of McAlmon puts into question the adequacy of his masculinity and sexuality and the possible lurking motives behind whichever type of gender or sexual deviant he may be. McAlmon is judged to neither be one of the inverts from his "fairy tales," who adopted feminine attire and mannerisms, nor a sufficient approximation of the rugged masculine ideal that Hemingway's entrance into the story embodies. While Glassco's initial impressions of McAlmon interprets the possibility that his intentions can retain some sense of purity, the impeccable heterosexual masculinity of Hemingway comes to dispel that notion and interrogate the assumed ulterior motives of the queer "tricks" McAlmon looks to play.

Glassco insinuates by the end of his narrative of their first night out partying that McAlmon's drinking to incapacitation may indeed have been a trick to get into bed with the young men. After having been taken to a couple gay bars where McAlmon dances with fairies, which McAlmon omits from his own narrative, Glassco and Taylor soon have to assume responsibility over a violent and disruptive McAlmon after he is slipped a barbiturate to get him to stop singing his infamous shrieking "Chinese Opera." In the aftermath of McAlmon's bacchanalia, Glassco writes "Waking uncomfortably a few hours later, however, I found he had made his way between Graeme and me and I began to wonder if he had been quite as helpless as he appeared to be in the Coupole bar" (1995, 51). Much like how McAlmon's own narrative exploits his alcohol-erased memory as an excuse for not explaining how or why he ended up in bed with the boys, Glassco suggests that a similar manipulative spirit compelled him to feign incapacitation in order to trick the boys into sharing a bed. In both accounts, McAlmon's homosexuality is present as a series of tricks and masquerades. In his own narrative, these tricks are implicit in the silence of what he does not include as an author, while in Glassco's tale, these tricks of his sexuality are based in his foundational queerness where he does not fit a specific paradigm of homosexuality common to the era and does not announce his attentions, preferring to remain opaque, illegibly queer.

Regardless of the real or imagined sexual desire between McAlmon and the boys, Kit's most profoundly queer influence over the boys is the initiation into the ways of life in Montparnasse that conflicts with the norms of heteropatriarchy. Kit's mentorship encourages what Kathryn Bond Stockton terms "growing sideways," which accounts for the kinds of queer, nonnormative behaviors and growth that children undergo that conflict with the imperative to "grow up" according to the prescriptions of heteronormative society. McAlmon's concept of the expatriate lifestyle represents a certain period of arrested development where the artist resists growing up and into the normal, supposedly respectable lives of an average American citizen and instead grows sideways, pursuing pleasure and arts without a thought toward the future. McAlmon sets the balance of the boys' time in Paris within a tension between the sideways growth of enjoying the opportunity for drunken debauchery and the time and space to concentrate on writing and the imperative to "grow up" and pursue a more conventional path of conforming to their fathers' expectations to cease their juvenile preoccupations, return to Canada, find employment, marry, and reproduce the lifestyle of their fathers. For McAlmon himself, the latter course of action was never a possibility and thus he found himself with the queer "nightinghouls" of the Quarter like Djuna Barnes and her lover Thelma Wood remaining after his compatriots one by one returned home either as failed artists reverting to tried and true American middle-class lifestyles, or like Hemingway and Fitzgerald, cashing in on their fame. While these normative standards of living did not bother the truly Lost Generation that remained in Paris, McAlmon wonders in his narrative if the new arrivals could resist "growing up" into fixity and middle-class security as he had:

> I had misgivings about my lost generation, which is thwartedly illusioned and in revolt to such an extent as to be incapable of detachment. Our lostness consists in knowing ourselves lost while viewing older or younger generations and types as unaware of their lostness and mediocrity. Were the boys of the new generation free of the sentimental complexities that once bothered us? With youth still in me I didn't want to feel a grandfather while readjustment and flexibility were possible. (McAlmon 2007, 11)

In addition to Glassco's suggestion of a narcissistic desire to be seen with young men, accompanying this new generation gave McAlmon a chance to take stock of what his generation had accomplished and perhaps, with decided measure, look forward toward merging his sideways growth with theirs.

Yet, as the fictional Sudge and Ross struggle as writers to produce anything and experience a string of failed attempts to romance women, they become somewhat disenchanted with Kit's expatriate style of living. McAlmon as Kit reflects:

> Ross might have been declared a true product of the after-war genera-
> tion, but it's probable he was another repetition of a biologic-psycho-
> logic type which exists and recurs. In his mental attitudes he had no
> patience with the lost-generation, barren-leaves-on-the-wastelands ap-
> prehension of life. Somewhere in him was hardness and disdain. His
> attitude toward Sudge was perhaps not so much sentimental as calcu-
> lating. He wanted, maybe needed Sudge, but more important, he in-
> tended to avoid coping with economic situations if he could. At times,
> his belief in himself as an artist was so supreme and his contempt for
> money as any kind of a standard so complete that, however he solved
> the economics of life, he was justified to himself. But now, he was
> merely a helpless wreck. (McAlmon 2007, 131)

McAlmon's narrative portrays Ross as lost in a world that offers him only the aimless indolence of the expatriates and the static materialism of his home in Canada. Compounding this unhappiness is his mostly unsatisfied desire for Sudge. Although Kit initially thinks of the boys as one and the same "twittering like love birds" in their own youthful language, and everyone they meet gets the impression that they are in love with one another, it becomes apparent over the course of the narrative that the love is decidedly one sided. While Sudge eventually admits a certain form of love for Ross, he never demonstrably pines for Ross like Ross does for him. Because of the disequilibrium of their desires and the lack of a social discourse through which to make sense of their feelings or put them into productive action, their relationship falls into a state of dysfunction that the fatherly Kit constantly counsels.

Without the language to directly confront their feelings, the boys end up creating what Eve Sedgwick calls an "erotic triangle," effectively projecting their desires for each other onto a series of other people.[5] The first of these, is of course, Kit who encourages their sideways growth. Kit also becomes a confessional figure and an intermediary in the boys' relationship. Thus, they confide in him the details of their other objects of triangulation. In an early conversation with Kit, Ross confesses, "Last spring we were broke, and ran into a dirty old Englishman who wanted to see a show. We took him to our room and staged a pose for him and he gave us two hundred francs. . . . The old fool," Ross scoffed, "didn't know we were only pretending. We made noises and the idiot pranced around having a great time" (McAlmon 2007, 25). Although at first Kit believes they saw it as a joke, it becomes apparent that such a fond memory for Ross may have been based on the fact that within the imaginary space of performance, he was able to approach some form of physical intimacy with Sudge. Ross further explains that with part of the money, they hired a prostitute to share. "I took her first, but just played around till Sudge got excited and wanted me to hurry." Analyzing Ross's statement, Kit thinks to himself "It was probably always 'just playing around' for Ross with the girls they picked up, I suspected." Here, according to Sedgwick's model of the triangulation of homosocial and homoerotic desire onto the body of a woman, Ross derives pleasure from the experience not out of his own desire for the prostitute's body, but from the desire Sudge invests in it and can experience through her body as a conduit. Ross's narrative also hints at a certain level of sexual attraction to himself on Sudge's part insofar as watching Ross "play" with her can arouse him.

While the experience with the lecherous man and the prostitute speak to mere physical desire, Ross and Sudge's final triangulation of desire which they structure around a young Greenwich Village type named Sanka is an interplay of romantic desire. Speaking to Kit for the first time about her relationship with the boys, Sanka says "Each of them thinks he's in love with me, and last night I told Ross it was him I loved. He's mad at me because I flirted with Sudge all day. . . . I feel sorta lousy horning in on them, because—I didn't see it at first—they're in love with each other. Ross is with Sudge, and I just mess things up" (McAlmon 2007, 130). While Sanka sees her presence as messing things up, despite how much she enjoys playing with their hearts, for Sudge and Ross, her presence is a decoy onto which they mutually sublimate this love for one another that even she can detect. Even though she lacks serious intentions, Sanka plays along with the idea of marrying Sudge which outrages Ross, shouting "To hell with him! . . . He'd be festering away with that cheap family of his if it wasn't for me. He wouldn't know anybody if it wasn't for me. He'd be married to some little slut like his brother is by now" (130). Ross's outrage over Sudge winning Sanka's affections over him has nothing to do with any desire he may feign to have for the girl, but that the coupling threatens to disrupt his relationship with Sudge. In Ross's quote, we see a stark opposition between the normal life route of heterosexual configured as an anchoring into a fixed, patriarchal space back in Canada and the more queer life he had shared with Ross.

The question of Sudge eventually getting married looms as a specter throughout the novel. Ross and Sudge live off a $100-a-month allowance from Sudge's wealthy father, yet Sudge knows that he stands to inherit a much greater sum were he to return to Canada married. For Sudge this looming proposition creates a constant existentialist dilemma. A natural desire for the security of economics and stability of identity that would come from cementing his place in the patriarchal structure of his family would come at the foreclosure of his more queer desires—his unspoken love for Ross and his literary passions. This tension comes to a violent rupture in the bar when an enraged Ross pushes Sanka off her stool and Sudge comes in to defend her, striking Ross in the process. The punch pushes a sudden realization into Sudge's consciousness as he reacts with instant remorse seeing Ross with a cut below his eye: "Ross, precious, forgive me. You know I didn't want to hit you. You know I don't care for her. It's you I love, but you don't leave me alone, ever. I want to take care of you, but you don't work, and you don't let me know anybody" (133). For the first time, Sudge puts into language his feelings for his compan-ion.

After Ross flees the scene, a disconsolate Sudge confesses to Kit, still fixed on the idea of synthesizing some form of marriage where he can somehow factor in his relationship with Ross. "I want to get married, but who will look after Ross if I do? Sanka wouldn't mind if he stayed with us, but most girls would." "Rot, you don't want marriage at your age." "It would look better, and people wouldn't have rotten ideas about Ross and me" (134).

At this moment Sudge reveals that he had similarly been triangulating his desire for Ross on the body of Sanka, basing his wish to marry her on the fact that she would continue to consent to this triangulation and tailor the parameters of their married life to include a space where his relation-ship with Ross remains intact yet remains closeted for the public as monogamous. This hysterical confession on Sudge's part speaks to the difficulty of placing into language and into social expectations a kind of queer relationship that lacked visible or socially acceptable examples to emulate. In the space of a few minutes, Sudge publicly outs his love but then immediately reveals his hidden shame, stating that he does not want people to have "rotten ideas" even if these ideas may be true. He cannot conceptualize his desire outside of the normative framework that con-demns and marginalize it; he has only negative discourse to work within order to construct some sort of paradigm for realizing his desire.

After his violent scene where he defends heteropatriarchy in the form of Sanka's body against the encroaching queerness of Ross only to imme-diately regret his impulse, Sudge becomes more openly hostile to the compulsory heterosexuality foisted upon him in all directions. Later in the novel, Sudge tells Kit of visiting his parents vacationing in England where an argument with his father over the direction of his life comes to blows:

> When he asked me what I was going to do with my life, I asked him what he had done with his and hoped I'd avoid being such a dull fart as he is. . . . He said how much money he had made in the last year, investing money Pinky, my sister and I inherited in trust from mother's family. I broke loose and told him that every cent he had he'd inherit-ed, married, or had thrown at him and that he was such a rotten lover,

> mother had to take on sea captains to escape him. That jolted him. He
> didn't realize I knew, or that I knew he'd kept his ugly secretary as a
> mistress. (155)

Sudge's criticism of his father deflates the power that he lords as the
patriarch by connecting his failure at normative heterosexuality with his
failure to produce anything of his own. Sudge pulls back the curtain that
shrouds the real sources of patriarchal power, finding that the emphasis
placed on reproduction and stability forecloses on the individual's ability
to produce anything of their own. Patriarchy grants each generation with
the same privileged resources of capital and the inheritors are merely
tasked with managing their domination long enough for the next generation to inherit the burden. Growing up means growing out of the creative
agency and individual freedom that characterizes the sideways child in
exchange for security rooted in generations of inherited repression.
Sudge's eventual choice to reject this inheritance of patriarchy and instead choose to inherit the legacy of the Lost Generation turns the tables
on patriarchal norms, revealing that the supposed sloth and licentious-
ness of Paris as a queer space pales in comparison to the shell game of
patriarchy that masquerades its inertia by shuffling capital around to
make it look like production and masking failed sexuality behind the
respectability of marriage.

EPILOGUE

By the end of the novel, it is actually Ross that breaks up their relationship by taking a teaching job in Canada while Sudge remains in Montparnasse still writing and looking for romance. McAlmon's novel concludes
with everyone's lives still very much in motion, without any resolution or
vision toward the future. Because this novel is an unpublished manuscript and it is possible McAlmon could have had further plans for the
narrative, one can only speculate if this sudden end was purposeful or if
he had simply run out of steam. In the mid-1940s when he wrote *The
Nightinghouls of Paris*, McAlmon was fully aware that the story of Ross
and Sudge's separation that ends the novel on a melancholic note would
soon be mended in real life. Shortly after this initial separation left Glassco alone in Paris, he would return to Canada and resume his companion-
ship with Taylor until Taylor's death in 1957 (Gnarowski 1995, xii).

Why does McAlmon end the novel during their short-lived separation? Perhaps this was McAlmon's way of ending the expatriate movement with Ross's decision to "grow up" and yet to simultaneously per-
petuate it through Sudge's decision to continue his sideways growth. In
the final chapter, Kit returns from a short trip to America to find Sudge
alone in the Quarter waiting for his newest female object of desire, Katherine to arrive. Sudge tells Kit that he thought he had settled permanently

in Mexico, to which Kit responds "No, I won't be settled anywhere for many years, if ever until the old boy pops off." McAlmon patterns his novel's narrative arc without a resolution according to his nomadic life-style that also resists a locatable destination. While the McAlmon that wrote this story in the 1940s probably knew where and when his itinerant lifestyle would retire, he nonetheless retains the spirit of nomadism by resisting a fixed destination for the narrative to arrive to. He leaves Sudge's life as an author and a young man in a similar state of limbo. As Kit says to Katherine: "What's his next phase to be? He's skeptical about most writers, and literature in general; and a bit scornful of philosophy" (181). While the real-life Glassco would eventually establish a formidable literary career for himself, the young Sudge is placed in a moment of doubt where his future remains uncertain. Sudge tells Kit that he and Katherine are planning a trip to Morocco, to which Kit replies "Good idea. Perhaps you've both done too long a siege of Paris without varia-tion" (181). Kit's last piece of fatherly wisdom blesses Sudge's nomadism with an almost "like father, like son" attitude. Then with the last lines of the novel, Kit similarly sends his self off, telling a newly arrived English-man to Paris "Let's go on to the Quarter. There's an Irishman, several Russians, and a Pole there, all of whom delight in talking religion, mathe-matics, higher thought, and the power of evil. I'll locate one of them for you surely, and then I must be on my way, doing my rounds" (183). McAlmon encapsulates his entire expatriate identity into that last piece of dialogue. He etches into that period one last image of himself as benevo-lent patron of art, a weaver of social relations, and a wanderer off to find drink and merriment.

NOTES

1. Among those who are starting to bring attention to McAlmon as a writer are Richard E. Ziekowitz with his essay "Constrained Liberation: Performative Queerness in Robert McAlmon's Berlin Stories" and Craig Monk in his recent book *Writing the Lost Generation: Expatriate Autobiography and American Modernism.*

2. Furthermore, Stearns writes "For moral idealism, if it means anything, means fearlessness before the facts and willingness to face them, intellectual integrity, emo-tional honesty, the attempt to win a moral order out of the jungle of experience with-out bias, without any axe to grind, without native prejudice. This kind of moral ideal-ism the younger generation has in large measure and it is just the kind of moral idealism which the younger generation finds nowhere existent in America today.

3. McAlmon writes in *Being Geniuses Together* that upon arrival in Paris, Sylvia Beach, the famous proprietor of Shakespeare and Company, warned him against go-ing to Montparnasse, calling it "ghastly, a hangout for pederasts" (McAlmon and Boyle, 1984, 30).

4. In his original publication of *Memoirs of Montparnasse*, Glassco claims that he wrote the first few chapters during this time in Paris, finished it in a sanitarium in the early thirties and forgot about it until he decided to publish it in 1970. In reality, the majority of the book was written in 1964 (Gnarowski 1995, xiii).

5. This idea of the erotic triangle between ostensibly heterosexual men projected onto the body of another was first and most eloquently advanced by Eve Sedgwick in her 1985 book *Between Men*. Sedgwick argues that in nineteenth-century novels, unspoken homosocial desire between male characters is frequently projected upon a female body for which they compete. The woman's body becomes increasingly attractive as they sense the desire that the other man invests in it.

REFERENCES

Cowley, Malcolm. *Exile's Return*. New York: Penguin, 1994.

Glassco, John. *Memoirs of Montparnasse*. Toronto: Oxford University Press, 1995.

Gnarowski, Michael. "Fiction for the Sake of Art: An Introduction to the Making of Memoirs of Montparnasse." in *Memoirs of Montparnasse*, by John Glassco, x–xxv. Toronto: Oxford UP, 1995.

Knoll, Robert E. *Robert McAlmon: Expatriate Publisher and Writer*. Lincoln: Nebraska University Press, 1957.

McAlmon Robert. *Miss Knight and Others*. Albuquerque: New Mexico University Press, 1992.

———. *The Nightinghouls of Paris*. Urbana: University of Illinois Press, 2007.

———. *Village: As It Happened Through a Fifteen-Year Period*. Albuquerque: New Mexico University Press, 1990.

McAlmon, Robert, and Kay Boyle. *Being Geniuses Together 1920–1930*. San Francisco: North Point Press, 1984.

Sedgwick, Eve Kosofsky. *Between Men: English Literature and Male Homosocial Desire*. New York: Columbia University Press, 1985.

Smoller, Sanford J. *Adrift Among Geniuses: Robert McAlmon: Writer and Publisher of the Twenties*. University Park: Pennsylvania State University Press, 1975.

———. Introduction. In *The Nightinghouls of Paris*, by Robert McAlmon, xi–lii. Urbana: Illinois University Press, 2007.

Stearns, Harold. *America and the Young Intellectual*. New York: George H. Doran Company, 1921.

Stockton, Kathryn Bond. *The Queer Child or Growing Sideways in the Twentieth Century*. Durham: Duke University Press, 2009.

Vidal, Gore. Forward. In *Miss Knight and Others*, by Robert McAlmon, ix–xiv. Albuquerque: New Mexico University Press, 1992.

SIX

Miller's Henry and Henry's Paris

Katy Masuga

Leaving behind a meager existence with an abusive, prostituting wife and her neurotic female lover in New York, a man called Henry Miller set sail in February 1930 for London on the *Bremen* with nothing more than a few dollars in his pocket. He already had his sights set on Paris, determined finally to live out his dream of becoming a writer. Against the odds, and not without much difficulty, particularly in terms of finances and the incredibly long-term censorship of his work, Miller ultimately did succeed in becoming a published, and noteworthy, writer that commenced during his ten years in Paris. Yet what he ultimately came to produce as a writer was by no standards conventional literature. Instead Miller developed an innovative style that came in direct relation both to his departure from America for Paris to fulfill his self-declared writerly destiny and to his profound interest in his self-appointed ancestral influences, notably including a collection of French heavyweights: Rabelais, Hugo, Rimbaud, Proust, Cendrars, and Céline.

In *Nexus* (1960), the third installment of *The Rosy Crucifixion Trilogy* Miller writes, "I might become interested in sewers, the great sewers of Paris, or some other metropolis, whereupon it would occur to me that Hugo or some other French writer had made use of such a theme, and I would take up the life of this novelist merely to find out what had impelled him to take such an interest in sewers" (239). Miller was charmed by French history, culture, and the arts in general. Miller first read Proust, for example, in New York shortly before sailing to France and again in French in 1932 while miserably working as an unpaid assistant English teacher in Dijon. In a letter to his lover at the time and lifelong literary comrade Anaïs Nin, he writes, "The man seems to take the words out of my mouth, to rob me of my very own experiences, sensations, reflections, introspections, suspicions, sadness, torture, etc. etc. etc." (Miller 1965, 18). Miller was not only a Francophile, but he was determined to become French himself.

His first encounter with a sense of the real Paris came through the stories of his lifelong friend Emil Schnellock in New York, who had visited Paris during his formation as an artist in the 1910s (and gave Miller the tenner in his pocket on the day he bid America a semi-permanent adieu). Schnellock's stories captivated Miller.[1] Already over forty years old, Miller finally left his native Brooklyn for Paris for two good reasons: to actualize his own imagined Paris as a writer and to escape his impossible life in New York: the fruitless struggle to survive on his art, in a disintegrating second marriage, often jobless, penniless and living in squalor. Miller remained in Paris roughly ten years before being forced to abandon his adopted homeland in 1939 at the onset of World War II.[2]

In a letter to Schnellock dated April 1932, at which time Miller had already been in Paris two years and had nearly completed *Tropic of Cancer* (published 1934), Miller writes: "in a word that coincident with my leaving America I chucked overboard all my preconceived notions about literature" (Miller 1989, 94). Having already struggled for decades to find his literary voice, Miller found that his relocation to Paris was what ultimately gave him the best tools for forging the persona by which we now know him. Apart from his very Francophile interests, this idealized construction of the literary life was based on Miller's deliberate assimilation of various sources: readings in philosophy (Nietzsche, Spengler, Lao-tse), in the history of European literature (Dostoievsky, Nostradamus, Plutarch) and American literature (Whitman, Emerson, Twain), in contemporary European literature (Hamsun, Mann, Cowper Powys) and American literature ("Doc" Williams, Ezra Pound, Dreiser) together with his awareness of Paris as the previous decade's literary mecca (Joyce, Hemingway, Stein). Because Miller was attracted to the very lifestyle of his contemporaries but also heavily rejected it (in part due to envy, to be sure), he took it upon himself to reimagine and thereby re-create a Paris that included his often contradictory model, both incorporating and fundamentally rejecting its literary traditions.

When Miller eventually settled on something he could publish, the results were controversial. *Tropic of Cancer* was immediately banned in the English-speaking world on grounds of obscenity.[3] Thus, a thorough analysis of Miller's writerly relationship with Paris requires the consideration of two different approaches: the first must account for Miller's biography and his personal interests as a person first and as a writer second. There is an obvious danger in this approach, which is the necessary psychoanalytic perspective that it demands, investigating Miller's motives and personal life. The second approach must account for the significance of the fact that much of the information on Miller comes to the reader directly from Miller's fiction, which is often mistakenly taken to be factual information that is merely couched in literary language. Miller ultimately weaved a deceivingly complex web of narratives in which the unsuspecting reader is inclined to conflate the writer with the author. Taking the personal writing style of his idols such as Rimbaud, Proust, and Céline to such an extreme, Miller then cleverly made it very difficult for the reader to distinguish between the writer and the figure of the literary creation.

Consequently, then, Miller's tremendous oeuvre on the whole—nearly fifty published texts, numerous letters, essays, reviews and other various fragments—tells the story of a fellow named Henry Miller whose great ambition is to be a successful writer in Paris. It is therefore significant to consider not only how French literature, and living in Paris particularly, serves as inspiration for Miller in his writing but precisely how it becomes an ideal to emulate in his own life, resulting in the very subject matter of his writing: an extensive image of Miller's literary life as an emulation of various French writers and their imaginary or imagined lives. Consequently, tracing the presence of Paris in Miller's work involves examining two vastly complex questions: First, how does Miller imagine Paris as viewed from within his texts? This question requires not only distinguishing between the autonovels and personal letters but also accounting for how Miller-the-writer and Miller's character Henry Miller distinguish them.[4] Secondly, how does actually being in Paris shape Miller's writing? That Miller's writing is itself about being in Paris furthers the already evident metatextual dynamic. Thus, once again, in looking to Miller's autonovels for the answer, the reader must carefully distinguish between Miller's impressions as a character and, externally, as a writer—with the latter, of course, being more difficult to decipher, since it is both outside the text but clearly informed just as well by what the reader discovers within the text. It may prove more useful, therefore, to answer this question by looking at Miller's nonfiction in conjunction with the impressions that his fiction imparts.

Additionally, this study tackles two themes. The first unveils the more readily available analysis of Miller's interests in Paris, which here includes answering the first question above strictly in relation to Miller's character Henry and answering the second in relation to Miller-the-writer and Miller's Henry in order to produce the most tangible and clear picture of Paris by Miller. Because the reader understands that the figure speaking the narratives of the autonovels is Miller's Henry and not Miller-the-writer, impressions of Paris come from his diegetic world and not the author's, even though the author himself is in Paris. At the same time, to subsequently evaluate the affect of Paris, both Millers and Parises must be considered, since the real Paris of Miller-the-writer in fact creates the Paris of Miller's Henry, but the reader is mostly only privy to the former through the latter.

The second approach serves to understand the significance of Paris in Miller's use of a technique that tempts the reader to conflate the writer with the character. This analysis examines how Miller-the-writer was influenced by French writers who often used a similar technique to create what Steven G. Kellman calls "the self-begetting novel." In his critical work on the subject, *The Self-Begetting Novel* (1980), Kellman explains that the writer of such a form creates a protagonist whose journey ultimately is to write the very novel that is being read. Thus, the second endeavor in this study explores both Miller's proclamations and his writing style as it developed in Paris.

SEEING PARIS

The first question of the first approach, then, is an explication of how Miller sees Paris, which is examined from within the perspective of Miller's Henry.[5] With the theory of the self-begetting novel in mind, Miller's reader first discovers that the experiences of the character Henry are representative of lived experiences (potentially those of the author) but also deliberate descriptions, or abstracted creations, of those experiences. In other words, the Paris that Henry encounters is also the Paris that Miller constructs. This doubling, or joining of visions, may seem an obvious literary structure, but indeed what it reveals, beyond the simple relation between author and subject, is the desire to sustain the image of a location as simultaneously actual and abstract. In particular, Miller regards Paris paradoxically as both a real and ideal location. In this way, he is able to sustain an image of Paris as a fantasy world coming to life. Miller uses this approach to represent Paris concomitantly as the ancient artist's mecca, full of wonder, mystery, and intrigue, and to highlight its squalor, decrepitude and decay.

In *Tropic of Cancer* (1961) Miller describes his sense of discovering the "forgotten world" of nineteenth-century Paris, pairing together what he currently sees with what once was: "Indigo sky swept clear of fleecy clouds, gaunt trees infinitely extended, their black boughs gesticulating like a sleepwalker. Somber, spectral trees, their trunks pale as cigar ash" (6). A few passages later he adds: "For the moment I can think of nothing—except that I am a sentient being stabbed by the miracle of these waters that reflect a forgotten world" (6). It is not just the old Paris that retains the enchanting allure of a literary dream; it is also the current Paris that Miller himself experiences, which he sets in opposition to the old, romanticized view. At the same time, Miller's actual lived experiences themselves, though depicting a harsh reality, often do so with a surprising positive slant.

It is, in fact, Miller's imaginative wanderings that are usually coupled with deeply physical, sordid, everyday experiences. Thus, the passage cited above from *Tropic of Cancer* is immediately followed by a blunt, unapologetic sexual episode (an analysis of various "cunts") that moves from seemingly overt description to surreal metaphor while including snippets of the "real" Paris, such as in the following passage: "At the confluence of the Ourcq and Marne, where the water sluices through the dikes and lies like glass under the bridges. Llona is lying there now and the canal is full of glass and splinters; the mimosas weep, and there is a wet, foggy fart on the windowpanes" (7). Miller begins by writing of a possible real sexual encounter in this passage, but it quickly transforms into a description of the world at large in Paris and the connection between this mystifying yet earthly urban space and the sexual experience: its mystery, charm, and eroticism but also its corporeality, stench, and discombobulating effect. Miller's experience of Paris is often imagined sexually: it retains a lofty allure and mystique while also revealing an often crude baseness.

For Miller, Paris represents his gateway into the new perceived literary life, but because the reader comes to this "new life" in medias res, there is always already automatically a paralleling of the ideal Paris with its real experienced self. They are sometimes nearly indistinguishable in his writing. More significant than even the effects of this paralleling, however, is its actual presentation. Still within the first pages of *Tropic of Cancer*, Miller describes, with equal measure of calm and frenetic speed, his scraping together a living during his wife's first troubling visit to Paris. Living momentarily in a dingy motel, they awaken to a bed crawling with bedbugs and so sneak out in the early morning. Without pause or transition, Miller suddenly describes the beauty in the dawn of the new day: "The day opens in milky whiteness, streaks of salmon-pink sky, snails leaving their shells. Paris. Paris. Everything happens here. Old, crumbling walls and the pleasant sound of water running in the urinals. Men licking their mustaches at the bar. Shutters going up with a bang and little streams purling in the gutters" (21). On top of the collision of the beautiful with the repugnant (a passage on swarming bedbugs immediately preceding one on the magnificence of the dawn), the reader can never be sure of Miller's tone regarding his descriptions of each of the highlighted elements; for what is sordid is beautiful (e.g., dirty gutters), and what is base is music to the ears (e.g., urinal sounds). The reader eventually senses that detecting when Miller is and is not ironic is next to impossible.

Nevertheless, through each street-level experience, Paris retains its pure, dreamlike quality. Curiously, its mythic status grows even larger, looms greater, and propels Miller forward toward his goal of becoming a writer. In the chapter entitled "Walking Up and Down in China" from his second work *Black Spring* (1936), a collection of partly surreal vignettes, he writes, "I look to the right of me and there on a slanting street is precisely the Paris I have always been searching for. You might know every street in Paris and not know Paris, but when you have forgotten where you are and the rain is softly falling, suddenly in the aimless wandering you come to the street through which you have walked time and again in your sleep *and this is the street you are now walking through.*" (Miller 1963, 199). For Miller Paris sustains its dreaminess, its largess of charm, ambiguity, and experience, and it is precisely through each gesture, each attempt to describe Paris that the aura of the city grows larger and that Miller makes his mark as a writer. Each image of Paris reconfirms its magical status as the writer's dream but also as a crumbling old city that often cruelly lets him go hungry and exacerbates his struggle to become the artist he knows himself to be.

As is well evident, Miller frequently includes the sexual side of Paris in his work, often describing the prostitutes, their working districts and his dalliances or those of his friends and acquaintances. Miller uses the sexual scene as another metaphor, or even as a synecdoche, for the allure of the city itself, commingling its erotic and ignoble qualities:

> To walk from the Rue Lafayette to the boulevard is like running the gauntlet; they attach themselves to you like barnacles, they eat into you like ants, they coax, wheedle, cajole, implore, beseech, they try it out in German, English, Spanish, they show you their torn hearts and their busted shoes, and long after you've chopped the tentacles away, long after the fizz and sizzle has died out, the fragrance of the *lavabo* clings to your nostrils—it is the odor of the *Parfum de Danse* whose effectiveness is guaranteed only for a distance of twenty centimetres. (Miller 1961, 158)

Miller's view of Paris is an intricate web of mixed descriptions that turn conventional imagery and perception on their heads and that explore and speak the once unspeakable of the time. Through an image of Paris as an ancient yet vibrant and pulsing city of culture, sexuality, humanity, and the arts, Miller accepts his self-appointed carte blanche with full force and outright announces his desire for both the high and the low, often not distinguishing between the one and the other, leaving it to his reader to make meaning or cajole value from his words.

Most every description of the city deliberately involves, conflates, and encourages these two aesthetic poles of the high and low. In *Tropic of Cancer*, Miller writes, "In the blue of an electric dawn the peanut shells look wan and crumpled; along the beach at Montparnasse the water lilies bend and break. When the tide is on the ebb and only a few syphilitic mermaids are left stranded in the muck, the Dôme looks like a shooting gallery that's been struck by a cyclone. Everything is slowly dribbling back to the sewer" (161). The imagery of each phrase brings together the beautiful and the hideous: electric dawn/wan and crumpled, water lilies bend and break, syphilitic mermaids. Through the descriptions themselves, Miller attributes this dichotomy to the rhythm of the city. Precisely, though, because it is not just any city, but Paris, these opposing primordial components are seen to pervade every element within its structure.

This endless back and forth occurring simultaneously in Paris, this clashing of forces of the old and new, the beautiful and unsightly, the sexual and pure, these otherwise unimaginable and contradictory networks are what Miller desires to express in his writing—because it is this dynamic that he finds in Paris and also because it is that which he seeks From one paragraph on the "varieties of sexual provender" in Paris. where "any misfortune that aggravates the natural homeliness of the female, seems to be regarded an added spice" (162) (including such things as missing body parts or facial features), Miller moves into an incredibly intricate and serene ekphrastic episode, sweeping the reader away into a colliding synesthetic vision conjuring Proust summoned through a viewing of Matisse in a gallery. The lengthy passage includes the following evocation of *A la recherche du temps perdu*: "On the beach, masts and chimneys interlaced, and like a fuliginous shadow the figure of Albertine gliding through the surf, fusing into the mysterious quick and prism of a protoplasmic realm, uniting her shadow to the dream and harbinger of death" (163). Moving freely from crippled prostitutes to high art, Miller defines what he sees as the nature of Paris: it is only Paris that can evoke this kind of observation of harmony through discordance but also discordance in harmony. After all, it is not necessarily (or always, perhaps) a peaceful or even coherent portrait Miller is painting, but one that is simultaneously congruent through its vibrancy while also corrupted and regularly dissonant.

For Miller, then, Paris is the ultimate source of inspiration in that every element, every minute component is the most tangible material for his writing. In *Tropic of Capricorn*, published just before Miller left Paris in 1939, he notes the significance of Paris upon him and lack of America: "I did not open my eyes wide and full and clear until I struck Paris. And perhaps that was only because I had renounced America, renounced my past" (Miller 1978, 45). In the previous paragraph Miller reminisces in detail on the distinction between the Paris he imagined before leaving New York and the one he sees now each day.

> What a thirst I had! Every slightest detail about the other world fascinated me. Even now, years and years since, even now, when I know Paris like a book, his picture of Paris is still before my eyes, still vivid, still real. Sometimes after a rain, riding swiftly through the city in a taxi, I catch fleeting glimpses of this Paris he described; just momentary snatches, as in passing the Tuileries, perhaps, or a glimpse of Montmartre, of the Sacré Coeur, through the Rue Laffite, in the last flush of twilight. (44)

The Paris that Miller sees is a combination of this real and imaginary. It holds all possibilities as a malleable source to be viewed from diverging perspectives simultaneously. Miller's Paris is both contemporarily alive and sentimentally ancient, influencing him through his own creation of it as that very source of influence in the way that he imagines it and constantly manipulates that imagining.

EFFECT OF PARIS

Paris both as an actual location and as a potential writing theme have of course had a profound impact on the formation of Miller's style. Not only is Paris Miller's subject matter, but the feel that Paris exudes for Miller also becomes the heart of his own style. What this means is that this elusive aura of Paris, again sustaining the real and mythical, comes to serve as the very substance of Miller's writing. His chief concern becomes attempting to capture the essence of what makes Paris sometimes literally painfully attractive, as the ideal city for writers as well as for bums. The point of focus of this section is on the fact that Miller's writing is itself about being in Paris, specifically about struggling to be a writer in Paris. In the way that Miller creates the Paris in which he resides, so too does the real Paris shape Miller. This section thus also incorporates Miller's explicitly nonfiction works in order to consider the impact of Paris on him from a distance that is less accessible in his autonovels.

The most direct text of Miller's for exploring the influence of Paris on him and his work is his collection of letters to his lifelong friend Emil Schnellock that begin in 1922 and continue until Schnellock's death in 1958. Their relationship is also fictionalized throughout Miller's work, with Schnellock being credited with Miller's increasing excitement over the possibilities of moving to Paris. While pouring over a map of the city sprawled on the floor of his dingy basement apartment in New York, Miller writes in *Plexus* (1953), the second installment of *The Rosy Crucifixion Trilogy*: "We all got down on hands and knees to wander through the streets of Paris, visiting the libraries, museums, cathedrals, flower stalls, slaughter-houses, cemeteries, whore-houses, railway stations, bals musette, *les magasins* and so on" (15). Ulric, the character based on Schnellock, brings the map over that initiates the imaginary walkabout. Through this episode Miller takes Paris to a new level in his work by bringing it to life in the literary text through a mode decipherable only within the text itself. The characters are obviously not traipsing across Paris, but for the intents and purposes of the reading encounter, they in some way are, in the same way that Miller's Henry has a life of his own. The reader enters the text in New York and follows Miller to an imaginary, yet tangible, Paris.

Miller's reader is often privy to his process of creative invention, experiencing not simply the world of the imaginary but of the imaginary of the imaginary. The reader observes as Miller constructs the universe that he is going to write about. In "Third or Fourth Day of Spring" from *Black Spring* Miller describes himself sitting at a café but shortly afterward confesses to the reader that he "really" isn't at a café at all. "You thought I was sitting at the Place Clichy all the time, drinking an *apéritif* perhaps. As a matter of fact I *was* sitting at the Place Clichy, but that was two or three years ago" (31). This crossing of spatial and temporal thresholds is a recurring theme in Miller's work, particularly in relation to Paris and the dual nature that Miller sustains through using it in his work as much as an actual location as a metaphor for creative possibilities.[6]

As evident in the nature of his peripatetic lifestyle, Miller places great importance on location throughout his entire oeuvre, particularly on the significance of his displacement in Paris as the nexus for his development as a writer. He summons the entire sense of human geography through his descriptions of lengthy wanderings among its streets. In "Walking Up and Down in China" from *Black Spring* he writes: "In Paris, out of Paris, leaving Paris or coming back to Paris, it's always Paris and Paris is France and France is China" (Miller 1963, 185). Again, Paris the real is also metaphor. It is emblematic of the space of influential culture on the eager writer. Shortly after the above passage, as Miller begins describing his walk back home on the outskirts of Paris, he writes:

> Afternoons, sitting at La Fourche, I ask myself calmly, "Where do we go from here?" By nightfall I may have travelled to the moon and back. Here at the crossroads I sit and dream back through all my separate and immortal egos. I weep in my beer. Nights, walking back to Clichy, it's the same feeling. Whenever I come to la Fourche I see endless roads radiating from my feet and out of my own shoes there step forth the countless egos which inhabit my world of being. Arm in arm I accompany them over the paths which I once trod alone: what I call the grand obsessional walks of my life and death. (186)

Miller creates a Paris that represents the entire world, hence permitting him to see himself in it and his own detached place within that world. This viewing of the self is from the outside, as far as Miller can manage, so that he deliberately identifies as the outsider, allowing Paris to affect him as an external source that he can explore like a fly on the wall: "to wander endlessly unbodied, unhooked, a nameless identity, or an unidentified name, a soul unattached, indifferent to everything, a soul immortal, perhaps incorruptible, like God—who can say?" (201). From this perspective as the peripatetic, Miller identifies with life in Paris as an other and as himself culturally separate from his surroundings.

At the same time, this identification does not mean Miller does not feel he belongs to Paris and to France. On the contrary, living in Paris gives Miller a sense of perspective on his identification with his origins, and therefore, it gives him the courage to write with a new freedom and experimentation, focusing on the fissures that being in Paris opens up for him artistically. In one instance in *Nexus*, contemplating his new future in Europe while taking a walk through a familiar neighborhood in New York, Miller calls himself "a tourist now" (Miller 1960, 308), as he feels foreign in a formerly familiar location. Paris and its artistic possibilities instead become Miller's home, to be sure, even before his relocation. As pointed out earlier, however, what makes this incident most curious is the fact that the publication of *Nexus* came many years after Miller actually lived in Paris even though the novel depicts the period before his departure. Writing that he feels "a tourist now" is actually accurate in light of Miller-the-writer, who is no longer a resident of New York in any sense, as opposed to Miller's Henry who has distanced himself from New York mentally—having moved to Paris already in his mind—but who still walks the streets of Brooklyn.

In *Letters to Emil*, which spans the years 1922–1934 but focuses on Miller's first years in Paris from 1930 to 1934,[7] Miller writes almost entirely of the significance of Paris in his writing. The year 1930 begins with Miller's first entry from Paris where he declares his joy, by the next entry praising the French people as though already discovering himself in their culture: "They seem to be enjoying each day as it comes along, finding their pleasures simply and naturally" (Miller 1989, 20). The entry is entitled "First Sunday in Paris" and also includes the following passage: "It is tranquil and beautiful along the Seine. So many bridges, each of them christened with an imposing name. They look this morning as they have often looked to me on a canvas. The water is slightly ruffled and the shadows under the arches waver and tremble" (20). Paris compels Miller immediately to adjust his style to the centuries-old beauty that he sees around him. As he begins to write as an artist, so too does he begin to live as an artist, to see as an artist, to regard the world around him as a painted canvas, to use the language of the mythical painter wandering the streets of Paris.

Adopting this new way of seeing, which he discusses much later in *Nexus*, Miller describes the tools he would begin to develop and incorporate from the environment around him. He writes: "Thus, not so strangely, I developed a kind of painter's eye. Often I made it my business to return to a certain spot in order to review a 'still life' which I had passed too hurriedly the day before or three days before. The still life, as I term it, might be an artless arrangement of objects which no one in his sense would have bothered to look at twice" (Miller 1960, 242). This sense of the world as a canvas becomes particularly poignant in Paris, where Miller is now literally surrounded by millions of art objects. But the city itself becomes an art object and entices Miller to adopt a more literary—if incredibly subversive and experimental—style through which to portray it. Influenced greatly by the letters of Van Gogh, for example, Miller identifies not only with his artistry and expatriatism but also with the very unreality in Van Gogh's reality. For Miller too is guilty, deliberately guilty, of conflating the imaginary and with the real in the name of art and life.

Moving to Paris was clearly a monumental turning point in Miller's literary career. It was in Paris that Miller was first published, but it was also because of Paris that Miller finally had the right kind of resource and inspiration to harness his desire to write. Prior to coming to Paris, Miller had obviously not been successful as a writer, having written two manuscripts that remained unpublished (*Clipped Wings* and *Crazy Cock*), were poorly written, derivative, and reactionary to his negative surroundings. Paris finally gave Miller the freedom to imagine himself away from his origins, to dissociate himself from his American roots and to find his notable literary voice. With the publication of his first book around the corner, in a 1933 letter to Schnellock he announces: "France is where I belong. Or somewhere here in Europe. I am no longer an American. I can swear to that" (Miller 1989, 113). From his position in Paris, Miller could be critical of America, but, more importantly, he could recreate himself as writer and as a European simultaneously. In 1933 dramatically he writes to Schnellock: "It is a classical fate for such as myself. (Vide—Gauguin, Van Gogh, Strindberg, Nietzsche, Lawrence, Proust, Dostoievsky.) Just enough strength to convey what they wanted—and then finis! Well, that's me. Life hasn't been too kind to me, as an artist" (122). With earnest affection, Miller aligns himself with a European literary heritage, choosing for himself his own lineage, encouraged to an inscrutable degree by his residence in Paris.

INFLUENCE AND CONFLATION

One of the greatest twists that Miller adds to his narrative curiosities is the fact that *The Rosy Crucifixion Trilogy* was completed long after Miller had already left Paris for good, even though it describes the life of Miller's Henry in the ten years leading up to his ten-year sojourn abroad. Miller's Henry could suddenly write about his excited apprehension of moving to Paris to become a writer, with Miller-the-author building in all of the anticipation that ten ultimately positive years in Paris produced in him. Such literary techniques of manipulating space and time allow for new paths to form in literature, which would not otherwise be particularly problematic, but that Miller is often conflated with his main character. Of course this "mistake" itself is part of Miller's innovation, and, in a study of the significance of Paris in Miller's work and life, it is necessary to maintain an awareness of these often vaguely yet also quite distinct

tracks and the various literary and possibly social consequences that result from them.

Kellman's extraordinary study, *The Self-Begetting Novel* (1980), traces
this modernist technique of writing a novel in which the protagonist
himself writes the work that is being read. Kellman asserts that this technique, although indeed having a much older history, has taken a particular foothold in French literature since Proust, such that Proust combines
the *Künstlerroman* and *Bildungsroman*, bringing a new theme into the self-
begetting novel: that of the "self-evident sham" of writing (Kellman 1980,
4), in terms of its limitless ability to express itself, which is the nothingness of itself. It is this form of the self-begetting novel that Kellman suggests is carried out most strongly in Proust's American and English literary inheritors of the twentieth century, Henry Miller specifically among
them.

What would we know of Henry Miller if he did not write about "Henry Miller"? (And why would it matter?) Strangely, the reader's engage-
ment with Miller-the-writer exists solely due to the development of Miller's Henry, which is not to say that biographical information also does
not enter into the process of analysis, but it is precisely that Miller is a
writer, specifically a self-begetting novelist, that makes the reader interested in Miller's life. Setting this question peripherally aside for the moment, here we firstly follow the path of the figure called Henry Miller
from his beginnings as "just a Brooklyn boy" (Miller 1978, 45) to his
adventures in Paris in order to uncover the impact that the city and its
culture had upon his literary developments.

More accurately, however, our introduction to Miller's Henry, again,
begins in medias res with *Tropic of Cancer*: "It is now the fall of my second
year in Paris. I was sent here for a reason I have not yet been able to
fathom. I have no money, no resources, no hopes. I am the happiest man
alive" (Miller 1961, 1). Miller's first pronouncement is one of his greatest:
provocative and encouraging, simple and confrontational. The reader immediately assesses that Miller's plight is both dire and exuberant, defining the state of things for Miller's Parisian experience as he adopts the
persona of happy beggar, living life "to the full," as they say, regardless
of his lowly means, thereby opening a world for the reader that spreads
into the life of the real world and re-colors one's own personal vision of
that world. Indeed, it is this disposition of Miller's Henry from page 1 of
Tropic of Cancer that also characterizes Miller-the-writer's entire personality into the pages of history.

The passage above has become one of Miller's best known, serving as
the crux for an unfortunate popularized assessment of what is often tak-
en as Miller's own personal philosophy: "All I ask of life, he says, is a
bunch of books, a bunch of dreams, and a bunch of cunt" (Miller 1961,
103). Incidentally, this particular passage, also from *Tropic of Cancer*, is
spoken by a particularly seedy character called Van Norden. The history

of writing shows us that Miller is not particularly unique in developing such a potentially controversial structure, but it is a significant point for analysis when discussing anything to do with Miller and his writing, particularly in terms of influence, because of the quality of the material, namely, the type of content. It is true enough that the culturally rich and foreign environment around Miller gave him the courage and motivation to develop his brass and personal style, and, as explained in the previous section, Miller at once identified with and felt entirely removed from the very French society in which he immersed himself. Yet, simply conflating Miller-the-writer with Miller's Henry overlooks what Miller himself was aiming to achieve, namely, among other things, a provocative form of literature that undermines conventional structures.

In *The Secret Violence of Henry Miller* (2011) I argue that this controversial and experimental form of writing can be read through Deleuze and Guattari's concept of a minor literature. Such writing as Miller's designates a writing style that subverts the structure of the major language in which it is written, thereby disrupting its linguistic, cultural, and moral codes. For the first near ten years of his career, Miller wrote in English while physically within the framework of Parisian society. Paris gave Miller a sense of native removal, outsider status and cultural artistic support to develop his writing in the minor key that he did. Moreover, the writing itself embarks on an investigation of the nature of writing, of language, of literature, and of man's relation to the world and relation to literature and language as separate entities. Not only was the conventional structure on the chopping block, but the new material became the very process of questioning and dispatching with the old. In *Tropic of Cancer* he writes: "There is only one thing which interests me vitally now, and that is the recording of all that which is omitted in books" (Miller 1961, 11). A bold statement that is later reconfirmed in *Black Spring*: "In the street you learn what human beings really are; otherwise, or afterwards, you invent them. What is not in the open street is false, derived, that is to say *literature*" (Miller 1963, 3). The mother tongue is placed in check; used not for communication but to explore the periphery of language, of literary language and possibly of the limits and possibilities of communication itself.

Kellman specifically defines the self-begetting novel as "an account, usually first-person, of the development of a character to the point at which he is able to take up his pen and compose the novel we have just finished reading" (Kellman 1980, 3). Beginning with Proust's *A la recherche du temps perdu* (1913–1927) and extending to Beckett's trilogy, Kellman's tracing of the self-begetting novel's more recent lineage focuses on the influence of nineteenth-century French literature upon modernist American and British literature in which the novel itself is the story of the protagonist's development of his writerly craft. Kellman includes Miller's *Tropic of Cancer* and *Tropic of Capricorn*, implying Miller's indebtedness to Proust but also, for example, to Joris-Karl Huysmans and *À rebours* (1884). Indeed, Miller includes Huysmans's self-begetting novel in his list "The Hundred Books That Influenced Me Most" from *The Books in My Life* (1952). *À rebours* may serve as the epitome of the decadent self-begetting novel that elevates this idea of its own creation out of itself, thus missing the point taken up by modernists of the dependency of that concept on the forces that compel it. For Kellman, Proust affects this dilemma in the self-begetting novel, thereby creating the modernist's melancholy in the years to come.

Miller and other Francophile Anglo-modernists then reject the idea of the self-begetting novel as "the triumph of literature over time" (Kellman 1980, 10), what Kellman claims Proust enacts, by moving towards the veritable yet ironic emptiness of the endeavor. Kellman states: "Miller's Henry recognizes that infinity is generated out of ciphers, and it is the negative capability of figures like Marcel and Darley that permits them to create a self and a world" (136). For this reason writers like Miller and Beckett use the metaphor of sex (or sexlessness) to highlight this paradoxical task of the novelist. Kellman writes, "Whether nest or dungeon, the self-begetting novel begets both *a self* and *itself*. It recounts the creation of a work very much like itself, but it is also the portrait of a fictive artist being born" (7). Referencing Miller and Beckett, he then writes: "Sex preoccupies the self-begetting novel's lonely and aging hero, who somehow succeeds in giving birth to twins — self and novel" (8) Miller directly uses this trope directly in multiple passages across his work. In *Tropic of Capricorn* he writes, "I felt all the books I would one day write myself germinating inside me" (Miller 1978, 191), and "the book has begun to grow inside me. I am carrying it around with me everywhere. I walk through the streets big with child and the cops escort me across the street" (26).

This image of being pregnant with literature is also in contradistinction to the passages in which the sex act is done not for procreation or even pleasure but for the sake of trying to create something from the gesture itself, while often failing miserably. "As I watch Van Norden tackle her, it seems to me that I'm looking at a machine whose cogs have slipped. Left to themselves, they could go on this way forever, grinding and slipping, without ever anything happening. . . . It's like watching one of those crazy machines which throw the newspaper out, millions and billions and trillions of them with their meaningless headlines" (Miller 1961, 143–44). Like a cipher, the sex act is done for the sake of canceling itself out, thus producing the same paradox of the image of the literary pregnancy: neither one can fulfill itself, as it perpetually relies on its own state in order to exist at all.

In a strange twist Miller makes clear both the paradox of the self-begetting form and of a kind of anxiety of self-influence, stating in *Nexus*: "Every author I fall in love with I want to imitate. If only I could imitate myself!" (191). The affirmation not only of imitation but also in a sense of "bad" imitation becomes one of Miller's innovations. After all, Miller's Henry, in creating the book being read, states his writerly project in *Tropic of Cancer* at the outset: "This is not a book. This is libel, slander, defamation of character. This is not a book, in the ordinary sense of the word. No, this is a prolonged insult, a gob of spit in the face of Art, a kick in the pants to God, Man, Destiny, Time, Love, Beauty . . . what you will" (2). In true Proustian form, Miller tries to transcend all previous books and even overcome art but manages only to create another book and another new form of art. The triumph contains within it its own failure.

This form of writing "a gob of spit" also takes writers like Céline and Cendrars as its precursor. Miller cites Céline and Cendrars on his list "The Hundred Books That Influenced Me Most," as well as Rimbaud, Rabelais, Flaubert, Stendhal, Hugo, Proust, Balzac, and numerous other French writers, as well as, of course American, Russian, German, English writers and so on.[8] Nevertheless, the French influence and the literary climate of the time made a great impact on Miller's interest in settling in Paris. In *The Books in My Life*, Miller writes: "With Cendrars, I have the feeling that in switching from active life to writing, and vice versa, he replenishes himself" (Miller 1952, 69). Miller most admired those writers who injected themselves into their work and injected life as much as possible into art. Writers like Rabelais, Rimbaud and Hugo all sought to incorporate the underside of life into their work, to envision a work of art that did not shy away from embracing life *en toto* in writing as much as possible.

Miller finds these same writers at odds, like himself, faced not only with the limits of writing but with the desire to overcome the impossibility of life in art, making his pursuit both perpetually incomplete and eternally compelling. In *Nexus* he writes: "That *histoire* should be story, lie and history all in one was of a significance not to be despised. And that a story, given out as the invention of a creative artist, should be regarded as the most effective material for getting at the truth about its author was also significant. Lies can only be embedded in truth" (Miller 1980, 246). Miller is fascinated with how language, and the French language in particular, entices the writer to engage with this grappling of its own limitations but also with the paradox of the beauty in that futile endeavor. Truth is revealed in words, in explanation, but explanation is itself only another incomplete form for addressing the impossible limits of being—like Rimbaud: aware of using arbitrary signs within a systematic, very non-arbitrary structure.

Interestingly, it was the live-in, antagonistic female lover of Miller's wife who first introduced him to Rimbaud in New York during the final years before he left for Paris. Miller recounts this period in relation to Rimbaud's own life, writing in his critical study of the poet, *Time of the Assassins* (1946): "If that period in Brooklyn represented my Season in

Hell, then the Paris period, especially from 1932 to 1934, was the period of my Illuminations" (3). He goes on to compare specifically their approaches to writing: "Rimbaud restored literature to life; I have endeavored to restore life to literature. In both of us the confessional quality is strong, the moral and spiritual preoccupation uppermost. The flair for *language*, for music rather than literature, is another trait in common" (5–6). Miller sees his own interest in literature as a way for exploring life. It was an affinity in this pursuit that he found in the French, from Abelard and Heloïse to Rimbaud and Balzac, and from Proust and Céline.

Miller identified with France and French writers not only because he felt at odds with his homeland, but also because that primal alienation itself made him attracted to the literary culture of France, which seemed to have a visible audacity to explore the nether regions of language at the level of the everyday. In "Walking Up and Down in China" from *Black Spring* he writes:

> I am here in the midst of a great change. I have forgotten my own language and yet I do not speak the new language. I am in China and I am talking Chinese. I am in the dead center of a changing reality for which no language has yet been invented. According to the map I am in Paris; according to the calendar I am living in the third decade of the twentieth century. But I am neither in Paris nor in the twentieth century. I am in China and there are no clocks or calendars here" (191).

Miller's affinity with French literature can certainly be overemphasized or overdramatized, to be sure, as he was clearly very interested in other world literature beyond his American roots. Focusing on French literature and the effect of Paris on Miller and his work in this study has not been meant to limit the reader's view of the nature of Miller's ancestral influence and interest in other national literatures. On the contrary, as the passage above demonstrates, location in many ways serves as a metaphor for Miller; one that he uses to explore the boundaries of language and thought itself.

This metaphoricity of location may be why Deleuze and Guattari rely so heavily on Miller in their two-volume, all-encompassing critical and cultural behemoth *Capitalism and Schizophrenia: Anti-Oedipus* and *A Thousand Plateaus* (*Capitalisme et schizophrénie: L'Anti-Oedipe* [1972, in English 1980]; *Mille plateaux* [1980, in English 1987]).[9] Indeed, if any conclusion can be made about the significance of Miller's physical location as a writer, it would simply be to reassert the argument proposed by the editors of this volume, which is to say that a writer's time away from his or her origins appears to encourage creativity. Miller's decade abroad certainly affected his creative output, giving him a concrete source of inspiration to write the auto-novels that are often considered to be his best.

As to the causal relation between place and creativity that may be relevant here, it is difficult to say whether Paris instilled something in

Miller or whether it was Miller who instilled that something in Paris. In other words, was Miller the creative artist who brought himself into that community in order to develop his talent? Or can it be concluded that Miller would not have flourished without Paris as his backdrop? It probably would be a grave limitation to assume an answer either way. What can be surmised is that Miller gives us a Paris that is the furthest thing from what we might imagine, insofar as it is perpetually escaping itself as a real and concrete location even while being a very real, tangible place. Just as Miller through writing escapes himself as a concrete body or personality—both through language that itself escapes beyond rational limits and through the elements of space and time that demand we re-think the parameters of what defines a place, an object, a body, a person.

NOTES

1. Schnellock's Paris stories themselves became writing material for *The Rosy Crucifixion Trilogy* (1949–1960), written many years after Miller had left Paris.

2. He spent the second half of his life in California as a reputed writer yet with cult-like status due to the necessary underground circulation of his work: from its first publication in 1934 and until 1961, Miller's entire oeuvre was banned in the English-speaking world for obscenity. Thus, the ban on his works and his public reputation as pornographer inhibited Miller from ever living a financially comfortable life, despite his underground reputation as a proto-Beat and progenitor of the new literary and cultural sexual revolution. Once the ban was lifted, devaluation of the franc left Miller with a modest sum that itself was difficult to obtain, leaving him perpetually in a financially difficult state for much of the rest of his life.

3. It was accepted in France, where it was first brought out, although in 1945 it did face a lawsuit that was ultimately dropped due to the support of well-respected figures in French arts and letters including Jean-Paul Sartre, Simone de Beauvoir, Georges Bataille, André Gide, Albert Camus, André Breton, Paul Éluard, Gaston Gallimard, and Robert Queaneau.

4. From here on, when it is necessary to overtly make a distinction between author and character, the former is called "Miller-the-writer" and the latter "Miller's Henry," to borrow Steven G. Kellman's phrase in *The Self-Begetting Novel* (1980).

5. This topic is explored in greater detail in the chapter "Our Changing Geography" of *The Secret Violence of Henry Miller* (Masuga 2011), in which the urban space as metaphor is examined, specifically including Miller's writings on Paris, New York, and America.

6. See *The Secret Violence of Henry Miller* (Masuga 2011) for an analysis of locations (along with bodies and other things) as metaphors.

7. Although Miller ends the collection with a letter from Paris before his departure to America, it would not be his final adieu. Miller left for New York in January 1935 and returned to Paris in September, remaining until late 1939. He spent several months in Greece with the Durrells, then returned to America, living permanently in California until his death in 1980.

8. Not all can be named here, but several notable works on Miller and his influences include my work *Henry Miller and How He Got That Way* (2011), Karl Orend's *Henry Miller's Red Phoenix: A Lawrentian Quest* (2006), Maria Bloshteyn's *The Making of a Counter-Culture Icon: Henry Miller's Dostoevsky* (2007), John Parkin's *Henry Miller, the Modern Rabelais* (1990) and Bertrand Mathieu's *Orpheus in Brooklyn: Orphism, Rimbaud, and Henry Miller* (1976).

9. See *Henry Miller and How He Got That Way* (2011) for a much longer discussion of Deleuze and Guattari's use of Miller in their monumental work, particularly in terms of its application in their reading of Proust.

REFERENCES

Deleuze, Gilles and Guattari, Félix. *L'Anti-Oedipe: Capitalisme et schizophrénie*. Paris: Editions de minuit, 1980.

———. *Mille plateaux : Capitalisme et schizophrénie*. Paris: Editions de minuit, 2006.

Kellman, Steven G. *The Self-Begetting Novel*. New York: Columbia University Press, 1980.

Masuga, Katy. *Henry Miller and How He Got That Way*. Edinburgh: Edinburgh University Press, 2011.

———. *The Secret Violence of Henry Miller*. New York: Camden House, 2011.

Miller, Henry. *Black Spring*. New York: Grove Press, 1963.

———. *The Books in My Life*. London: Villiers Publications, 1952.

———. *Henry Miller's Letters to Anaïs Nin*. Ed. Gunther Stuhlmann. New York: G. P. Putnam's Sons, 1965.

———. *Letters to Emil*. Ed. George Wickes. New York: New Directions, 1989.

———. *Nexus: The Rosy Crucifixion, Part III*. London: Panther Books, Granada Publishing Ltd., 1980 (1960).

———. *Plexus: The Rosy Crucifixion, Part II*. London: Panther Books, 1969.

———. *Time of the Assassins*. New York: New Directions, 1962.

———. *Tropic of Cancer*. New York: Grove Press, 1961.

———. *Tropic of Capricorn*. London: Panther Books, Granada Publishing Ltd., 1978.

Proust, Marcel. *A la recherche du temps perdu*. Paris: Gallimard, 1913–1927.

SEVEN

Chicago Adventures in Paris

The Revelation that Sparked
Bellow's Creative Opposition

Matthew Crowe

While *The Adventures of Augie March* (1953) is predominantly set in Chicago, as Saul Bellow noted, not "a single word of the book was composed" there (Bellow 1954). Bellow began and wrote much of the text while living in Paris on a Guggenheim Fellowship, and the foreign circumstance had a significant influence on the germination process of the narrative. During the first period of his stay in Paris—until the revelation that allowed him to begin writing in earnest—Bellow found himself depressed, melancholic, and culturally alienated in the French capital. The author's disappointment with Paris was galvanized on a particular occasion when, while contemplating a gutter stream created by Parisian street-workers, he experienced the artistic revelation that his concerns as a novelist lay with the city he had abandoned: Chicago. The first sentences that came to him that day would become the opening lines of *The Adventures of Augie March*, and this paper examines the creative function of Bellow's cultural estrangement in France, a subject that is textually interpolated through Augie, the narrator-protagonist of the book, who ultimately reveals that he is writing his memoirs while based in Paris. Augie's attitude towards the city, like Bellow's, demonstrates his symbolic position as a character defined in cultural opposition to his surroundings. The sense of displacement Bellow experienced while living in Paris catalysed his developing sense of his identity and his objective as a novelist, and functioned as a literary and thematic resource, one which enabled him to write with a creative latitude that had previously escaped him.

DEPARTURE

Originally Vilnius Jews, Saul Bellow's family emigrated from Saint Petersburg to Montreal where Bellow, the youngest of four children, was born. During his childhood the Bellow family moved to Chicago, where Saul would spend most of his life. By 1948, Bellow was married, a father, and had published two critically respected novels. He had lived in Minneapolis, New York, and Acatla, Mexico, and the latter two had influenced his early writing.[1] Bellow and his wife, Anita, had speculated on moving to several places in the United States and Europe, but when Bellow was awarded a Guggenheim grant, France became the leading candidate for their new residence (Taylor 2010, 54, 57, 58–59, 61). While Bellow ostensibly resisted moving to Paris, or indeed anywhere in Europe: "I have been opposing her [Anita]. I don't like to hazard a year of writing, and France or Italy may be too exciting or disturbing" ("Letter to Melvin Tumin," Taylor 2010, 58); he would later note that he had gone to Paris with certain hopes and expectations, though they were not solid: "I thought I understood why I had come to Paris" (Bellow 1983).

ARRIVAL

Upon his arrival Bellow discovered that Paris was undergoing a tumultuous period as the community struggled with the hardships of the postwar environment. He found the city saturated with Americans from all walks of life and he sensed that their presence added to the woes of the proud French: "the city defeated and recently occupied by the Germans was experiencing a second and even more disgraceful occupation by the dollar-proud Americans, moronically happy, stupid and mal élevés" (Bellow 2005). From the beginning Bellow's interactions with the French were difficult. "Prices are doubled as soon as one opens one's mouth," he wrote in his first letter from the city ("Letter to Henry Volkening," September 27, 1948, Taylor 2010, 68), and he would maintain throughout his career that Americans were not warmly welcomed in postwar Paris: "The French hated us" (Bellow 2005).

Bellow interpreted the anti-Americanism of the French as influenced by an attitude imbued by their cultural heritage. Bellow categorized the French into two groups:

> the workers and the other French. The workers are infinitely superior and are, really, what we at home have always considered *French*, the others what we meant by bourgeois. You see then what it's like . . . it's

anything but warm. ("Letter to Oscar Tarcov," December 5, 1949, Taylor 2010, 90)

For Bellow, the French working class were the more authentic group, but they did not attract his interest, as he claimed that they differed only superficially from the American working class, which he knew well from his Chicago youth ("Letter to David Bazelon," Taylor 2010, 87). Bellow scorned the French bourgeoisie, and in 1955 he wrote "The French as Dostoyevsky Saw Them," in which he expressed a degree of affinity with Dostoevsky's fervent hatred of bourgeois Paris. Like Dostoevsky in his time, Bellow saw the French bourgeoisie as hypocritical, acting in contradiction to the noble image and values they exported (Bellow 1955, 42). Bellow complained often of the impermeability and exclusiveness of French society, and its strict rules that hindered newcomers (Dommergues 18; Bellow 1955, 41; Bellow 1983). He thought that the French only accepted those who had "done everything possible to become French" (Bellow 1983). Bellow refused, and described how he was "constantly aware that [he] was not a Frenchman. Americans at that time were forever being told what they were or were not" (Bellow 1954). Though he claimed to have had French friends, in his first two years in Paris Bellow was never invited into a single French-person's home (Atlas 2000, 142). Bellow considered the French and American attitudes diametrically opposed:

> Americans find it hard to believe that foreigners are unalterably foreign, for they have seen generations of immigrants become Americans. But old cultures are impermeable and exclusive—none more so than the French. (Bellow 1955, 41)

Coming from an immigrant society (and an immigrant family), Bellow saw Parisian exclusivity as a negative attribute with weak premises. He found the romantic myth of Paris false and therefore hypocritical, and when a friend spoke of "The City of Man, The City of Light," Bellow "took his rhetoric at a considerable discount" (Bellow 1983). The prenihilistic era of Balzac that Bellow admired was well gone, and the remnants of what Bellow considered the nihilistic modern era, which had culminated in World War II, were still present, hanging in the ashes in the air. The French themselves were undergoing internal violence coming to terms with the new world. Hollow attempts to manifest anything prestigious about French society, or to recover the Glory of France, only amounted to "museum custodianship" in Bellow's view ("Letter to David Bazelon," Taylor 2010, 87). French society's exclusivity was evidence of the detrimental attachment of the custodians to their own past and myths: "If there's anything that dwelling in this French Park has shown me it is the blindness that a great cultural inheritance bequeaths" ("Letter to Herbert and Mitzie McCloskey," Taylor 2010, 92). According to Bellow's outlook, the French attempted to claim prestige through inheri-

tance and exclusivity, but exclusivity rendered a society of petty haughti-
ness. In previous decades Paris had also garnered attraction as an artistic
hub where expatriate writers thrived, but Bellow found no such community during his time. Instead he ridiculed those Americans who believed
in the literary myth of Paris and labelled the rest of the literary contingent
as "collapsed Americans" ("Letter to David Bazelon," Taylor 2010, 80).
He had less respect for the native artistic scene, as he was of the opinion
that French intellectual and cultural life had suffered firstly due to the
ideological thirties and then due to the subsequent and even less inspir-
ing postwar movements: "Marxism, Eurocommunism, Existentialism,
Structuralism, Deconstructionism could not restore the potency of French
civilization. Sorry about that. A great change, a great loss of ground"
(Bellow 1983). In his view none of the "marvellous" that made French
culture famous remained. As a result Bellow found himself disappointed
in his choice of Paris as a destination for a writing residency, as he came
to believe that "Paris was deader than a doornail for an American writer"
(Illig 1973, 106).

PART WEAKNESS TO STRENGTH

Bellow believed that French civilization had left the Parisians full of
"melancholy and bad temper," and the city with a pervasive atmosphere
of gloom (Bellow 1955, 43). Paris, with its hereditary culture, was overciv-
ilized, which resulted in custodianship, hollow and static dynamism, and
arrogant self-assurance. Living amid this gloomy and obstinate condition
led Bellow to exclaim in a letter that he was "sick and tired of all that sort
of melancholy and boredom"; France had given him "a bellyful of it"
("Letter to Oscar Tarcov," Taylor 2010, 89). Living in a custodian civilisa-
tion also made Bellow aware of the hindrance of tradition to individual-
ity and creativity. According to Atlas, Bellow

> regarded European culture as an oppressively dominating institu-
> tion—another bullying authority to resist. A resource, yes, but also a
> geographic and historical version of his brothers. The fact that he was
> forced to struggle with a society that he felt excluded him proved tonic.
> (Atlas 2000, 146)

The longer he spent in France, the more he became aware, through
contrast, of his own upbringing and character. In post-Holocaust Europe,
Bellow developed a keen awareness of what it meant to be an American
Jew (Bellow 1983). The environment also made him perceive fundamental differences between the European and the American outlook. In Bellow's view, in their nation of immigrants, Americans learned that "cultures were not indispensible" (Bellow 2005), and those who built and
strived to belong in the nation gained a type of energy: "An effort was

required. One made oneself, freestyle" (Bellow 1983). By the time he was writing *The Adventures of Augie March*, Bellow "badly miss[ed] American energy" (Letter to Dave Bazelon, Taylor 2010, 86). He had "learned in Europe" how "deeply involved" he was with the United States, but also that as a writer he should be there:

> After the Second World War all the action seemed to be on our side of the Atlantic. No getting away from it. Paris was no longer the home (or locus, if home is too sentimental a word) of international culture. You had to reconcile yourself to life in commercial-technological-etc. America. (Gray, White, and Nemanic 1984, 200)

A writer, particularly an American writer, had to engage with the "new" frontier and "theatre" of the modern experience. Bellow had come to Paris on a "wild-goose-chase" (Gray et al. 1984, 200) to find energy, only to discover that his energy derived from his experience and place in America.

As he became more aware of who he was, Bellow realized that he was not meeting his own expectations: "I had come to great humanistic Paris to reach what was deepest in my nature and the best I was able to do was to begin to realize the scope of my failure." Bellow had become a writer hoping to express his "singular reactions to existence." His first two books had fallen short of this expectation, and were in fact more closely aligned with the stifling European styles, tones, attitudes, and values that he had come to resent in Paris. Bellow had initially worked on a novel entitled *The Crab and the Butterfly* ("Letter to J. F. Powers," Taylor 2010, 79), which was "even more depressing than the first two. Two men in a hospital room, one dying, the other trying to keep him from surrendering to death." The novel had Bellow "tied in knots," and he considered it another shortcoming: "the French were not more unhappy than I was when I began to recognize the scope of my latest failure." Thoroughly disappointed, he began to realize that his writing had missed, and was missing again, something essential—his own original vision.

Walking towards his studio one morning, feeling the "atmosphere of misery or surliness," Bellow experienced a sudden breakthrough:

> Parisian gutters are flushed every morning by municipal employees who open the hydrants a bit and let water run along the curbs. I seem to remember there were also rolls of burlap that were meant to keep the flow from the middle of the street. Well, there was a touch of sun in the water that strangely cheered me. . . . [I]t wasn't so much the water flow as the sunny iridescence. Just the sort of thing that makes us loonies cheerful. I remember saying to myself, "Well, why not take a short break and have at least as much freedom of movement as this running water."

A new path presented itself immediately. Walking away from the stream Bellow spoke under his breath, "I am an American—Chicago-born"—the opening line of *The Adventures of Augie March*. The line did not refer to Bellow, who was born in Montreal, but to a childhood friend whose last name was August or possibly lived on Augusta Street.[2] Bellow returned to his writing studio reminiscing about this boy: "The gloom went out of me and I found myself with magical suddenness writing a first paragraph." *The Adventures of Augie March* was born.

Reflecting on Chicago from Paris as a creative framework, Bellow accessed a profound writing source and was able to work more quickly than he ever had before ("Letter to Monroe Engel," Taylor 2010, 85). Letters from the period indicate an almost overwhelming enthusiasm for writing: "For the time being I think it is best to stall, stall everyone except Augie" ("Letter to Henry Volkening," Taylor 2010, 75). In a 1953 interview Bellow said, "The great pleasure of the book was that it came easily, all I had to do was be there with buckets to catch it" (Breit 1953, 4). The enthusiasm led to a lack of objective restraint that Bellow later regretted, though at the time he responded to similar reservations on the part of his editor: "I'm having such an enthusiastic labor with it that it hadn't occurred to me . . . how a reader might feel about risking limbs in the clearing" ("Letter to Monroe Engel," Taylor 2010, 98). Writing *The Adventures of Augie March* was an enjoyment, due to its ease, and also its escapism: "In Paris I enjoyed a nostalgic Chicago holiday" (Gray et al. 1984, 217). Bellow found himself "independent of place" with the result that Paris suffered from "invariable normalcy" while Chicago "had grown exotic." Yet the task was more than an escape, as Bellow quickly sensed the work was the best thing he had "ever written" ("Letter to Henry Volkening," Taylor 2010, 83). He "had the triumphant feeling" that he had discovered what he "had been born for," and he broke out of his depressive state with enormous momentum: "back to strength from a position of extreme weakness: I had almost suffocated and then found I was breathing more deeply than ever."

AUGIE MARCH

Bellow's foreign residency in Paris induced powerful intellectual reflection as he confronted forces oppositional to his own experience and vision, and he responded by writing a novel that manifested this development. Bellow chose as his subject someone ontologically opposed to nihilism, suffering, and the rest of the "modern theme," to which Paris had given him exposure. The novel began as an imaginative biography of his childhood friend "Augie," as it was in his image that Bellow could recognize qualities of his own character, will, and artistic direction. Augie's nature had taught Bellow something more quintessentially "Bellovian" (Atlas 2000, 153):

Augie had introduced me to the American language, and the charm of
that language was one of the charms of his personality. From him I had
unwittingly learned to go at things freestyle, making the record in my
own way—first to knock, first admitted. (Bellow 2005)

Bellow harnessed Augie as someone who, like himself, would never
accept being held down by depressiveness and tradition, and who would
only be satisfied by experiencing and expressing his own "singular reactions to existence." The personality and the language of such a character
allowed Bellow to move into a subject and style that were more organic:
"The language was immediately present—I can't say how it happened,
but I was suddenly enriched with words and phrases." As Atlas notes,
through *The Adventures of Augie March* Bellow made a leap toward capturing "a voice capable of registering both his mental states and the into-
nations of his native speech—a voice of his own" (Atlas 2000, 152). It was
Augie, perceived through the cultural distance of a Parisian walk, which
released Bellow's artistic voice and subject matter.

Beyond his characterisation as Bellow's childhood friend, Augie also
manifests elements of Bellow's developed self-awareness in Paris. The
stronger awareness of the Jewish American experience directly influenced *The Adventures of Augie March*: "Much of 'Augie' was for me the
natural history of Jews in America." The "ethnography" of the American
Jew, Bellow's story, had not been told, and he wished to give his version
(Gray et al. 1984, 209). For Bellow, the story of the American Jew meant
trying to be American. Like Bellow, Augie has a distinctly "American
outlook, superadded to a Jewish consciousness." Augie treats his Jewish
inheritance and presents it to the reader without comment, something
Bellow himself later criticized: "he wanted to enjoy his situation, wanted
to play the American naïf. There was a price to pay. He was unwilling to
pay it" (Gray et al. 1984, 209). Augie has the animism that Bellow identified in the American immigrant, without the trouble of socio-ethnic
alienation. At the time, Bellow was simply after energy and regarded the
immigrant idealism as a powerful source of dynamism, so he gave it to
Augie in unbalanced abundance.

In Bellow's view, the stagnancy and suffering of Paris was attributable
to overcivilization, so Augie March is the uncivilized type, more "stub-
bornly barbarian" than Bellow felt in relation to the French ("Postcard to
Samuel and Rochelle Freifeld," Taylor 2010, 64). When he wrote *The Adventures of Augie March* Bellow had "felt like doing the ingenu, that's all. It
genuinely corresponded to a kind of Americanism of the thirties—naive,
easy-going, tolerant, all-accepting, youthfully affectionate" (Roudane and
Bellow 1984, 279). His choice of an "ingenu" may have been influenced
by the man who lived below his writing studio, Caffii, "the very embodiment of the European intellectual émigré in Paris," a man who constantly
thought about "Goethe, Johnson, and Voltaire" and tried to imagine

"what it would have been like to drop in for a chat with Diderot" (Atlas 2000, 145). *The Adventures of Augie March* can be regarded as an adaptation of Voltaire's *L'ingènu* (1767). Voltaire's novel tells the tale of a young, intelligent, handsome man, of European descent but raised away from "civilization" by Native Americans. He arrives in France where his naïve, honest, impulsive, and optimistic nature and organically pure reason are dealt continual blows by the corruption inherent in French civilization. The worst blows are dealt in Paris. Bellow no doubt found affinity with Voltaire's tale and chose it as the model for his own novel written in response to his Parisian experience. Augie possesses the same free will and goodwill as L'ingènu, and their stories follow similar patterns. The idealism, determination, and mobility of Augie have also been described as "pícaro" qualities, and these have led to comparisons with Don Quixote (Gericke 1990; Shaw 1987). The attributes are fitting given a letter in which Bellow remarked that facing up to all the modern "melancholy and boredom" was a "a kind of Quixotic job" ("Letter to Oscar Tarcov," Taylor 2010, 89). Bellow wanted Augie to have the character of L'ingènu, along with Quixotic determination. Through his fiction Bellow created the ultimate weapon to combat the obstacles and limitations he faced in Paris.

Augie is defined as passive in appearance but profoundly resistant in character. According to Atlas, Bellow shared the same quality: "Pretending to be at the mercy of others was a way of disguising his fiercely independent will. . . . Passivity in Bellow's hands was an instrument of freedom" (Atlas 2000, 124). Bellow himself admitted to experimenting with submission and resistance against domineering, powerful, Machiavellian people:

> The challenge was to emerge intact from the grip of these would-be dominators. To extract the secret of their powers from them while eluding their control became my singular interest. If I had any game it was the independence game. Perhaps it was not so much an interest as it was a spiritual exercise. I recognized that I did not have to do the will of others. (Bellow 2005)

Like Bellow, Augie also comes to define himself through his oppositional independence, as Einhorn, a character in the novel recognizes:

> "But wait. All of a sudden I catch on to something about you. You've got *opposition* in you. You don't slide through everything. You just make it look so."
> This was the first time that anyone had told me anything like the truth about myself. I felt it powerfully. (Bellow 1953, 117)

In Paris, Bellow learned that he had been limiting himself, and that these limitations and the very act of limiting were oppositional to his nature. Augie March is a character who refuses any limitations on his individual possibilities. "For a minute I felt rather insulted that he should laugh when he asked me what I was doing here. It might be incongruous but if it was for Man why shouldn't it be for me too? If it wasn't, perhaps that wasn't one hundred per cent my fault. Which Man was it the city of? Some version again. It's always some version or other" (Bellow 1953, 521). He will follow others, keen to broaden his experiences, but when they attempt to tie him down, he breaks lose into identities of his own device. Thus Augie March, like Bellow, defines himself by opposition and expansiveness.

Throughout the novel, Augie jumps from adventure to adventure, falling into and out of the control of other people. With each adventure he gains further insight into who he is and what he wants. Some of the adventures are brutal or tragic, but Augie never abandons his optimistic spirit. His adventures take him through various jobs such as dog groom-er, book thief, shoe salesman, and unions man. He goes to Mexico where he trains an eagle and almost meets Trotsky. He joins the merchant navy and survives the destruction of his ship at sea by a U-boat. Eventually his adventures take him to Paris where he is living with his newly wed Stella, an actress who has difficulty with honesty. He is employed by an Armenian businessman as a black-market entrepreneur and is often on the move around Europe. It is from this latest setting that Augie is writ-ing his memoirs, *The Adventures of Augie March*: "I sat at a table and declared that I was an American, Chicago born, and all these other events and notions" (Bellow 1953, 519).

Since Augie was created as a response to Paris, he expresses the same opinion of the city as Bellow. Bellow claimed that Paris was his wife's choice for their residence, and Augie similarly claims that he is living there at the will of Stella. Augie finds that the so-called "City of Man" is not in cohesion with his own nature, which therefore renders the title hypocritical and nonsensical. The city has its own, and a limited, "ver-sion" of man, which indicates a flawed civilization. Constantly good-natured and optimistic, Augie, the "blue-eyed *ingenu*" (Simmons 1979, 162), cannot hold a grudge for too long against Paris or his friend's sur-prise that he should be there:

> But who could complain of this pert, pretty, Paris when it revolved like a merry-go-round—the gold bridge-horses, the Greek Tuileries he-roes and stone beauties, the overloaded Opéra, the racy show windows and dapper colors, the maypole obelisk, the all-colors ice-cream, the gaudy package of the world.
> I don't suppose Frazer meant to hurt my feelings; he was merely surprised to see me here. (Bellow 1953, 521)

In this passage Augie seems to have what subsequent returns to Paris gave Bellow: "*les yeux passagers* of a tourist" ("Letter to Henry Volken-ing," Taylor 2010, 108). Brian Way argues that the final chapter is itself too much on the side of tourism (Way 1964, 44). However, Augie, like

Bellow, is still aware that there is an underlying suffering and struggle beneath the superficial appearance of Paris: "Everybody gives me a line about Paris being a place of ease and mentions *calme, ordre, luxe, et volupté,* and yet there is this toil being done" (Bellow 1953, 523). Nor has Augie gained any reprieve from the arrogant and pretentious assertiveness of others: "I'm good and tired of all these big personalities, destiny molders, and heavy-water brains, Machiavellis and wizard evildoers, big-wheels and imposers-upon, absolutists" (524).

At the end of *The Adventures of Augie March* it is revealed that Paris has given Augie the opportunity to sit down and express an understanding of himself through the writing process, just as it did for Augie's creator, Bellow. Throughout his adventures, Augie expresses the desire to find the "axial lines" of life, which can be found beyond striving, and which give life its most essential and beautiful meaning: "When striving stops, the truth comes as a gift—bounty, harmony, love, and so forth" (Bellow 1953, 514). For someone like Augie, or Bellow, the striving never stops: "Maybe I can't take these very things I want" (514). However, by writing his memoirs Augie, the Quixotic ingènu, has affirmed who he is and how he sees things. He claims that man's "fate, or what he settles for is also his character" (514). Therefore Augie's character, his fate, is his opposition and determination to keep striving, and this discovery is Augie's access to the truth, to the axial lines. Augie's Parisian discovery reflects Bellow's revelation that led him to write *The Adventures of Augie March*, and thus released his original voice and subject matter as a novelist.

In Atlas's opinion *The Adventures of Augie March* represented the "garrulous, high-spirited, life-hungry" half of Bellow's personality (Atlas 2000, 153). Previously dormant, this half of him awoke with such strength when he wrote the novel that in 1984, with the objectivity of decades-long hindsight, Bellow had critical misgivings:

> There were two things wrong with *Augie March* as I see it now. It got away from me, for one thing. I had found a new way to write a book. It was my very own. But I had no control over it. I couldn't say no to any of the excesses. I didn't know how to check myself. Up to a point it was effective. Americans who read it felt liberated by its excesses, but I don't think *The Adventures of Augie March* is going to wear well. Its other fault was disingenuousness. I really knew much more about darkness than I let on. I knew perfectly well what nihilism was. I had no excuse for being such an ingenu. (Roudane and Bellow 1984, 279)

His newly found half escaped Bellow's control, and drowned out the more restrained and "dark" side. Bellow's weapon was too powerful, and Augie, the narrator of the novel, governed an inaccurate image: "It's not really the way it was; it's just the way Augie wanted it to be" (Gray et al. 1984, 216). The shortcomings meant that it was "not a true book, not fully true" (217). However, Bellow admitted that "the best part of" him was "formed in jumps" ("Letter to Herbert and Mitzie McCloskey," Taylor 2010, 93), and despite the shortcomings, critics universally agree that *The Adventures of Augie March* marked a sharp breakthrough in Bellow's career. At the time Bellow saw that he had put his hand "strongly on a good thing and was making it resound" ("Letter to Monroe Engel," Taylor 2010, 102), and he never changed his opinion that *The Adventures of Augie March* was his first true work as a novelist.

Bellow travelled to Paris hoping to find an environment sympathetic to writers in which he could discover a greater sense of his uniqueness and potential as a novelist. Ironically, it was his disappointment with the Parisian environment that led to this self-discovery. Paris was suffocating—the weight of the city's custodial culture, the hollowness, exclusiveness, melancholy, and hypocrisy. The pervasiveness of the city's oppressive gloom cornered Bellow and propelled him to develop an oppositional self-awareness, and it was though the artistic expression of this position that Bellow achieved his breakthrough. By creating in Augie a character who refuses all limitations, Bellow broke through everything that had constrained him. *The Adventures of Augie March* served as both a vehicle for and a manifestation of opposition to the many forces Bellow found himself surrounded by in Paris. The critically important role of Paris is reflected in the ending to the novel, as it is in Paris that Augie, like Bellow, embarks on a writing process that reveals his interpretation of his unique experiences, and therefore of his character, which are based upon his opposition and his quest for a unique fate. *The Adventures of Augie March* released Bellow's "singular reactions to existence" (Bellow 2005) and his career as a novelist.

NOTES

1. Bellow wrote and set *The Victim* in New York, and Acatla was setting in *The Adventures of Augie March* and an earlier unpublished work named after the town (Saul Bellow Archives, Regenstein Library, The University of Chicago, Series B, Box 1, Folder 1). He first saw Paris with a group of college students on the way to Spain in 1947 (Atlas 2000, 120).

2. "I Got a Scheme!" is the publication of Bellow's notes that repeatedly recalls the same events in various iterations. For example, on one occasion Bellow attributes the origin of "Augie" to his friend's surname, and on another occasion to the street on which his friend lived.

REFERENCES

Atlas, James. *Bellow*. London: Faber & Faber, 2000.

Bellow, Saul. "Choosing the Necessary: Remarks by Saul Bellow to Padgett Powell's Graduate Class in Fiction Writing at the University of Florida, Gainsvile, February 21, 1992." Transcribed by Andrew Gordon. http://web.clas.ufl.edu/users/agordon/beluf.htm

Bellow, Saul. *The Adventures of Augie March*. 1953. London: Penguin, 2001.

————. "The French as Dostoyevsky Saw Them." In *It All Adds Up: From the Dim Past to the Uncertain Future*. 1955, reprint London: Penguin, 2007.

————. "How I Wrote Augie March's Story." *New York Times Book Review* January 31, 1954.

————. "'I Got a Scheme!' The Words of Saul Bellow." *New Yorker*, April 25, 2005.

————. "My Paris." *New York Times Book Review*, March 13, 1983.

Breit, Harvey. "A Talk with Saul Bellow." In *Conversations with Saul Bellow*, ed. Gloria L. Cronin and Ben Siegel, 3–5. Jackson: University of Mississippi Press, 1953.

Dommergues, Pierre. *Interview Manuscript*. Series B, Box 1, Folder 1. Saul Bellow Archives, Chicago.

Gericke, Philip O. "Saul Bellow's *The Adventures of Augie March* and Its Picaresque Antecedents." *Pacific Coast Philology* 25, nos. 1–2 (1990): 77–83.

Gray, Rockwell, Harry White, and Gerald Nemanic. "Interview with Saul Bellow."In *Conversations with Saul Bellow*, ed. Gloria L. Cronin and Ben Siegel, 199–222. Jackson: University of Mississippi Press, 1984.

Illig, Joyce. "An Interview with Saul Bellow." In *Conversations with Saul Bellow*, ed. Gloria L. Cronin and Ben Siegel, 104–12. Jackson: University of Mississippi Press, 1973.

Roudane, Matthew C., and Saul Bellow. "An Interview with Saul Bellow." *Contemporary Literature* 23 no. 3 (Autumn, 1984): 265–80.

Shaw, Patrick W. "History and the Picaresque Tradition in Saul Bellow's *The Adventures of Augie March*." *CLIO* 16, no. 3 (Spring 1987): 203–19. Actually a reprint 1–9.

Simmons, Maggie. "Free to Feel: Conversation with Saul Bellow." *Conversations with Saul Bellow*, ed. Gloria L. Cronin and Ben Siegel, 161–70. Jackson: University of Mississippi Press, 1979.

Taylor, Benjamin, ed. *Saul Bellow: Letters*. New York: Viking, 2010.

Way, Brian. "Character and Society in *The Adventures of Augie March*." *Bulletin of the British Association for American Studies* 8 (1964): 36–44.

EIGHT

The Road to Paris in Tim O'Brien's *Going After Cacciato*

Nanette Norris

The Vietnam War took some fifty-eight thousand American lives and up to two million Vietnamese. The Paris Peace Accords that were designed to end it were negotiated in fits and starts over five years, during which time Richard Nixon authorized the "Cambodia Incursion," sending U.S. troops into Cambodia in an effort to cripple North Vietnamese supply lines. Home front tensions increased and four days after the Cambodia announcement the Ohio National Guard killed unarmed students at Kent State University. Tim O'Brien's *Going After Cacciato* figures the complexities of these times as a soldier named Cacciato goes AWOL in a bid to walk to Paris, and a squad is sent after him, into Cambodia, with orders to stop him in any way they can. It is a world gone mad, in which absurdities and ironies abound. Is it ever possible to walk away from a war, O'Brien asks? Can one simply leave? Under what circumstances can one—should one—end a war? And why Paris?

The journey to Paris takes place not in real but in imagined time, and yet it is the most important traversing of the concept of civilization, of that for which it is, ultimately, worth living, fighting, and even dying. Paris is the epitome of the urban—of intellectual, creative, and physical freedom in community. Although the journey to Paris, in the context of the story, takes place only in the imagination of Paul Berlin, nonetheless we are aware that Paris is there, is substantial; that life continues in Paris even as the war proceeds in Vietnam; that Paris has a long history of being a civilized, urban community; that Paris is, in the book, and was, in historical time, the seat of the peace negotiations and therefore the seat of hope for the end of the war. It is a simple equation: civilization is greater than the sum of barbarities. *Going After Cacciato* questions the nature of civilization as an evolving concept, in terms of the motivations and purposes of the nations involved in the Vietnam conflict, in terms of a first-world/third-world interaction, and in terms of the thoughts and actions of the soldiers themselves.

This essay looks at the journey to Paris in *Going After Cacciato* as the central metaphor of our time: contemporary life has become the jungle experience, bizarre and uncertain, demanding the conscious imposition of the values of civilized behavior in order to cope with, and perhaps overcome, the ever-threatening barbarity of the unknown and unknowable. O'Brien seems to suggest that participating in the call to war, even a seemingly unjust and nonsensical war such as Vietnam was seen to be, is, part of one's participation in the ultimate continuation of civilization. He suggests elements such as duty to one's country, expectations of the community, and so forth, but ultimately the fight is to be able to position oneself to get to Paris, for the civilized negotiation which will end the barbaric conflict.

However, attaining peace is by no means simple. Even reaching the bargaining table is a feat. The novel approaches this quest as a combination of the personal and the political: as an example of "the road" genre, defined for the 1960s generation by Jack Kerouac's *On The Road* but in fact as classic as Homer's *The Odyssey*, the trip questions and redefines the values by which we live—in this case, the values by which America fought in its "longest war" (so-called, and now surpassed by the involvement in Afghanistan).

In an article entitled "A Game—Theoretic Analysis of the Vietnam Negotiations: Preferences and Strategies 1968–1973," Frank C. Zagare looks at the process of the Paris Peace Talks through the lens of a tool of economics called "game theory," which focuses upon how groups of people interact (Zagare 1977, 663–84). He mentions that the first round of talks took place from 1968 to 1973, ended in a stalemate, and remain an enigma to researchers because the parties involved (and especially the United States) were able "to develop completely distinct public and private negotiating positions" (664). He goes on to discuss both the first and second rounds of talks, and attempts an interpretation of American actions, using game theory. In essence, his analysis of the "game" in play shows that both the stalemate of the first round of talks and the negotiated peace of the second round resulted from specific preferences for conclusion on the part of the participants. In the first protracted round of talks, there was a lack of willingness to embrace peace at any cost—each participant (the Americans, the Communist Vietnamese, and the Republic of Vietnam) clung to a particular requirement for peace, was unwilling to stop warring except under specific circumstances, and found the specific requirements of the other parties unacceptable. Between the first and second round of talks, Zagare posits, a change in the strategic order of preference occurred for the United States which, according to one version of the game, the United States was successfully able to disguise from its opponents.

> Under the second, this game was shown to be vulnerable to a deceptive strategy by the United States. Only by falsely communicating its willingness to continue fighting could the United States ensure its most-preferred outcome. Under either interpretation, the optimal strategy by the United States entailed announcing that it would prefer to prolong the war rather than capitulate to the communists. (684)

O'Brien's novel echoes the duplicity, the hesitancy, the belligerence of these strategic moves on the part of the United States, working from the perspective of the boots on the ground, who are asked to participate in a dangerous and unpopular war on foreign soil, and, sometimes, to perform the duties of SOGs (Special Operations Group) by moving beyond the borders of official belligerency, into Cambodia (and beyond, toward Paris), where, if caught, they would be persona non grata, without passports, without identification, without the soldier's orders which are (at some level) his moral immunity against trespass. Cacciato and the squad that goes after him, like the U.S. soldiers in (and around) Vietnam during the war, are on a mission to which they cannot confess, caught in a conundrum of irony and duplicity, where right and wrong are reversed, superimposed, well-nigh indistinguishable.

Going After Cacciato, published in 1978, was written shortly after O'Brien's 1969–1970 tour of duty, when the full history of the Paris Peace Talks had yet to be written. Although O'Brien says he came from "a town that congratulates itself, day after day, on its own ignorance of the world: a town that got us into Vietnam" ("President's Lecture"), and the politics in the novel are similarly broad and imprecise, nonetheless the novel reeks of the kind of ironies of politics of which each of us becomes aware without knowing all of the ins and outs, all of the details. Thus, there is a clear focus on the American perspective, and the main Asian character, Sarkin Aung Wan, represents all Vietnamese, as well as all refugees, and even the Chinese, rather than any specific group. She is both the girl-friend Berlin never had and whomsoever the U.S. got into bed with. However, if we were to pin it down, the novel as a whole would have to be representative of the first round of peace talks, which came to an ignominious end in 1973. As Gareth Porter points out, "The Paris Agreement could not end the war, because Thieu had been assured by the Nixon Administration that he would get full US backing for a policy of avoiding political accommodation and continuing the military offensive" (Porter 1975, 278, italics removed).

Thus, in the novel, the group arrives in Paris and pinpoints Cacciato's location, only to have him slip out from under once again. Paris disappears and we are left with Paul Berlin, in the war, at a decisive moment of reckoning, ordered by his superior to fire on one of his own (who is doing what Berlin/O'Brien wishes he could, in withdrawing from the war), an act which encapsulates the complexities of a war which killed *"four* civilians for every soldier" (Zinn 1967, 2).[1] Berlin experiences a total personal breakdown by shaking and firing his weapon in error: "A dozen rounds were off in the time it took to squeal" (O'Brien 1978, 331).

> Then there was a floating feeling, then a swelling in his stomach, then a wet releasing feeling. He tried to stop it. He squeezed his thighs together and tightened his belly, but it came anyway. (331)

Berlin's most humane act—the one that allows Cacciato to get away—affords him the most relief and, perversely, humiliation. The humiliation is equally the failure to trap Cacciato and the return to war. In a lecture given at Brown University in 1999, O'Brien described an experience he had during the summer he was trying to decide whether or not to obey the draft call:

> [S]omething exploded in my stomach. It felt like a water balloon that popped open inside of me. It was a leaky, gaseous, watery feeling—a feeling of, uh, real despair. (O'Brien 1999)

Relief or despair? In *Going After Cacciato* it is both—a postmodern conundrum in which things are not what they seem. More than mere fragmentation, the fragments of narrative (if that is indeed what they are) exist simultaneously: all exist, and none exist . . . all are true, and none are true. Paul Berlin is relieved, and he is humiliated. The United States is fighting a war, and it is promoting civilization; it is escalating fighting publically, and moving toward a negotiated peace privately.

At the heart of the novel is a collapse of the literary sense of modernism/postmodernism and the historic sense of modernity. The transformative dream that is the modernist desire to reunite the disunited in a new spiritual whole (peace for nations and marriage for individuals) is disrupted by the realist understanding of a reality dictated by science and politics—a reality which is the direct outcome of modernity. Thus, over three hundred years of Western striving for "civilization," reflected in enlightenment thinking and industrialization, have culminated in this ironic double vision of waging war to establish peace, of destroying those you would save, of death that there may be life.

Structurally, the movement in the novel is from the separated units—of "The Observation Post," of the often painfully realistic memories of the war, and of the narrative of the journey to Paris—to a conflated overlapping or superimposition of these realities (O'Brien 1978, 326).[2] Where is reality? In some sense, only the poignant thoughts of "The Observation Post" can be counted on. A kind of short, narrative blog (before the word entered our vocabulary) interspersed between the other chapters/realities, "The Observation Post" offers a view of Paul Berlin, safe in a military observation tower between the South China Sea and the province of Quang Ngai (where the My Lai massacre occurred), concentrating on an idea that Paris might be attainable, and that the AWOL Cacciato was bearing the dream hence. "It was an idea. It was a working out of the possibilities. It wasn't dreaming and it wasn't pretending. It wasn't crazy" (O'Brien 1978, 29).

The life of the mind is quintessentially opposed to the soldier's accustomed or expected life, especially in Vietnam where "Bernie Lynn and Lieutenant Sidney Martin had died in the tunnels" and "rain fed fungus . . . grew in the men's boots and socks, and their socks rotted, and their feet turned white and soft so that the skin could be scraped off with a fingernail, and Stink Harris woke up screaming one night with a leech on his tongue" (O'Brien 1978, 1). O'Brien spares no nasty detail. The Doc calls Berlin's flight of mind in the observation post "an excess of fear biles" acting "as a soothing influence, quieting the brain, numbing, counteracting the fear" (21, 7). His contemplation of possibilities is deemed counterproductive, as it takes away the fear that keeps the men alive.

But someone has to think of the alternatives. Someone has to be involved in the search for peace, which is precisely who or what Cacciato is. Cacciato is an idea that, like a savior, is "[t]he light of the world" (O'Brien 1978, 21, 7) climbing "towards the clouds":

> Very slowly, deliberately, Cacciato was spreading his arms out as if to show them empty, opening them up like wings, palms down. The kid's face was fuzzy, bobbing in and out of mist, but it was a happy face. Then his mouth opened, and in the mountains there was thunder. (11)

The "winging motions" are "[a]wkward, unpracticed, but still flying," according to the visionary Paul Berlin. His compatriot, Stink, undercuts the grandiose view: "A squawking chicken, you see that? A chicken" (12)! It's all a matter of perspective.

Western ideology and religion cannot be separated (or rather, are separated at one's peril). Judeo-Christian values were fundamental to the development of Western ideology and continue to underpin the spirit of laws and social interaction. However, most of us don't really know what this means or when our behaviors and attitudes transgress in this sense. Lieutenant Corson, who constantly reminds us that he is ill, that he has "deteriorating muscle," and that this "wasn't his war" (21), represents a career soldier and an older generation which is baffled by Vietnam and its complexities; nonetheless, he is essential to the journey to Paris as he also embodies these almost-passé Judaeo-Christian values of "[m]ercy" and love (13). The text reiterates the pun, "mercy" for "merci," thereby linking French, France, Paris, and Judaeo-Christian values such as mercy (12–13).[3]

The novel expresses an era of confusion in values for the country that, politically, considered itself the seat of civilization and the protector of the world, and this confusion is imaged in the text as liminal space, in whose paradigm certain truths can emerge. The term *liminal* is most often seen in the context of fairy stories, where characters cross thresholds and have magical adventures through which they fulfill their hopes as heroes, returning to the world richer than they set out. The liminal space is betwixt and between. It exists out of time, being not clearly of this world. The rules of the so-called *real* world no longer govern and anything can happen—most often to the growth and development of the hero. In some sense, this novel takes place in entirely liminal space (Berlin's thoughts, the war narrative, and the mythical journey itself) because the truths it privileges are not valued in our society. Metaphysical experience (thought) is seen as suspect; memories can be altered; a journey that occurs only in the imagination is no journey at all. The effect of having liminality drive the story is that of turning the world upside down and exposing its madness and its lack of perspective.

The American perspective, manifested by the seven soldiers,[4] is quickly seen to be both crude and euphemistic, displaying a glaring ignorance of the people and the land of Vietnam, and an unwillingness to look their own actions in the face. For instance, the first meeting with Sarkin Aung Wan is under completely inauspicious circumstances: just as the jungle came to an end and the horizons expanded, Stink thought he spotted Cacciato. He readied his weapon:

> It happened instantly . . .
> Stink fired without aiming. It was automatic. It was Quick Kill. Point-blank, rifle jerking. The first shots struck the closest animal in the belly. There was a pause. The next burst caught the buffalo in the head, and it dropped.
> That fast. Every time, that fast.
> Someone was screaming for a cease-fire but Stink was on full automatic. He was smiling. Gobs of flesh jumped off the beast's flanks. (O'Brien 1978, 50)

As the dust clears, two refugee women are bawling over the death of their buffalo: "the girl gestured in the direction of the dead water buffalo. 'My aunts raised him from a tiny baby. Their own breasts, And now poor Nguyen—'" (52), and the suggestion is that the buffalo, raised at "their own breasts" from babyhood, was a person whose killing the soldiers euphemize in order to distance themselves from culpability: "I'm sorry about this. War's a lousy thing" (52).

Jane Jacobs has described the civilizing influence of boundaries in the jungle which is the urban landscape. Her sociological study looks at the influence of windows and sidewalks on behavior, along with other details of layout and accessibility.[5] The urban setting on one hand denotes civilization and the progress of modernity, but it also shows the break-down of civilizing influence, the maelstrom of modernity where values are relative and boundaries are sliding, whether national or behavioral. In this example from the novel, the soldiers have traveled beyond the jungle, beyond the clearly acknowledged space of uncivilized behavior, but their "automatic Quick Kill" (uncivilized) behavior has merely morphed into euphemism: "You VC?" he demanded of a little girl with braids. "You dirty VC?" (O'Brien 1978, 37).

Sarkin Aung Wan moves Paris out of the realm of barely–conceived crazy dream into possibility.

> "You will take me along, yes? As a refugee? Paris! Oh, I shall love to see Paris—Pont Neuf and the Seine, all the windows full of pretty things. We shall see it together!"
> Careful to choose his words, Paul Berlin tried to explain that it wasn't what it seemed. He told how Cacciato had walked away in the rain, a dumb kid with maps and candy and an AWOL bag. How they'd taken after him; a dangerous mission, nothing easy. How already they'd lost one member of the search party, Harold Murphy, and how they had marched many weeks through jungle and rain. A thousand hardships lay ahead.
> "But Paris!"
> "It's only a possibility."
> She looked at him, holding the brush to her nose and sniffing it. A dab of red paint gleamed on her cheek. "I am sure of it," she said. "Together we shall see Paris. Stroll through the gardens, visit all the famous mon-uments. Perhaps we shall fall in love there. Is that possible?"
> The oxcart swayed and pressed them together.
> "Paris," she whispered. Her eyes shifted to the horizon. "Yes, I should dearly love to see Paris." (58)

Paris materializes as euphemistic, a term for a complex package of desires for history, nobility of purpose, civilized behavior, emotional ful-fillment, commerce, technology, the best of the known and the unknown, but it is not static: it cannot be realized without great effort. Unlike the sugar-coating of a negative which characterizes the majority of euphe-misms, such as disguising a human death in memory as a buffalo, Paris emerges from imagination—the same imaginative process that can pro-duce the euphemism of the buffalo can "see" the way to Paris. "If you can imagine it, he tells himself, it's always real. Even peace, even Paris—sure, *it's real*" (O'Brien 1978, 291).

What, then, are the hardship and challenges of making it to Paris? First, there is the question of going beyond the American "tunnel vision" which insists on viewing the Vietnamese as an uncivilized, uncultured people, with whom discussion is impossible. This is the first-world/third-world clash. In the novel, this is imaged in the magico-realism of the chapter "Falling Through a Hole in the Road to Paris," in which Paul

Berlin, Sarkin Aung Wan, Oscar, Eddie, Doc, the old lieutenant, the buffalo, the cart, and the old women tumble "down a hole in the road to Paris," with "a series of enormous shock waves" (O'Brien 1978, 76).

The fall itself is reminiscent of Alice tumbling down the rabbit hole. The world Alice falls into is satirical and cleverly insightful of the functioning of the *real* world. Sarkin Aung Wan sees the fall as "having found the way," by which she means that the imaginative function is operating in a real and dramatic fashion, producing results which seem crazy from some perspectives but which open new possibilities. The so-called *real* world continues relentlessly, with Paul Berlin in the "Observation Post," thinking about courage, and Silver Stars, and how "the issue was how to act wisely in spite of fear"(O'Brien 1978, 80). In the war itself, Lieutenant Sidney Martin sends both Frenchie Tucker and Bernie Lynn to their deaths, going down into a tunnel that has to be searched. (Bernie Lynn does not *want* to go, but he volunteers angrily, while swearing "violently. He dropped his gear where he stood, just let it fall, and he entered the tunnel headfirst. 'Fuck it,' he kept saying, 'fuck it.' Bernie had once poured insecticide into Frenchie's canteen. 'Fuck it,' he kept saying, going down" (90).[6]

At the end of the fall, they find themselves in "a narrow tunnel with walls of hard red stone" (O'Brien 1978, 83). Up to this point, Paul Berlin has only known the tunnels as places of extreme danger, and he has never met "the enemy" face-to-face. He finds himself in an underground room that is technologically advanced, and fully provided for with furniture, food, and drink. He meets a major from the Forty-Eighth Vietcong Battalion who is gracious and socially adept, and to whom he poses the many questions of his ignorance. He learns about *xa*: "It means community, and soil, and home . . . earth and sky and even sacredness. . . . But at heart it means that a man's spirit is in the land, where his ancestors rest and where the rice grows. The land is your enemy" (86). He learns how badly he and other Americans have misjudged both the place and its people. The civilization that the Americans think they are bringing (or preserving from the Communists) does not take into consideration the essential value system inherent in Vietnam.

Imagination enables getting out of the tunnel as well, as the Vietnam imaginary takes the squad and Sarkin Aung Wan to Mandalay—"even the name was musical" (O'Brien 1978, 112)—a Polynesian paradise with "women pushing baby carriages, people lingering, people chatting and laughing, bikes and Hondas and carts and buses and donkeys, date trees in neat rows, hedges trimmed and cut square. "Civilization," Paul Berlin said" (112). The question now becomes, what is civilization? How can one define it? Is it the beautiful simplicity of Mandalay, where the travelers can relax, "almost [making] love" (115), and reconnect with a kind of innocence? But the innocence of Mandalay is naivité: easily corrupted (a young boy "touched Oscar's weapon. Then he touched Oscar's hand.

Oscar knelt, and the boy touched his face. "Nigger," Oscar said. The boy lit up. "Nigger!" said the boy" [113]). When they finally spot Cacciato, he is dressed as a monk, hiding among them at the time of the *Cao Dai*, the evening prayers. When Paul Berlin goes into the crowd of monks to try to catch Cacciato, he is attacked: "A monk with gleaming green eyes was screaming and bending his arm double. Two others bounced on his chest." Cacciato is "a lighted jack-o'-lantern" (122), mischievous and mythical, leading and misleading. One might expect peace and nonviolence at the sacred hour among the monks of Mandalay, but in fact monks actively protested and were politicized during the war, involving themselves in horrific and dramatically violent acts of self-immolation in order to draw spiritual and secular attention to the governmental persecution of Buddhist monks in largely Catholic South Vietnam.

Next on the journey is Chittigong, then Delhi, and a train ride during which the squad searches the passengers, a shameful memory for Paul Berlin: "*Sorry papa-san*—and he meant it truly, deeply" (O'Brien 1978, 138). The word *responsibility* enters the journey, and the path is revealed. We don't as yet know what responsibility means, except that it cannot mean the shameful searches of old men, women, and children, nor the confusion as to who are the "*Savages*" (139). In Delhi, the old lieutenant falls in love with Jolly Chand, and the movement away from war, toward civilization (complexified), toward Christian values such as love, seems like desertion or running away. Can you walk away from a war by embracing differences, loving "the other," as Lieutenant Corson wants to do? The question is answered when they grab the drunk lieutenant and pull him away with them, on the grounds that "he's among the walkir' wounded . . . [you] don't never leave your wounded behind" (139). Love is not the answer, and neither is giving up. The personal is *not* more important than the political. Neither do the squad members accept the idea that they are in any way deserters. There is a mission: that mission is capturing Cacciato, and thus the trip continues.

Space permits only the briefest look at the rest of the trip: Afghanistan, Tehran, Athens, Germany. As they move deeper into Western civilization, technology advances and behavior become organized, but no less barbaric. Iran deals with AWOL soldiers by beheading them, a fate which the unsupported, unofficial "peacenik"[7] soldiers would have shared had they not been able to get away. Not generally uncivil in behavior, the Iranians nonetheless deal with alternate perspectives in a brutal and intolerant manner. A thought-provoking view of pre-Revolutionary Iran which, ironically, shows that not much has changed in the Iranian manner of dealing with opposition, this section also highlights the special nature of the soldier in society, who operates in some sense outside the normal rules: "As soldiers we are exempt. In fact, it is our solemn duty to enforce the curfew. One of the pleasures of soldiering, yes? We shall drink and enforce curfew till dawn" (O'Brien 1978, 195). After this state-

ment on the part of Captain Rhallon, the discussion about moral purpose
rings hollow. There is something not quite right about the ideas that wars
are fought to win, and that soldiers are above the laws of the nation.
Their discussion about why soldiers don't run points not to some grand
sense of moral purpose and the *justness* of their cause, but, according to
Doc, to self-respect and fear—the soldier's own ego and reputation.

As the war narrative points out, the soldiers themselves "fought the
war, but no one took sides." "They did not know even the simple things:
a sense of victory, or satisfaction, or necessary sacrifice" (O'Brien 1978,
270). The mission, the going after Cacciato, is not about some grand moral purpose, nor is it about victory. It does not even come down to a
conviction, expressed by Captain Rhallon, that "desertion is a most serious offense" (201). But, of course, Captain Rhallon doesn't mean desertion as in a refusal to do a soldier's duty (although he does mean that,
too). He includes dissension with the means and purpose, dissension
with the ideology that brings about the warfare in the first place. To be
AWOL is to dissent, even more than it is to be absent or to desert in a
manner that implies cowardliness. (Is it cowardly to not want to abuse a
weaker and potentially innocent population?)

Athens, the "wharves of Western Civilization" (O'Brien 1978, 272), is
followed by the German heartland:

> The end was coming. He could feel it. Already he anticipated the tex-
> tures of things familiar: decency, cleanliness, high literacy and low mo-
> rality, the pursuit of learning in heated schools, science, art, industry
> bearing fruit through smokestacks. Wasn't this the purpose? The goal?
> Some vision of virtue? Weren't these the valued things? Wasn't free-
> dom worth pursuing? If civilization had meaning, weren't these the
> reasons? Hadn't wars been fought for these very promises? Even in
> Vietnam—wasn't the intent to restrain forces of incivility? The *intent*.
> Wasn't it to impede tyranny, aggression, repression? To promote some
> vision of goodness? (277)

All of these thoughts appear to be ironic as the squad rushes "through the
German dark" (278), alluding to the efforts of one of the world's so-called
most civilized of nations to impose their brand of civility and organiza-
tion through repression and brutality.

The journey, then, is through the mistakes of history and via the pre-
tenders of peace. Cacciato is the soldier who walked away from the war,
in the simplistic sense a deserter. He is also the one who refused to fight:
"Two little kings, playing at games, they threw a war and nobody
came."[8] However, O'Brien's vision of the path out of the war begins with
a denial of this idealistic view—"Can't just waddle away from a war,
ain't that right, sir? Dummy's got to be taught you can't hump your way
home" (O'Brien 1978, 10)—and moves to a more sophisticated sense of
how the war could come to an end. In this sense, Cacciato is the leader,

the idea which shifts, changes, and moves in the approach to a viable solution. As Carl Sandburg wrote, in "Washington Monument by Night," "The republic is a dream. / Nothing happens unless first a dream."[9] Peace is a dream which cannot come about unless "first a dream." The idea *is* of peace, but the form of that peace needs first to be manifested mentally. It is *not* simply ditching the whole effort; it is *not* settling for a soft life and turning one's back; it is *not* employing totalitarian and vicious methods to keep people in line; it is *not* terrorizing the innocent. Most of all, peace in any form is elusive: it will not "just happen"—it has to be pursued relentlessly. "He looked for meanings. Peace was shy. That was one lesson: Peace never bragged. If you didn't look for it, it wasn't there" (294).

The distance from conception of the idea (in the person of Cacciato walking away from the war) to destination ("gay Paree") is great: Paris is as amorphous an idea as peace. In keeping with postmodern ambiguity, Paris has multiple meanings. In the most superficial sense, each person views Paris differently. The lieutenant is glad simply to have reached a place with creature comforts and recognizable culture. He is happy to drink coffee and read a newspaper. Sarkin Aung Wan sees it as a place where a refugee can make a home, end the moving about. Only Oscar maintains his soldierly vigilance, pressing to keep them all focused on the mission. The arrival in Paris is no guarantee of the achievement of peace, albeit it is a peaceful place.

Paris has so much history in its buildings and streets. This history, like the history of the journey, is the trial-and-error of the process toward civilization, the pains of industrialization, "the soot and coal dust, all the artifacts of industry strewn like a child's toys along the tracks—rusting flatbeds and switching gear, timbers, heaps of mangles iron, incinerators, tin cans, crushed old automobiles, tank cars and abandoned warehouses and barbed wire" (O'Brien 1978, 289). The detritus is no excuse for dismissing the process of civilization, and neither can it weigh one down. Mistakes have been made. Paul Berlin ignores it all in his desire to reach "the peace of Paris."

Paris is the search for meaning, the attention to detail, "the order of things. Simple courtesies" (O'Brien 1978, 294). Every aspect of Paris speaks to the search for peace, from day-to-day living in which the pace of life is easy, open, to the special use of Paris as the host of the Peace Talks. Paris embodies everything that we take for granted as well as the hope for the future.

But it is also like the field of poppies in which Odysseus and his men found themselves: soporific, leading to an inclination to stop searching, to stop trying so hard to find Cacciato aka peace. "Can't you simply forget them?" asks Sarkin Aung Wan. "We could find a splendid apartment. . . . Be happy!" (O'Brien 1978, 297). Hard-won civilization, all the things Paris stands for and which we take for granted on a day-to-day basis, cannot be maintained by simply stopping, any more than it can be maintained in the jungles of a war zone.

Two events occur which shake the squad, out of its lassitude: the death of Eisenhower, former president and supreme commander of NATO forces in Europe during World War II, credited with orchestrating Operation Overlord, the D-Day landings, and the subsequent invasion of southern France which was decisive in bringing the war to a close, and President Richard Nixon's decision to *drop* "the number of B-52 missions over the North . . . from 1,800 to 1,600 a month. . . . Ike was dead and an era had ended" (O'Brien 1978, 302). This last places the novel squarely between the two Peace Talks, and before the Nixon decision to enter Cambodia and to escalate the war. Paul Berlin calls Eisenhower "[a] hero" (303), suggesting that his boldness in the face of the threat to civilization and freedom as we know it, by using war to end war, was strategically responsible. Cacciato, peace, evades capture as the B-52 missions abate and the reality of Paris becomes the dream of Paris as the soldiers return once more to the jungles of Vietnam and the narrative of history prepares for the escalation that, perversely, must come in order to capture the peace. As George Washington said, "If we desire to secure peace, one of the most powerful instruments of our rising prosperity, it must be known, that we are at all times ready for War."[10]

Thus, Paul Berlin's moment of humiliation is also his moment of triumph. When he does not shoot Cacciato, when his hand shakes and his aim slips, he maintains the illusion of war while preserving the possibility of peace—the soldier's double-bind and civilization's responsibility.

In *Going After Cacciato*, Paris represents not the end of the road, but a plateau on the road to peace for all nations and peoples. Its history encapsulates the great movements of modernity, the essays of pain and pride by which the world has moved forward, through modernity, toward civilization and civilized behavior. Paris held a position of prestige in the attempts to negotiate peace during the Vietnam War. However, as O'Brien points out, peace itself is slippery, complex, and hard to pin down—the difficulties of its realization are exacerbated by the conundrums of warfare: the gaming, the private versus public personas, the gap between have and have-not nations, differences of culture, and of language. Never, he seems to say, can it be found by turning one's back and resting on one's laurels.

NOTES

1. Howard Zinn, *Vietnam: The Logic of Withdrawal* (Boston: Beacon Press, 1967) 2. "A Chicago newspaper, asked by a reader if it were true that for every enemy soldier it killed in Vietnam the United States was killing six civilians, replied that this was not true; we were killing only *four* civilians for every soldier."

2. "The night seemed to move. Paris, Paul Berlin was thinking, but the feeling was Quang Ngai" (326).

3. Corson is refusing the offer of artillery and gunships from a joking radio voice that he refers to as a "monster." When he finally gets his refusal accepted, he gives his thanks, "Mercy." The word is reiterated by Corson when they are in Paris, when he is asking to be left out of yet another search for Cacciato, a search which is "a responsibility" (311–12). Although not prolonged or emphasized in the text, this could be seen as the turning moment of duplicity, when politically the United States was of two minds, escalating the war on one hand, and wishing for the end on the other. It raises questions about the metaphoric interpretation of Cacciato as *peace*, as the link is by no means straightforward, remaining postmodern in its lack of closure.

4. Note the number 7, which is often associated with divinity and transformational power.

5. Jane Jacobs, *The Death and Life of Great American Cities* (New York: Vintage, 1992).

6. A student of mine, an officer-cadet who had already served a tour of duty in Afghanistan, once told me that he spent most of his tour volunteering angrily for missions that were dangerous but that he felt were his duty to perform.

7. The name that has been given to protesting soldiers and draftees in Israel.

8. Bill Chadwich and John Chadwich (w), The Monkees (p), "Zor and Zam," *The Birds, The Bees & The Monkees* (Rhino/Wea, 1968).

9. Carl Sandburg, "Washington Monument by Night," in *The Complete Poems of Carl Sandburg* (New York: Houghton Mifflin Harcourt, 2002), 282.

10. George Washington, "Fifth Annual Address to Congress, Dec. 13, 1793" *Presidential Speech Archive*, www.Millercenter.org. (accessed August 30, 2011).

REFERENCES

Chadwich, Bill, and John Chadwich (writers), The Monkees (performers). "Zor and Zam." *The Birds, The Bees & The Monkees*. Rhino/Wea, 1968.

Jacobs, Jane. *The Death and Life of Great American Cities*. New York: Vintage, 1992.

O'Brien, Tim. *Going After Cacciato*. New York: Broadway, 1978.

O'Brien, Tim. "President's Lecture, April 21, 1999." *Writing Vietnam*. www.stg.brown.edu/projects/WritingVietnam/obrien.html (accessed July 17, 2011)

Porter, Gareth. *A Peace Denied: The United States, Vietnam, and the Paris Agreement*. Bloomington: Indiana University Press, 1975.

Sandburg, Carl. "Washington Monument by Night." In *The Complete Poems of Sandburg*, 282. New York: Houghton Mifflin Harcourt, 2002.

Washington, George. "Fifth Annual Address to Congress, Dec. 13, 1793." *Presidential Speech Archive*. www.Millercenter.org (accessed August 30, 2011).

Zagare, Frank C. "A Game-Theoretic Analysis of the Vietnam Negotiations: Preferences and Strategies 1968–1973." *Journal of Conflict Resolution* 21, no. 4 (December 1977): 663–84.

Zinn, Howard. *Vietnam: The Logic of Withdrawal*. Boston: Beacon Press, 1967.

NINE

"What Keeps You Here?"

Paris, Language, and Exile in The Book of Salt *by Monique Truong*

Daniela Fargione

In the summer of 1984, at the age of sixteen, Monique Truong fell in love. Her object of attraction, however, was not an individual but a place: "That July," she writes in "The Season de l'Amour," "I broke my heart and gave both halves to the city of Paris" (Truong 2003c, par. 1). Published in *The New York Times* in August 2003, this essay is a condensed recollection of Truong's first encounter with the French city and with her own body. What is evident from the outset of her narration is that both her spatial and physical mappings are preparatory to the recognition of a form of "topophilia," a condition that according to geographer Yi-Fu Tuan reflects "an affective bond between people and place or setting" (Tuan 1990, 4). Tuan also claims that the sensory stimulus that we decide to attend among the many provided by the environment "is an accident of individual temperament, purpose, and of the cultural forces at work at a particular time" (113). Being a teenager, Truong's "particular time' highly affected her perception of the city: Paris, in fact, was soon identified as an "accommodating" lover, whose affectionate embrace allowed her "awkward limbs" and her tied tongue for a gradual easing, eventually marking the passage from paralysis to mobility, "from language withheld to language *exchanged*" (Truong 2003c, par. 6, emphasis added).

Puberty was an unknown condition that Truong needed to explore, and her attempts at being in command within an alien space were not new. Ten years earlier, in fact, the writer had been forced to move from

Vietnam to the United States as a precautionary and temporary measure to escape bombings. When some weeks later Saigon fell to the Communists, her father, a high-level executive for an oil company, left on a boat to join his family. Of course, as Truong admits in an interview (Apte 2003), "the departure, the loss of home, that act of refugee-seeking" are all intertwined and recurrent themes of her work.[1]

In "The Season de l'Amour," Monique Truong's narrative is told from the vantage point of a tourist who engages linguistic complexity and cultural difference, while finding solutions in what Tuan defines as a *"dualism of dominance and affection,"* not a dichotomy but a dialectic (Ley 2001, 3). Eventually, Truong establishes a dynamic of continuous and mutual exchange between herself and the unknown city: she gives her heart to Paris, but Paris reciprocates by offering her an unexpected gift: the necessary coordinates to come to terms with herself and with her personal geography. Truong concludes this essay stating that Paris "seemed knowable and promising, like a detailed map spread before a traveler," her experience was an internal compass, and she saw in the city "a summer of possibilities" (Truong 2003c, par. 10).

Monique Truong's "The Season de l'Amour" underscores and anticipates the same crucial issues and concerns that trouble Binh, the main character and narrating voice of *The Book of Salt* (Truong 2003a). The novel chronicles the invisible existence of a gay Vietnamese cook, who works in the Parisian kitchen of the renowned lesbian couple Gertrude Stein and Alice B. Toklas. The book is thus an exploration of the forced exilic condition of a colonial subject, whose life in France is a savvy attempt at reconciling past and present, domesticity and domestication, linguistic confinement and culinary creativity. In this sense, "The Season de l'Amour" may be read as an ideal prologue to the novel, a savory appetizer introducing to a luscious meal.

Although Monique Truong's previous production was highly praised,[2] *The Book of Salt* was an auspicious novelistic debut. The germ of the book dates to her college days, when she bought a copy of the *Alice B. Toklas Cook Book* (1954) to find a hash-brownie recipe (Apte 2003). With great surprise she found out that it was not a Toklas recipe and that the book was more a memoir than a traditional cookbook. However, in a chapter called "Servants in France," Toklas writes about the numerous cooks—many of them nameless—who worked for her and Gertrude Stein at 27 rue de Fleurus. After reporting Stein's lamentations on "a servant, a complete stranger, [who] entered your home one day and very soon after into your life and then left you and went out of your life" (Toklas 2010, 186). She narrates how she decides to put an ad in the local newspaper: "Two American ladies wish to retain a cook . . ." (Toklas 2010, 186, Truong 2003a, 11). "It was then," Toklas continues, "that we commenced our insecure, unstable, unreliable but thoroughly enjoyable experiences with the Indo-Chinese," where by "Indo-Chinese" she refers to a broad and unitary category of undifferentiated people. In this sense, Toklas's *Cook Book* posits one of the main questions that postcolonial theories have tried to undermine, and one that Truong's novel constantly challenges: the false argument that "Asians" or "Orientals" constitute a fixed, unchanging, and homogeneous group, whose subjects conform to stereotypical representations generated by a dominant cultural logic (Chambers and Curti 1996; Lowe 1996; Eng 2001; Nguyen 2002; Xu 2008). Thus, to the degree that the discourse generalizes Asian identity as an anonymous body, Binh, the main character of *Book of Salt*, is rendered invisible. In this way, he is compared to the other outcasts in the homes of the dominant: "I am but one within a long line of others. The Algerian orphaned by a famine, the Moroccan violated by his uncle, the Madagascan driven out of his village . . . these are the wounded trophies who have preceded me" (19). What is also significant is the fact that the two ladies "wishing" to "retain" a cook are American, thus situating the two expatriates within the hegemonic domain of colonizers. Their choice to use a language and a register that do not conform to the style of a newspaper advertisement reveal their hypocritical attitude: the two women's linguistic mode is an indication of their persistent assumed superiority. Language, Truong seems to suggest, is a tricky tool: it can conceal, but it can also betray.

Binh is thus a fictional combination of two real Vietnamese cooks: Trac and Nguyen. Toklas describes the first one as a person whose French was made up "of a couple of dozen words" (Toklas 2010, 186), although his creativity extended from the gastronomical to the linguistic fields.[3] Furthermore, we are told that he would not work for his *Mesdames* on Sunday nights, since on his day off he used to cook for a rich bachelor (192), a role that in *The Book of Salt* is assigned to Lattimore, the bookish mixed-blood iridologist with whom Binh has an illicit affair. Nguyen, on the other hand, "had been a servant in the household of the French Governor-General of Indo-China" (187) and, like Binh, is taken to Bilignin to spend one long summer vacation with Toklas and Stein. Because of the numerous cross-references, the *Cook Book* represents an inspirational source for the construction of the main character in Truong's novel, which, as Ann Linzie has argued, "must be considered as an intertext of the Toklas autobiographies and a contribution to (reiteration and rearticulation of) the ongoing legend of Alice B. Toklas" (Linzie 2006, 184). *The Book of Salt* foregrounds a "dualism of dominance and affection," to continue using Tuan's expression, that also exhibits the value of interchange that it embeds. Notably, Truong shows how migrants are subject to different metamorphoses that are enacted by displacement and that respond to a dynamic of loss; at the same time, however, they can transform not only the new spaces they end up inhabiting,[4] but also the stories and the languages used to narrate them. Binh, for instance, exemplifies the condition of the silenced affective laborer, but he also challenges the idea of colonial imposed invisibility by creatively inventing a

unique gastronomical language. In this way, he can translate (thus transform and re-write) his own story both within the Parisian space and in
his employers' domestic place. It is my contention that Toklas's and
Stein's narrations of their years spent in Paris on the one side, and Truong's fictional rewriting on the other, are not only intertextual but also
complementary and compensatory: one supplements the unsaid of the
others and of History's official recordings. As I will demonstrate, Binh's
and his Mesdames' roles are the opposing sides of the same photography: exile in the Paris of the late 1920s and early 1930s and the reconstruction of the self through corporeal and linguistic mobility.

The novel opens with two photographs taken in October 1934, just
before Gertrude Stein and Alice B. Toklas's departure to the United
States, where Stein is to embark on her famous lecture tour. In the first,
Mesdames are sitting at the Gare du Nord; the second is set on the deck of
the SS *Chaplain* just before its sinking. "It captures my Mesdames perfectly" (Truong 2003a, 261) comments Bihn, their cook for the past five years,
who has accompanied them and who now faces the hard decision of
whether to follow them to America, to go back to Vietnam, or stay in
Paris. Truong engages her readers with both the recollection of those five
years in France and of Binh's previous life in Saigon before revealing his
final decision.

As for Monique Truong, at the time of her adolescent trip to France,
the body/text of Paris projected to Binh as a riddle that needs to be deci-
phered. He arrives in the City of Light by chance and without choosing it:
"I never meant to go this far" (250), he confesses to Bão, his shipmate on
the *Niobe* that takes him from Saigon to Marseilles. Through a series of
flashbacks that reconstruct Binh's days in Saigon, we find out that he is
twenty years old and works as a kitchen boy for the governor-general at
the time of his relationship with Jean Blériot, the French head chef whose
"reign" begins in 1923. When his father is informed of his son's "condition" (127), Binh's dismissal from the governor-general's kitchen pairs his
father's disownment and his expulsion from the Old Man's House, which
also marks the beginning of his inevitable exile. For Binh, Paris is not an
elected place and yet it has already tickled his curiosity, so that his imaginary (re)construction of the city starts even before he leaves his country:
"I found my way to the city that the Governor-General's chauffeur had
made vivid with his stories, his cigarette waving about in excitement of
the *retelling*" (257 emphasis added).

In the economy of Truong's novel, the governor's chauffeur plays a
significant role. In one of the last chapters of the book, Binh identifies the
chauffer as the one who betrays him and the real culprit for his dismissal.
In his last conversation with him, Binh finds out that he attended medical
school in Paris and "prided himself on being cosmopolitan, a man of the
world via Saigon and Paris" (128). Moreover, not only is he thought to be
a "poet," but his stories about the French city are also narrated to provide

"scientific" advice for the treatment of Binh's "disease." An example comes from his insistence in telling Bihn how cafés and dance halls in Paris are crowded with men *like him*—"*lai cài*" in Vietnamese (133)—that he has never visited, but that he knows about through "the writings of those doctors who were trying to find a cure" (128). The chauffeur's iteration of the same stories about the French city offers insight in the perpetuation of a tradition that through the twentieth century posited Paris as "an ideal place to explore queerness" (Durham 2005, 182; Troeung 2010, 123; Kennedy 1993, 79–141). His narrations, in fact, transmit a variegated palimpsest of shared assumptions that also convey and reinforce false cultural values and stereotypes, so that the supposed distinctiveness of Paris only equals a dominant popular image (Kennedy 1993, 6) that "Dr. Chauffeur" is not able to deconstruct and transform. Moreover, his "poetic" inclination is counterbalanced by his "scientific" education, so that Binh soon concludes that poetry and science lie in the same ways and that trust is easily disrespected.

The ironic effect achieved by using stereotypical popularized images and expressions—Paris as the capital of ambivalence and deviation; homosexuality as a condition that requires normative correction—is matched and reinforced by the fact that the two "Mesdames" he ends up working for suffer from his same "disease." However, while Stein and Toklas find a solid position in history as the iconic lesbian couple of literary modernism and as "exemplars of queer liberalism" (Eng 2010, 19), Binh is completely excluded from history. While Stein and Toklas's romance is not questioned and is englobed in literary tradition, Binh's love can be narrated only as fiction.

To the extent that retellings of the same stories immortalize socially conservative, ethnocentric, and androcentric generalizations, they only intensify Binh's desire to escape heteronormativity as epitomized by his father's patriarchal and dogmatic religious control. As Troeung affirms "for subjects such as Binh, unhomeliness is a condition that precedes migration" (Troung 2003a, 123), but in the same way, Paris unconsciously becomes the idealized, spatial, pretextual context for his own narration and identity reformulation. Moreover, crystallized and canonized versions of the city of Paris exist as perpetuated via identical and univocal retellings, they also resonate with critiques of the rationales of trust and faithfulness that the novel challenges in its various declinations: historical (we are reading a fictionalized story that fills real historical and literary omissions), sociopolitical (migrants in the text are constantly required to provide guarantees of their own loyalty), linguistic (Binh, who cannot speak but Vietnamese, re-narrates his own story in English and through food, eventually becoming a self-translator, who asks his readers to trust him). Even in this first approach to the French world, language plays a central role for Binh's discourse on subjectivity, since through language the concepts of loyalty and betrayal are brought to the fore: "after all, the tongue is an organ of truth" (178). His relationship with Chef Blériot clearly illustrates Binh's gradual acquisition of both verbal and body language knowledge that is pivotal, once in Paris, to negotiate his presence in the host country while reinventing himself in the new culture. In view of his (future) transformation, this episode acquires relevance and foregrounds its premises.

The new *chef de cuisine*'s arrival from France is an arrogant political statement and Anh Minh, Binh's oldest brother, has to accept the brutal reality that his aspirations to cook for the governor-general have come to an end. "Minh *Still* the Sous Chef" (60) has to experience the impositions of a colonial and capitalist logic that annihilates his wishes: his alienation from his own kitchen *and* in his own land is a first important lesson on the political dynamics at work in Vietnam and on the weight of its binary formula of inclusion/exclusion. Binh instead, despite his scarce command of the French language, becomes Blériot's translator, since he knows more French words than the chef does of Vietnamese. His duty is to take him to the market and be the interpreter of his culinary needs. In little time, of his sexual needs as well. Intimacy, Binh narrates, is soon spun through the streets of Saigon, but what Binh mistakes for love is colonial exploitation, here legitimized by their asymmetrical positions in relation to power. Blériot's movement into the body of the other finally reveals itself to be an act of dominance that perpetuates well-established practices of subjugation and racial misperceptions. Moreover, as a consequence of his ambivalent position, Binh is soon forced to provide evidence of his loyalty: natives start "wondering where my allegiance lay" (63). The account of Binh's affair with Blériot inquires into the links between verbal/body language and subjectivity on the one hand, and nationalism and colonialism on the other. Both incapacitated to use verbal language to communicate with each other, the two cooks find in their respective bodies a universal code of mutual (mis)understanding. However, it is exactly because of this "linguistic transparency" that their illicit liaison is exposed. French is the language of power; it affirms the colonial imperatives of possession and cultural hegemony, but the language of sex—so easily identifiable from the outside—is marked by a semantic opacity that Binh cannot grasp. Blériot, in fact, does not hesitate to betray him by denying their relationship when it becomes public. Exile is for Binh the only way out.

After three years of navigation on different ships, Binh finally realizes that it is time to "shit on land again" (256). He arrives in Paris at the age of twenty-three, knowing that cooking is his "only legitimate skill" (257), and that a position as a live-in cook would provide him with food and a place to sleep for the night. Clearly, Binh's decision to interrupt his sea travels is a physiological necessity that soon requires a physical exploration of the new space through a dynamic of movement: "When each day is mapped for me by a wanton display of street names congesting the pages of the help-wanteds . . . , I am forced into an avid, adoring courship with the boulevards of this city" (15). Yet, the alluring, insistent wooing that Binh employs to encourage the city's interest does not resonate with any romantic overtones. His first reading and interpretation of this urban context, in fact, rely on previous information of other people's experiences and, especially, on the chauffeur's implications that the city has a licentious disposition. That Paris is seen through the lenses of profitable activity, a reality suggested by the commercial nature of his initial interchanges (these allude to sentimental and emotional intercourse rather than prostitution). After all, his knowledge of the French character derives from both his personal and collective experience of colonial domination in his homeland. Paris, as a crucial node of Binh's identity construction, discloses itself through an abrupt unveiling unlike the seductive rituals of lovers' undressing. Binh's final "intimate knowledge of the city" (15)—which is far from being the "accommodating" beau of Truong's "The Season de l'Amour"—soon allows him to realize that Saigon and Paris are specular images, one the double of the other: "Most Parisians can ignore and even forgive me for not having the refinement to be born amidst the ringing bells of their cathedrals, especially since I was born instead amidst the ringing bells of the *replicas* of their cathedrals" (17, emphasis added).

As Panivong Norindr has eloquently illustrated, French colonialism assumed many different forms: "from the physical domination of native space in cartographic practice to a slightly more subtle form of cultural subjugation elaborated in the policy of 'acculturation'" (Norindr 1996, 5). Indochina was regarded as an empty space to be filled with symbols of progress, as a white page that a benevolent hand could mark with its elegant copying of a sophisticated and civilized original. The paradigms of duplication and movement are displayed in the text in terms of forceful penetration, offered by Binh's brief description of his brother Anh Hoàng, who works as a porter for the railroad. Carrying, the vanity cases of French government-clerks' wives visiting Saigon, Anh witnesses how both real and imagined mapped spaces spring from a desire of control: "The French had tattooed the countryside with tracks, knowing that mobility would allow them to keep a stranglehold on the little dragon that they called their own. Every day, mobility pounded on the shoulders of my second oldest brother" (Truong 2003a, 43). If the colonial conquest is inscribed on the body of Vietnam with permanent signs, the map of the country fosters further interrogation on its multifold functions. This is an empirical description that delineates open spaces, limits, and boundaries as a result of historical events; it is also an image, a seductive iconic representation of a space where "desires, aspirations, affective memory, the cultural memory of the subject can be projected" (Norindr 1996, 94), eventually producing enduring myths.

Monique Truong seems particularly concerned to demystify the idea of an imaginary Indochina,[5] a colonial fantasy that lingers in the picturesque nostalgic representation of a land filled with exotic overtones and erotic allusions. She consistently questions this notion both in *The Book of Salt* and in other works. In her essay "Into Thin Air" (2003b), for example, the writer expresses her aggravation, when traveling, at being immediately recognized as Vietnamese by other tourists and implicitly invited to speak as an assumed expert of the history and culture of her birth country. However, if Vietnam is "not a home but a green dragon tattoo somewhere on my torso, metaphoric and absent," the United States "is not a real home" either (Apte 2003). Caught between two countries, neither of which she can really call "home," Truong expresses her personal feeling of permanent "in-betweenness" through the oxymoronic Binh, an invisible walking map in the streets of Paris:

> My body marks me, announces my weakness, displays it as yellow skin. It flagrantly tells my story, or a compacted, distorted version of it, to passersby curious enough to cast their eyes on me. It stunts their creativity, dictates to them the limited list of who I could be. Foreigner, asiatique, and, this being Mother France, I must be Indochinese. Every day, when I walk the streets of this city, I am just that. I am an Indochinese laborer, generalized and indiscriminate, easily spotted and readily identifiable all the same. (Truong 2003a, 152)

The permanent racial tattoo imprinted on Binh's skin stigmatizes him and relegates him at the margins of the French society. In the streets of Paris, he is one of the many foreigners that Gertrude Stein describes in some of her works—in *Paris, France,* in particular—the presence of whom details her topophilic relationship with the city. Stein's lifelong preoccupation with ideas of nationality as an index of identity is echoed all through Truong's novel and her personal journey to Paris functions as a counterpoint to Binh's exile. As we have seen, the Vietnamese cook is forced into an existence of isolation; Stein's "separateness" (Benstock 2002, 13) from her country instead is a personal need that triggers and fuels her writing.

As noted in a review of *The Book of Salt*, Truong resists the temptation "to round up the usual Stein entourage of Hemingway, Picasso, and company" (Benfey 2003). Still, one of the writer's best achievements is the exploration of foreigners' lives in the Paris of the moveable feast, here rendered in its several forms and with aching authenticity. Although the reconstruction of that historical moment is wisely left to the background, the novel succeeds in offering a complex inventory of distinct displacements whose meanings vary according to the subjects' motivations to leave "home" and to their conditions in the new ad(o/a)pting country.

Whether we talk about exile, emigration, expatriation, we always talk about distances, transits, transformations, which convey some sort of estrangement. In an essay on the lives of American women who contributed to the book world of Paris during the 1920s, Mary Niles Maack reminds us that American residents were different from most other immigrant groups. In general, they had better economic conditions, which did not force them to seek work, their education was above average, they were not political refugee, and rarely were they eager to be assimilated in the French society. In most cases, this freedom allowed them to keep their nationality, their language, even their American passports, thus creating and protecting a "city within a city" (Maack 2005, 400), the same one in which Toklas and Stein (both real and fictional) take residence. In *What Are Masterpieces*, Gertrude Stein affirms: "America is my country and Paris is my home town" (Stein 1970, 62–63), while in a passage of *Paris, France*, she confirms her urgency to set distance between herself and her home country: "writers have to have two countries, the one where they belong and the one in which they live really" (Stein 1971, 2). Nevertheless, her statements are predicated upon the privileged condition of a well-off intellectual who lives in a city that has "traditionally called to the American heart" (Fitch 1983, 162): not only is Paris an international "cultural capital," but it also displays tolerance, if not real love, for those artists that America rejects. As a consequence, both the real Gertrude Stein and her character in the book are not forced into the same rituals of courtship that Binh has to engage in with the boulevards of this city; for artists, Paris is a lover that reciprocates their affection. This, at least, until December 1929, "a terrible month to be in Paris" (Truong 2003a, 5).

In one of the first scenes of the book, the narrator evokes the atmosphere of that December, while he is sitting, almost drunk, in a crowded café. The city is in ferment, the talk of the day is that "the Americans are going home" (5), while the tangible signs of the end of American excesses are well expressed by their need to pawn their winter clothes or to deal with "skipped-out hotel bills or overdue rents" (6). In *Women of the Left Bank*, Shari Benstock analyzes different causes that brought Americans to lose their fortunes, underscoring the ambivalent social dynamics at work between the French and the Americans. Until that year, "Americans flourished at the expense of Parisians, the whole question of the invading American hordes with their fat bankrolls and big cars led to ambiguous threats and the potential for ugly street scenes" (Benstock 2002, 118). Binh depicts the same frustration with wry irony, highlighting how Parisians, at the beginning, "even felt charitable toward them," but they soon realized that Americans "traveled here in order to indulge in the 'vices' of home. First, they had invaded the bordellos and then it was the cafés. Parisians could more than understand the whoring and the drinking, but in the end it was the hypocrisy that did not translate well" (Truong 2003a, 7), to the effect that "the Parisians missed the money all right, but no one missed the Americans" (6). What is worthy of note in the brief sketch that Truong offers of the American Depression and of its consequences in

Paris is the inference that hypocrisy is ultimately a common trait of both the French and the Americans, thus aligning the two peoples in a symmetrical position of power in relation to Vietnam in general and to Binh in particular. A couple of examples may support this point.

In chapter 14, Binh discusses trust, one of the main factors that contribute to a solid relationship between a domestic servant and an employer. Economic immigrants are constantly pressed to offer continuous evidence of their social hypercorrectness and of their unfaltering will to adhere to a system that is imposed on them by virtue of their hosts' patronizing generosity. "The worst," says Binh, "was a Monsieur who locked up the kitchen knives at night and wore the key around his waist. . . . You, Monsieur, do not trust me with your life, but you trust me with your meals? Absurd, *n'est-ce pas?*" (148). Moreover, Truong's extraordinary ear for languages often allows her to reveal cultural features that she voices through Binh's comments. The French hypocrisy, the cook suggests, is even ingrained in its people's language. For instance, they call their busy pawnshops "*mont-de-piété,*" "mountains of mercy," "so French, so snide to use a heaping load of poetic words to refer to pawnshops, places filled with everything of value but never with poetry" (6). Or, they use the expression "*coup de grâce,*" "the finishing stroke," to refer to a brutal action such as the killing of a pigeon to concoct one of Toklas's recipes: "While I may never master the French language," Binh argues, "I have learned that the true faces of its lofty expressions are often found on their most literal meanings. It is a perverse way of hiding something right in the open, very French in its contempt and cruelty for those who are not" (69). The French penchant for figurative language and their inclination to attach hidden meanings to the surface rather than behind the words discloses another parameter of constraint that migrants, in their role of learners, must address in the process of language acquisition: each language carries an information load, a cultural background that serves as a metatext. Since this is the result of many juxtaposed layers, Binh is induced to believe that the real character of Parisians may be revealed by peeling off their language as he would do with an onion. But in this case, hypocrisy is paired to arrogance, since it is the literal meaning that can best illustrate what should not be exposed with such proud ostentation: assumed superiority disguised in benevolent, poetic articulations.

In contrast with most other employers, Stein and Toklas "are too trusting" (148), although Binh suspects that their attitude can possibly be attributed to negligence. In the end, however, the same hypocrisy of the French emerges through their false but appreciated generosity that extends him "the right to eat what they eat. . . . My Mesdames do not even demand that I wait until they have finished, that I scrape together my meals from what is left of theirs" (209–10). Yet, there is always a wall between them, that delimits a space and marks the boundary between dominance and affection and reminds him that the apartment at 27 rue de Fleurus is "a temple, not a home" (23) like the Old Man's house, and that every time he behaves like "a cad" he gets "excommunicated yet again from that perfect circle that is at the center of every home" (103) Binh's sense of "insideness" results from his perception of this sheltered place from which he keeps being excluded. Binh knows that "belonging" is just an asymptotic state, achieved only at infinity.

In addition to the inquiry on the circumstances that prompted the different types of outsiders to choose Paris as the locus for their exiles, the writer seems very intrigued by the opposite question: what are the main reasons for remaining? "What keeps you here?" is the insistent question that we hear throughout the novel. As seen, the motivations that bring American artists and Binh to Paris differ extensively; their reasons to stay, instead, perfectly coincide: creativity and the awareness that Paris could offer the right stimuli to transform an innate gift into craft. If the main characters of the novel share the same exilic condition, they all demonstrate that separateness from their home countries, cultures, and languages is not necessarily a renunciation of their own vocations; on the contrary, displacement here serves as a spur to creative acts.[6] The examples offered by Truong's characters provide ample evidence of this theory and of the fact that their artistic products are not only intertextual but also complementary in the reconstruction of their identities. As we shall see, language plays again a crucial role in this process.

With unflinching authority Gertrude Stein repeatedly affirms the essential position of (fluctuating) nationality in the perception of the self and in the elaboration of one's own identity.[7] Gertrude Stein[8] is the priestess of her own Parisian temple, where over the years her intimacy with English has grown to the point to consider it as "a language reserved to genius and creation" (30). Curiously, her creativity—that Binh sees at work for a quarter of an hour each day (146)—is thought to be enhanced by the motion of her automobile, her "mechanized muse" (182). In this scene, Truong focuses on one of the most significant dicta of Stein's modernism, mainly her notion of mobility as the main incentive for change. This concept is best expressed in *The Making of Americans*, where Stein claims that it is "something strictly American to conceive a space that is . . . always filled with moving," and that she "made a continuous effort to create this thing in every paragraph" (Stein 1995, 291–92). Her rejection of a linear writing structured in time, which she substitutes with a spatial, process-oriented one, yields an experimental narrative whose technique engages repetition, rewriting, playful combinations, recycling of words collated in a performative fluctuation of meaning. Therefore, the obscurity of her prose[9] is the result of an oxymoronic tension between sameness and difference within the text, that she punctuates with imperceptible variations of the same unchanging pattern. The difference in the repetition is the condition for the movement to come alive[10]: "no matter how often you tell the same story if there is anything alive in the telling the emphasis is different" (291). Evidently, Stein engineers textual landscapes that she explores through repetitive incursions, and if English is the domain within which she achieves mobility, French provides her with a "linguistic otherness" (Kennedy 1993, 72) that she needs in order to come to terms with her native language. Kennedy pinpoints how Stein finds in the exclusion from the city the ideal condition to create, since this separation avoids obtrusions upon her consciousness (73). Yet, this is not absolute: her masculine penetrations into the body of the city are tantamount to her infiltrations into the body of her narrative. Paris eventually emerges not as an actual physical place, but as "an imagined space of writing, a city of words" (44), within which she can only move forward. In *The Book of Salt*, Truong reminds us that Stein cannot drive in reverse; she keeps driving until she can turn her automobile around, "That way, she is *technically* always going forward" (Truong 2003a, 29, emphasis added).

It is clear, at this point, that Gertrude Stein does not *need* to speak the local language, or it is better to *not* speak it. Besides, her French—"a shoe falling down a stairwell" (33)—is soon identified as the ambit that aligns her with Binh. The impairment that they both experience with the language of their host country not only equates them, but even becomes a mutual source of inspiration. Her French, "like mine, has its limits. It denies her. . . . I think *this* we have in common" (34, emphasis in the text). Likewise, for Binh this language is "a dry inkwell" that has made him "plummet into silence" (17), although Gertrude Stein takes an interest in his "interpretation" of the French language, in his use of negatives and repetitions. The dismantling and disruptive strategy that Binh applies in the (dis)articulation of a language that he "interprets," is very similar to the one that Stein devises for her experimental writing practices, particularly for her literary portraits. The performative quality of Binh's utterance confronts Stein with the possibilities of alternative uses of language and with its creative potential to refigure subjectivity. Their complementary roles, then, are particularly evident within the linguistic domain, although Binh's communication finds its best performance when it moves from the verbal to the gastronomical system.

In "Four American Impressions," a fanciful account by Sherwood Anderson of his visit to 27 rue de Fleurus, Gertrude Stein is compared to a "wholesome cook" who works in a "kitchen of words" (qtd. in Mellow 2003, 258). Similarly, Binh's cookery provides him with a thesaurus that neither French nor English can grant him: words, in those languages, are wielded "like a rusty kitchen knife" (Truong 2003a, 18). However, this "linguistic" empowerment emerges gradually; Binh's metamorphosis, in fact, is a slow achievement that will finally guarantee, if not complete agency and visibility, at least the awareness of its potentiality.

In the Parisian kitchens where he is employed, Binh keeps tasting the bitter savor of the French arrogance that he experienced before leaving his country and that permits him to confirm and refine his understanding of the colonial divide. When he works for those hosts that he calls "collectors," his cookery complies with the expectations of these "ravenous" people, who "crave the fruits of exile" (19) and "covet the honey that lies inside my scars," the tattoos that they have contributed to imprint on his body as well as on his country map: at every bite, "even the most parochial of palates" is overwhelmed by "a nostalgia for places they have never been" (19). Therefore, a phantasmagoric Indochina is evoked and served through Binh's dishes, whose "Asianness" exposes but never satates the French colonial lingering saudade.[11] After all, a nostalgic tone also invades him while cooking: "Every kitchen is a homecoming . . . , a familiar story that I can embellish with saffron, cardamom, bay laurel, and lavender" (19), but nostalgia, as Truong warns us, starting with her choice of the book's title,[12] is treacherous since her main character gets stuck between two worlds: a lost one that he keeps in his memory, and a new one, where he needs to reconstruct, transform, and translate himself. He lives, in short, the condition of "in-betweenness" theorized by Homi K. Bhabha (1997), a space that enacts multifold alternatives of resistance against the notion of identity essentialism, that features both the nationalistic and the ethnocentric colonial discourses. It is in this liminal space of transit that an ambivalent dynamic of translation and/as rewriting can be implemented. Indeed, if cooking for Binh means to retell an old story while resuming an absence (a past time and a faraway country), his repetitions (just like Stein's) propose a textual tension between sameness and difference that eventually prompts metamorphoses of perception and signification. His culinary "embellishments," for instance, modify traditional recipes and challenge Miss Toklas's demands. Binh tells us that "her cook has to adopt her tongue, make room for it, which can only mean the removal of his own" (Truong 2003a, 211), and yet Toklas's recipes start being modified by new flavors, by imperceptible adaptations: "Neither of them seems to notice that Miss Toklas's 'apple pie' is now filled with an applesauce-flavored custard and frosted with buttercream or that her 'meat loaf' harbors the zest of an orange and is bathed in white wine" (27). Some sort of transformation of an original flavor is already at work and functions to slowly erode a long-standing tradition.

Moreover, Alice B. Toklas's *Cook Book* adds interesting details on the use of recipes and ingredients at 27 rue de Fleurus. For example, she laments that Trac is never willing to share his culinary secrets and that he cooks "with unmeasured and unwritten ingredients" (192). Similarly to the real cook, Binh variously thematizes and negates the imperatives of gastronomical formulaic repetition. His refusal to use recipes serves to question the notion of identical equivalence that he extends to the verbal domain ("Words . . . do not have twins in every language. Sometimes they have only distant cousins, and sometimes they pretend that they are not even related" [223]), but also to validate the chef's personal variations and creativity, which may be used to resist the dictates of both a "national" taste and the expectations of the patronizing receiving palate. Eventually, Binh cooks/translates to create a "différance" and to undermine the authority and the supposed superior status of an original text.

As stated by Lefevere (1992), translation is certainly one of the most efficient acts of *rewriting* an original text; however, it is "never innocent" (Bassnett and Lefevere 1990, 11), since it operates selectively and encompasses narratives that rework other narratives, while offering critical commentary on sociohistorical contexts. In other words, far from being a smooth and transparent process, translation is a complex activity that, in the recognition of the writing of the other also involves a process of *re-citing*—that is, a linguistic, historical, and cultural dislocation, that implies a *re-siting*, a relocation within an elsewhere, hence a betrayal of the "original" intentions (Chambers and Curti 1996, 49). As a consequence, the assumed superiority of the original text solicits interrogation, since it has already been subject to different *mani*-pulations[13] even before being translated.

Binh modifies traditional French recipes, nostalgically adding Vietnamese flavors to them; in the same way, Gertrude Stein "translates" his Indochinese cook's life story when she writes Binh's literary portrait, the fictional "Book of Salt" written in English and kept in her unlocked cabinet. Binh agrees to steal it for his lover, Dr. Lattimore, who eventually reveals himself to be just another exploiter, leaving the city in a hurry after writing a brief note for him: "Bee, thank you for *The Book of Salt*. Stein *captured* you, perfectly" (Truong 2003a, 238, emphasis added). The lady wishing to *retain* a cook finally *captures* him in a book.

However, in this circumstance Binh confirms his intuition that cooks and writers share common ground: "Writers, I suspect, are . . . like cooks. We practice a craft whose value increases tenfold once its yield is shared and consumed. A notebook inside a cupboard is a cake languishing in an oven" (236), thus alleviating his sense of guilt for his theft, but also suggesting that any artistic product needs to nurture a logic of exchange, the only valid dynamic for mutual understanding and respect. Instead of using his hands to purposefully corrupt dishes in a form of satisfactory and undetectable revenge against his Mesdames,[14] Bihn investigates into his margins of freedom and starts using his labor as a platform for identity reformulation and disenfranchisement: "During these restorative intervals, I am no longer the mute who begs at this city's steps. Three times a day, I orchestrate, and they sit with slackened jaws, silenced" (19). Binh's assertion of agency finally comes through a rewriting of his own story via food and culinary practices, a strategy that *exceeds* language and gives him unexpected (although still limited) power.

Bihn's metamorphosis begins in 1927, three years before reading the ad of the two American ladies. On a bridge on the Seine, while contemplating the water and maybe his suicide, Binh meets a fellow countryman, the Scholar-Prince of his mother's stories.[15] He, on his turn, immediately recognizes him as a Vietnamese cook, not because of his marked skin, and neither because of his language (although their conversation proceeds in their mother tongue), but because: "Cooks have a vocabulary all their own" (87) which comes from their bellies. They spend just a few hours together sharing a meal, their feelings for their home country and for the complexities of their diasporic existence, sharing their bodies in a park made private by the mist. But on that bridge, the man asks a question that will linger in Binh's mind for a long time: "What keeps you here?" "Your question, just your desire to know my answer, keeps me, is the response" (261). On that bridge, Binh takes the decision not to leave Paris:

> The only place we shared was this city. Vietnam, the country that we called home, was to me already a memory. I preferred it that way. A "memory" was for me another way of saying a "story." A "story" was another way of saying a "gift." The man on the bridge was a memory, he was a story, he was gift. Paris gave him to me. And in Paris I will stay, I decided. (258)

For Bihn, Paris finally becomes "a madame with a heart" (15), a place that can both separate and connect at the same time, exactly as the bridge where he meets his friend, "something akin to love," that "could happen again. After the man on the bridge departed, Paris held in it a promise" (258). As for Monique Truong at the height of Notre Dame, Paris offers Binh a "summer of possibilities" (Truong 2003c, par. 10). And if we agree with Casey's reading (Casey 2009, 65), according to which Truong's secret history might be seen as "a commentary on language and place" (66), then Paris, one of the most stimulating epicenters of creativity in the 1920s and 1930s, functions as a "bridge-city," a "translation hub" (Cronin 2006, 120): Gertrude Stein finds her national identity there, Binh his translatorial power.

NOTES

1. Monique Truong's evacuation from Saigon in 1975 and memories of her childhood in North Carolina are narrated in "Kelly" (1991), a short story in which a Vietnamese refugee girl confronts the fragile negotiation between assimilation and distinctiveness.

2. After her graduate studies at Columbia University School of Law, Truong coedited *Watermark* (Tran, Truong, and Khoi, 1998), an anthology of Vietnamese American poetry and prose. On that occasion, she submitted a piece to her coeditors, who rejected it. Strongly inclined to prove that her grandfather was not the only writer in the family, she rewrote her story ("Seeds"), which placed her on the American literary scene as a talented young writer.

3. A witty example comes from his definition of a pineapple as "a pear not a pear," while "a lobster was a small crawfish" (Toklas 2010, 186, Truong 2003a, 35).

4. "To migrate," affirms Salman Rushdie, "is certainly to lose language and home, to be defined by others, to become invisible or, even worse, a target. . . . But the migrant is not simply transformed by this act; he transforms his new world" (Rushdie 2010, 210).

5. The act of aggression that France operated in Vietnam is manifested not only through physical penetration into geographical spaces, but also through a more subtle colonization of the imaginary. The first *Exposition Coloniale Internationale* held in Paris in 1931 was crucial in its representation of the colonial territory but also in the sublimation and justification of French cultural prejudices. See Norindr (1996).

6. That living in foreign countries enhances this condition has been amply proved by the many artistic products generated at various times. Recently, however, new systematical multimethod approaches in the study of the relationship between living abroad and creativity have added empirical evidence to anecdotal, while showing how economic gratification and personal rewarding may result from enhanced inventiveness. Cf. Maddux and Galinsky 2009.

7. Phoebe Stein Davis demonstrates how in *The Autobiography* Stein recasts the terms through which the link between nationality and one's own birth country is configured. The notions of authenticity and legality are also questioned, eventually showing how "nationality is an aesthetic that can be adopted" (Davis 1999, 39).

8. Her name, suggests the concierge when Binh meets the woman for an interview, needs to be pronounced as if it were one word (21). This spelling is used to refer to the fictional Stein.

9. "Readers can feel as if they are freewheeling in space as the writer 'hasten[s] slowly forward'" (Taylor 2003, 29).

10. Stein believes in Henry Bergson's equation of reality as mobility: "There do not exist *things* made, but only things in the making, not *states* that remain fixed, but only states in process of change" (Bergson 2002, 274).

11. In their lucid analysis of the shaping of a "colonial subject," Winston and Ollier underline the centrality of a manipulative process that was often put in force through mere propaganda of Vietnam and that effected the French "collective unconscious." (Winston and Ollier 2001, 2).

12. Truong explains: "Salt—in food, sweat, tears, and the sea—is found throughout the novel. . . . For me, the title is also a nod toward the Biblical connotation of salt, in particular to the turning of Lot's wife into a pillar of salt for looking back at her home, to the city of Sodom. That story says to me that the Catholic God, whom the cook is so wary of, disapproves not only of the activities of the Sodomites but also of nostalgia. Binh is a practitioner of both" (Apte 2003).

13. *The Book of Salt* is interspersed with references to the characters' hands (*manus* in Latin). Some examples include Alice B. Toklas's, that prepare the food as an act of devotion to Stein (27); Ahn Minh's, as the part of his body that better reflects his sorrow at the arrival of Chef Blériot (69); the ungloved hands of Lattimore, that do not "stay cold for very long" (40) but unravel his real story (187), and Binh's mother's, that teach him how to cook and to tell stories (80–82). Great attention is also paid to nails, under which different materials get stuck, thus functioning as the keepers of the specific "flavor" of the moment: from flour to dirt, from fig seeds to ear wax.

14. Binh mentions *chefs de cuisine* who never wash their hands, or pastry chefs who stick their fingers in their ears and then work "the wax into their buttery disks of dough" (Truong 2003a, 64).

15. Only later in the novel will the reader find out that this is a fictionalized Ho Chi Min.

REFERENCES

Apte, Poornima. Review of *The Book of Salt*, by Monique Truong. *MostlyFiction Book Reviews*, March 31, 2003. http:// mostlyfiction.com/world/truong.htm (accessed July 13, 2011).

Bassnett, Susan, and André Lefevere. *Translation, History, and Culture*. London: Pinter, 1990.

Benfey, Christopher. "Ordering In." Review of *The Book of Salt* by Monique Truong. *New York Times* April 6, 2003. www.nytimes.com/2003/04/06/books/ordering-in.html?src=pm (accessed July 13, 2011).

Benstock, Shary. *Women of the Left Bank: Paris, 1900–1940*. Austin: University of Texas Press, 2002.

Bergson, H., A. K. Pearson, and J. Mullarkey. "Introduction to Metaphysics." In *Henry Bergson: Key Writings*, 274–78. New York: Continuum, 2002.

Bhabha, Homi K. *The Location of Culture*. New York: Routledge, 1997.

Casey, Maud. "The Secret History: The Power of Imagined Figures in Historical Fiction." *Literary Imagination* 12, no. 1 (2009): 54–67.

Chambers, Iain, and Lidia Curti, eds. *The Post-Colonial Question: Common Skies, Divided Horizons*. London: Routledge, 1996.

Cronin, Michael. *Translation and Identity*. New York: Routledge, 2006.

Davis, Phoebe Stein. "Subjectivity and the Aesthetics of national Identity in Gertrude Stein's *The Autobiography of Alice B. Toklas*." *Twentieth Century Literature* 45, no. 1 (1999): 18–45.

Durham, Carolyn A. *Literary Globalism: Anglo-American Fiction Set in France*. Cranbury, NJ: Rosemont Publishing, 2005.

Eng, David L. *The Feeling of Kinship: Queer Liberalism and the Racialization of Intimacy*. Durham, NC: Duke University Press, 2010.

Fitch, Noel Riley. *Sylvia Beach and the Lost Generation: A History of Literary Paris in the Twenties and Thirties*. New York: W.W. Norton, 1983.

Kennedy, Gerald J. *Imagining Paris: Exile, Writing, and American Identity*. New Haven, CT: Yale University Press, 1993.

Lefevere, André. *Translation, Rewriting, and the Manipulation of Literary Fame*. London: Routledge, 1992.

Ley, David. "Landscapes of Dominance and Affection." Introduction to *Texture of Place. Exploring Humanist Geographies*, ed. Paul C. Adams et al., 3–7. Minneapolis: University of Minnesota Press, 2001.

Linzie, Ann. *The True Story of Alice B. Toklas: A Study of Three Autobiographies*. Iowa City: University of Iowa Press, 2006.

Lowe, Lisa. *Immigrant Acts: On Asian American Cultural Politics*. Durham, NC: Duke University Press, 1996.

Maack, Mary Niles. "American Bookwomen in Paris during the 1920s." *Libraries and Culture* 40, no. 3 (2005): 399–415.

Maddux, W. W. and A. D. Galinsky. "Cultural Borders and Mental Barriers: The Relationship between Living Abroad and Creativity." *Journal of Personality and Social Psychology* 96, no. 5 (2009): 1047–61.

Mellow, James R. *Charmed Circle: Gertrude Stein and Company*. New York: Henry Holt, 2003.

Nguyen, Viet Thanh. *Race and Resistance. Literature and Politics in Asian American*. Oxford: Oxford University Press, 2002.

Norindr, Panivong. *Phantasmatic Indochina: French Colonial Ideology in Architecture, Film, and Literature*. Durham, NC: Duke University Press, 1996.

Rushdie, Salman. *Imaginary Homelands: Essays and Criticism, 1981–91*. London: Penguin Books, 2010.

Stein, Gertrude. *The Autobiography of Alice B. Toklas*. London: Vintage, 1990.

———. *The Making of Americans. Being a History of a Family's Progress*. Foreword by William H. Gass. Normal, IL: Dalkey Archive Press, 1995.

————. *Paris, France: Personal Recollections*. London: Peter Owen, 1971.

————. *What Are Masterpieces?* New York: Pitman, 1970.

Taylor, Melanie. "A Poetics of Difference: 'The Making of Americans' and Unreadable Subjects." *NWSA Journal* 15, no. 3 (2003): 26–42.

Toklas, Alice B. *The Alice B. Toklas Cook Book*. New York: Harper Perennial, 2010.

Tran, Barbara, Monique T. D. Truong, and Luu Truong Khoi. *Watermark: Vietnamese American Poetry and Prose*. New York: Asian American Writers' Workshop, 1998.

Troeung, Y-Dang. "'A Gift or a Theft Depends on Who Is Holding the Pen': Postcolonial Collaborative Autobiography and Monique Truong's *The Book of Salt*." *Modern Fiction Studies* 56, no. 1 (2010): 113–35.

Truong, Monique. *The Book of Salt*. New York: Mariner, 2003.

————. "Into Thin Air." *Time*, August 18–25, 2003. www.time.com/time/asia/2003/journey/vietnam.html (accessed July 13, 2011).

————. "The Season de l'Amour." *New York Times*, August 22, 2003. www.nytimes.com/2003/08/22/opinion/the-season-de-l-amour (accessed July 13, 2011).

Tuan, Yi-Fu. *Topophilia: A Study of Environmental Perception, Attitudes, and Values*. New York: Columbia University Press, 1990.

Winston, J. B., and L. Chau-Pech Ollier. *Of Vietnam: Identities in Dialogue*. New York: Palgrave, 2001.

Xu, W. *Eating Identities: Reading Food in Asian American Literature*. Honolulu: University of Hawai'i Press, 2008.

Epilogue

The Futures of American Paris

Jeffrey Herlihy-Mera and Vamsi K. Koneru

"You can't escape the past in Paris," notes Allen Ginsberg, "yet what's so wonderful about it is that the past and present intermingle so intangibly that it doesn't seem a burden" (qtd. in Sawyer-Laucanno 2001, 264). For centuries Paris has been a forum to restlessly innovate, to rip apart convention, to shock and to revolutionize, to explore and to regenerate. The importance of Paris in art and literature—even art and literature "of" the Americas—is perhaps unrivaled; but what value has Paris had beyond those realms? Has writing in Paris changed the way we think, or the way we live? Has it influenced the way we read and write, the way we perceive distance and spaces, the way we think about ourselves and our society? Has it influenced the way we present the world to our children? How powerful is literature?

Creative writing—through design or chance—often outlines methods of communication, of comprehension, of forming limits of aesthetics and interpretation: writing can put structure to society and stand as a cultural pillar that describes our realities, relationships, ourselves. The thematic role of a foreign literary clime is an important dimension in this dialogue: at once a complementary and dialectic reality, the unfamiliar setting balances the home space and interprets it. In this way, Paris has opened American writing. The displaced character or writer in the city often transcends the aesthetic and the literary—forging a sense of new identity and (or through) difference—and at the same time, the phenomenon itself of using distance as a creative device approaches the construction of concepts like "we" and "they"; and in some ways interprets the looming obsoleteness of those terms.

Paris has been this place for many writers beyond those considered in this volume. Some names untreated here stand out as icons in American writing: James Fennimore Cooper, Henry James, Mark Twain, Djuna Barnes, Ezra Pound, F. Scott Fitzgerald, Anaïs Nin, James Baldwin, Richard Wright, and the Beats (Lawrence Ferlinghetti, Allen Ginsberg, William Burroughs, Jack Kerouac); of particular importance to note here is that the scholarly weight of contemporary authors—like Adam Gopnik, Jake Lamar, Elliot Hester, Harriett Welty Rochefort, Samantha Dunn. The diverse nature of their writing in and about Paris, underscores the eminent value of Paris as a scene of creativity and light. Our volume has endeavored to survey different time periods, literary techniques, and personalities, while recognizing the broadness and quality of the work which has gone untreated in these pages.

DISPLACEMENT STUDIES: BRIDGING EMPIRICAL AND RHETORICAL APPROACHES

Cultural displacement is an increasingly common circumstance. The empirical studies of migrants treat social displacement as a condition that influences our physical and mental health—and this is true regardless of the mover's motivation for their foreign residence. In the case of American migration, however, the cultural studies of the same phenomenon tend to read temporality and superficiality into the experience of foreign life; as though living abroad—for Americans—were the equivalent to an extended vacation in which there is little self-transformation or shaping consequences from cultural displacement. Because of this tendency, the word "expatriate" instead of "immigrant" abounds in this realm of scholarship. This is true even in the case of writers and artists abroad with permanence and who indeed eventually died in France, like James Baldwin, Gertrude Stein, and Silvia Beach. Despite Stein's assertions about her town and country, immigration was the defining characteristic of her reality: she and the others lacked the circular intention to return to their place of origin and thus the cultural estrangement of their adult lives should be an axis of inquiry—more precisely, these men and women should be read in the context of the physiological and psychological outcomes of foreign life.

As a field, migrant studies is rapidly expanding; the amount of studies on the social tendencies of emigrants, the economic trends in immigrant communities, and the political inclinations of foreign-born residents demonstrates the robust importance of this phenomenon. The psychology of cultural migration is a central component in each of these camps, and the amount of government grants and other public support of these studies underscores the rising value of these reports. The concepts that emerge from this scholarship are constructive in cross-cultural cooperation and also in broader social terms: they are useful for more comprehensive public policy measures, community development, and higher education. As the field expands, cultural analyses, too, will likely integrate the related empirical data, adding a new dimension to perceiving the process of artistic production. While such interdisciplinary approaches are relatively new to humanistic inquiry—they are becoming more common. Indeed, reading a literary text (and the process of its composition) as a behavioral outcome, as a function of a set of conditions to which a writer is exposed (conditions which are measured through a body of empirical data), is a rich complement to the established rhetorical methods of literary inquiry. It is a field that will, as a subfield of migrant studies, expand and develop, offering new insights on writers from the past as well as contemporary authors who travel and live abroad, in search of the stimulation of cultural distance.

Regardless of the approach we take to interpret it, and the social background of the mover, a migration is a major life event. It shapes who we are and how we perceive our communities. Migration as an experience often involves loss of control: our use of language, cultural ceremonies, pastimes and traditions, and so on, are all rather obligatorily shifted when one moves to a new place. But what can be even more complex to face are the new social expectations. Writing and painting (and other creative pursuits) are a method to sort out the new commotion of these experiences. The process of putting a pen to paper (or, perhaps more accurate today, fingers to a keyboard), then, might offer both a compensating stimulation and a way to understand the new reality.

ON DISTANCE

The writers and artists who will venture to Paris from other places in the coming generations will dialogue with the concepts articulated by Hemingway, Truong, and Wright; by Picasso, Van Gogh, and Cassatt; and their mimicry of their innovation will bring new cultural dimensions in both sentiment and subject. The migratory sense of distance will also inevitably erode: one hundred miles translated to ten days' travel and two weeks' wages not long ago; today, less than one week's salary (at U.S. median income) can translate into a round trip from New York to Paris—albeit in the winter's low season—and the Boeing 777 will have you in the customs line at Charles De Gaulle Airport in six hours. The newly displaced American can see a significant other back on Long Island or in Upper Michigan that very same morning, instantly and for free online—as long as their lodging has an Internet connection.

Displacement itself is being reshaped. While moving abroad in the past meant, essentially, leaving behind a society for a period of time; now, the availability and negligible costs of hyper-communicative technologies (Facebook, Twitter, peer-to-peer exchange, messenger programs, videoconference software, and the like) facilitate an unbroken connection with home and therefore, reduce the social distance from their place of origin—and all of this can be achieved through a handheld device. Whether or not these technological "advances" concomitantly reduce the contact that a person abroad has with the society of the new place is yet to be examined. If this is the case, our identities, regardless of our places of residence, might be becoming more static; the reduction of contact (even with those of the same town or city) is a perplexing outcome of digitization, and it is one that might have profound outcomes in our perceptions of selfhood in the future.

This reduction of space and distance, however, is relative. For many, the distance from home to Paris is growing: the Schengen Agreement (like the U.S. Visa Waiver Program) has blocked European visitation rights to all but the wealthiest Latin Americans, Asians, Africans, and citizens of nations with Muslim majorities. While some apologists celebrate the concept that technological advancement has made the world smaller or "flat" (Friedman 2005), for citizens outside the capitalist West, the world has recently become walled. These laws—passed in 1989 and 1986, respectively—have made Europe and the United States all but inaccessible to the supermajority of the world population, and for that, regardless of their place of origin, visitors to Paris today are all of a certain class: they tend to look alike, dress in similar fashions, listen to similar music; their formal educations are structured through comparable aesthetic concepts. Even the antiestablishment movements tend to grow along similar lines. While differences like language and cultural ritual might persist to some degree, and are often rigorously defended, Europe and the rest of the West is fading into cultural homogeneity. The restrictions controlling the movement rights of not-properly-situated world populations has stalled our collective cultural growth, while stratifying the communities of rejected citizens, creating a debilitating discourse of minoritization. Truong's relatives in Vietnam, unless they have success in the financial dimensions of their lives, cannot see Paris but in movies and television, or on the pages of Monica's novels. Those who migrate to live are often relegated to certain urban districts and asked for papers when strolling through tourist areas, and thus they exist outside the collective culture. What these political statues imply for art and literature is distressing: voices have been silenced; pages of text go unwritten; canvases are bought and painted on by others. And as a part of due course, the silencing of "other" voices amplifies the influence of those who *are* able to articulate their ideas through art, literature, and philosophy—thus exacerbating the politically constructed inequality.

THE LEGACY OF AMERICAN PARIS

In some sense the French capital—for Americans, at any rate—has become a caricature of itself. As Andrew Gallix observes, "It seems now that the stories shape the city as much as the city once shaped the stories" Gallix 2010, 1). American Paris as a cultural good has been seized in films like *Midnight in Paris* (Allen 2011) and *The Da Vinci Code* (Howard 2006), with lucrative results. In addition to the nearly two million American tourists who visit the city each year (a number slightly larger than the population of the urban sectors of Paris itself), the number of undergraduates studying abroad there has increased fivefold since the 1980s. The number of students in the city for semester or yearlong academic programs in France is nearly twenty thousand annually—and between classes these twenty-somethings can been seen jogging in the Luxembourg Gardens, standing in line for the Eiffel Tower, or contemplating a Da Vinci in the Louvre. The Paris of the tourist and student imagination drives the repetition and commodification of the pilgrimage; Gallix's assertion here about the development of Paris in the collective imagination is somewhat misleading—the stories, like the screenplays and the somewhat limited study-abroad impressions, shape the *impression* of the city for the foreigner. The city itself has changed in ways not yet comprehensively addressed in how Paris is imagined in writing or in film (or in the general tourist experience of Paris). Foreign writers often cling to a nostalgic idea of Paris that fails to embrace the intricacies of the cultural context, particularly with respect to the regional identities that cohabitate in the capital city.

The cultural portrayals of Paris aimed at the American market, in film and literature, tend to overlook the diversity of the Parisian landscape: in the last generation immigration has brought new ways of life to Clichy-sous-Bois and rich diasporas to the area around Chateau Rouge; and the intranational migrations, too, as noted in the introduction, have translated into working-class enclaves from Lille around Gare du Nord; displaced police(wo)men from Corsica who patrol every arrondisement, two hundred thousand or more Bretons reside around Montparnasse, a district colored by restaurants, bakeries, and increasingly, the language of Brittany ("Les Bretons et Paris," 1). Paris has long existed as a cauldron of cultural assortment, yet these textures tend to be overlooked by foreign writers in favor of a mainline literary and popular tradition, one that embraces the imagined reality of a static, homogeneous France. The selective treatment of Paris, however, does not take away from the quality of the work. Indeed, the intentions of Hemingway, Stein, and others of the often retreated days of Paris in the 1920s achieved a freshness of vision in theme and form, and the emulators of this period—tourists, writers and artists, alike—intend to recapture these progressive components of the period.

Moreover, expatriation (or aesthetic migration) can be part of a narrative of artistic myth-making. The disconnect between life in Europe and the perceived life in Europe for those yet in America is a forum that makes exaggeration and hyperbole possible—and also believable to the readers back home. Writers abroad can construct a literary life that fulfils their desired self-perception precisely because the reading public is innocent, to a certain extent, of the reality of Paris; the texts themselves are a vehicle of this construction. The foreignness of the literary-subject coupled with the domesticity of the audience leverages the writing and imbues it with qualities that might not be possible if they were written and took place in the home space. Through a foreign scene and a foreign life, the writer enjoys a latitude of creation that permits the projection of a vision of a mythic reality as though it were authentic. Thus, beyond the existential components of being a writer in a foreign residence—possibly becoming bilingual, falling in love in another language, or accessing philosophies untenable back home—displacement can also be instrument to manage the home identity, through the measured textual impressions of a foreign scene in memoir, bildungsroman, or thinly veiled autobiographical fiction.

FUTURES OF DISPLACEMENT STUDY AND WRITING PARIS

American literature from Paris has succeeded in broadening the concepts of "Americans" and "American Culture," such that the idea of the City of Light has expanded the collective culture of the United States, even deprovincializing the self-perception of those who are not artists and have never ventured to Paris. Searching for displacement is an inner part of this dialogue. While for financial reasons many of today's artists and writers choose Berlin or Prague, Mexico City or Quito, as places to work, the heritage of Americans abroad inevitably touches Paris. The new generations in other cities will undoubtedly read the giant authors of the past, and realize travel and distance as a realm of possibility and wonder.

The energy of cultural displacement makes the contemporary moment tangible. Narrating American lives from the distance of Paris stores the past and elevates the present. This space between the past and present exists as an overlay, one that challenges linearity and destabilizes convention. Writing Paris is thus a mapping of the self that penetrates space and time, that interlaces language, geography, and histories—it offers a new perspective of consciousness. This dimension of life-narration, albeit often through "fictional" registers, offers insight on social and cultural creolization of the actors. The merging of supposedly disparate realities is projected through the mover (and the writer), and the reader thus accesses reports on this: what is an increasingly standard circumstance of life—between cultures, languages, societies, realities. Though there are many others, Americans in Paris form an axis of this plane, one that presupposes degrees of mixing and, in the end, growth.

REFERENCES

Allen, Woody, dir. *Midnight in Paris*. Gravier Productions, 2011.
Gallix, Andrew. "The Expatriate Literary Scene in Paris" (2010). http://andrewgallix.com/2010/12/04/the-expatriate-literary-scene-in-paris/.

Friedman, Thomas. *The World is Flat: A Brief History of the Twenty-First Century*. New York: Farrar, Straus and Giroux, 2005.

Howard, Ron, dir. *The Da Vinci Code*. Imagine Entertainment, 2006.

"Les Bretons et Paris." Federation des societes bretonnes de le region Parisienne (2007). http://bretonsdeparis.gwalarn.org/baparis.html.

Sawyer-LauCanno, Christopher. *The Continual Pilgrimage: American Writers in Paris, 1944–1960*. Paris: City Lights Publisher, 2001.

Index

About the Contributors

Jonathan Austad is assistant professor of humanities at Eastern Kentucky University. His research interests include interdisciplinary aspects of cultural theory, art, pop culture, film, and literature, and his recent inquiries focus on the artistic influence on Hemingway's aesthetic and Marxism's influence on Richard Wright's *Native Son*. He has a doctorate from Florida State University.

Matthew Crowe is a doctoral candidate in European Studies at The University of Western Australia. His thesis explores the development of Saul Bellow's early fiction and its literary inter-texts. Matthew Crowe's research interests include the French and American postwar novel.

Chase Dimock is a PhD candidate in the Program in Comparative and World Literature at the University of Illinois Urbana-Champaign specializing in twentieth-century American, French, and German literature. His dissertation in progress is on queer American expatriate writers of the Lost Generation in Paris. He is a regular contributor to *Lambda Literary*, *As It Ought To Be*, and a coeditor of The Queer Psychoanalysis Society's publication *The Qouch*.

Daniela Fargione is a Fulbright Scholar and assistant professor at the University of Torino, Italy, where she teaches Anglo-American Language and Literatures. Her research interests include: translation studies, the interconnections between modern and contemporary American literature and the other arts (music and photography in particular), and eco-criticism. She is author of *Cynthia Ozick: Orthodoxy and Irreverence: A Critical Study* (2005), *Giardini e labirinti: l'America di E. A. Poe* (2005), and of several translations and critical essays. She is currently editing an international volume on "madness," and preparing a book on the artistic and personal relationship between Carl Sandburg and Edward Steichen.

Jeffrey Herlihy-Mera is assistant professor of humanities at the University of Puerto Rico and the National Endowment for the Humanities Endowed Chair of Migrant/Transnational Studies at Albright College. He has been a Fulbright Lecturer at Universidad del Azuay and the Ernest Hemingway Society's Smith-Reynolds' Fellow. Herlihy-Mera is the author of *In Paris or Paname: Hemingway's Expatriate Nationalism* (2011) and his work has appeared in *The Hemingway Review*, *Studies in the Novel*, *Journal of Social History*, *The Barcelona Review*, *European Journal of American Studies*, and other publications. He has a doctorate from Universitat Pompeu Fabra in Barcelona.

Vamsi K. Koneru is a licensed clinical psychologist at Community Mental Health Affiliates, Inc. in New Britain, Connecticut, where he specializes in cross-cultural psychology. After serving in the Peace Corps in Quito, Ecuador, and doctoral studies at the University of Miami, Koneru was a fellow at La Clínica Hispana at the Yale School of Medicine and Harvard Medical School/Veterans Affairs Boston Healthcare System. His fieldwork is focused on themes concerning culture, immigration, and acculturation, and culturally attuned adaptations of psychological treatments for migrants. His work has appeared in *Psychiatry Research*, *Interamerican Journal of Psychology*, *Applied and Preventive Psychology*, *American Journal of Psychiatry*, and other publications.

Katy Masuga is the author of *Henry Miller and How He Got That Way* (2011) and *The Secret Violence of Henry Miller* (2011). She has also published essays on other modernist figures including D. H. Lawrence, Samuel Beckett, and the Paris bookshop Shakespeare & Company. She holds a PhD in Comparative Literature and a joint PhD in Literary Theory and Criticism from the University of Washington, Seattle. Since 2010 she has taught Comparative Literature in Paris at The American University of Paris, Skidmore College, and the Sorbonne (Paris III).

Carl F. Miller teaches literature at the University of Alabama, where his courses include British and American modernism and postmodernism, existential literature, and children's literature. He has recent publications on the influence of the Cold War in the 1980s graphic novel, the significance of philosophical ethics in Dr. Seuss's *Horton Hears a Who!* and the role of sport as identity in Harper Lee's *To Kill a Mockingbird*. He also has forthcoming publications on the crisis of the Bildungsroman in *Winesburg, Ohio* and the parallel significance of horse racing in the work of James Joyce and D. H. Lawrence. He has a doctorate from University of Florida.

Marta Miquel-Baldellou is an associate lecturer at the University of Lleida. She is a member of DEDAL-LIT Research Group, the Institute of Research in Identities and Society, the Spanish Association of Anglo-American Studies, and the European Society for the Study of English. She was Fellow at Victorian Studies Centre of the University of Leicester in 2008. She is coeditor of *Anthology of Cultural Ageing: Testimonies from Catalonia and England* (2007) and her work has appeared in *Heroines and Heroes: Symbolism, Embodiment, Narratives and Identities* (2007), *New Litera-*

tures of the Old: Dialogues of Tradition and Innovation in Anglophone Literature (2008), *Flaming Embers: Ageing and Desire in Contemporary Literature* (2010), and *Ageing Femininities: Troubling Representations* (2012).

Nanette Norris is assistant professor of English Literature at Royal Military College Saint-Jean. She is the author of *Modernist Myth: Studies in D. H. Lawrence, H. D. and Virginia Woolf* (2008). Her work has appeared in *Images of the Child*, ed. Harry Eiss (1994), *Engaging the Enemy: Canada in the 1940s*, ed. Andrew Hiscock and Muriel Chamberlain (2006), and *The D. H. Lawrence Review*, among others. She coedited (with Colette Balmain) the e-book conference proceeding *Uneasy Humanity: Perpetual Wrestling with Evils* (2009), and is the editor of *"Unionist Popular Culture and Rolls of Honour in Ireland in World War I" and Other Diverse Essays* (2011). She has a PhD from l'université de Montréal.

C. R. Resetarits's work has been published in numerous journals and anthologies, including essays on Dickinson and the genome project in *Kenyon Review* and on Henry James, Gore Vidal, and lost love in *Gender Studies*. Her background in American studies and interest in natural history have recently combined to bring about *An Anthology of Nineteenth-Century American Science Writing* (2012).

www.ingramcontent.com/pod-product-compliance
Lightning Source LLC
Chambersburg PA
CBHW030649110726
47901CB00002B/637